DEAR
MAIMONIDES

DEAR MAIMONIDES

A Discourse on Religion and Science

Andrew Sanders

JASON ARONSON INC.
Northvale, New Jersey
London

First Jason Aronson Inc. edition—1996

Copyright © 1996, 1993 Andrew T. Sanders

10 9 8 7 6 5 4 3 2 1

Library of Congress Cataloging-in-Publication Data

Sanders, Andrew.
    Dear Maimonides: a discourse on religion and science / Andrew Sanders.
       p. cm.
    Previously published: Toronto : University of Toronto Press, 1993.
    ISBN 1-56821-925-3 (alk. paper)
      1. Judaism—Doctrines. 2. Maimonides, Moses, 1135-1204—Correspondence.
    3. Imaginary letters. I. Title.
    BM601.S26 1996
    296—dc20   95-48476

Manufactured in the United States of America. Jason Aronson Inc. offers books and cassettes. For information and catalog write to Jason Aronson Inc., 230 Livingston Street, Northvale, New Jersey 07647.

To my wife, Judith

FOREWORD

The author hopes that the kind Reader of this book will find it entertaining. Nevertheless, he intends it to be read as a serious work, a major effort to understand the "meaning of it all", using the viewpoint of someone far removed in space and time from our world, to eliminate all the "static" that we normally take for granted, never notice, yet which cloud our view of many facts that normally would be staring us in the face.

Should the opinions of the nominal writer of the letters annoy or insult some of the Readers, she or he is asked for forbearance: those opinions are not the author's, but necessarily those of a late 12th century Jewish intellectual. Please consider also that as the writer gradually adjusts to the 20th century, his views and opinions undergo a subtle change, as perhaps reflected in the way he signs his name to the letters.

For this reason, and also for the thoughts in this book to make sense, the author wishes to make an unusual request of the kind Reader: please try to read the book through from beginning to end, even if your reaction to the early chapters may be "well, but I know about those things".

In any case, the author wishes to thank the Reader for his/her willingness to share that special and somewhat unusual vantage point with him.

T A B L E   O F   C O N T E N T S

BOOK II.

Rambam, we don't agree with everything you said

BOOK III.

To understand God—and man

BOOK IV.

The Future

PREFACE

1. *Maimonides*

Moshe ben Maimon, usually called "Maimonides" (meaning 'the son of Maimon', 'of the family Maimon') or, by his Jewish admirers, "the Rambam" (an acronym of his name, *R*abbi *M*oshe *b*en *M*aimon) was the most illustrious Jewish sage, scholar, philosopher and teacher since talmudic times; the high regard accorded to him being eclipsed by none during the last nearly two millennia, not even by any of the 20th century scholars. A brief review of his biography may be in order.

He was born in Cordova, Spain, in 1135. His family was one of the most distinguished in that city and, indeed, in the entire region of Andalusia. His father, Maimon ben Joseph, was a highly regarded scholar, physician and judge; he was called the *dayyan*, or judge, of Cordova.

Maimon ben Joseph took it upon himself to educate his son, except for a few years when Moshe was sent to an outstanding rabbi for further enlightenment. His teachers must have been proud of the young man, who showed signs of unusual flair for all sciences then known—medicine, astronomy, mathematics—which were considered branches of philosophy. Yet the most important knowledge was that of the Bible and the Talmud, and nobody was more familiar with these than young Moshe.

Life was good for the Jews in Spain, but that bliss came to a sudden end when Muslim fanatics, the Berber Almohades, captured Cordova in 1148. They destroyed churches and synagogues, and forced all residents to convert to Islam, or leave immediately, upon threat of death. The Maimon family chose exile.

Curiously, we don't know where they went; it appears that they moved from one Spanish city to another for some ten years. In the end, they were forced to leave Spain for Northern Africa, also Muslim-ruled but more tolerant. They arrived at Fez, Morocco, in the year 1160.

The Muslims claim that the Maimon family actually converted to Islam. That is possible, many did so for form's sake only; but some of Maimonides' writings indicate that he personally rejected that option. In any case, the Head Rabbi of Fez was killed by the Muslims for refusing apostasy; probably as the result of this, the Maimon family escaped from that city in 1165. They boarded a ship for Palestine.

Having arrived at Acre, they made their headquarters there for five months, and Moshe visited all of the holy sites. But civilized life, especially for a businessman, such as Moshe's brother David, was impossible there; so they moved down to Egypt, Alexandria at first, and then to Fostat, a suburb of Cairo.

There, Moshe devoted his attention to his writings and studies; he could afford to do so comfortably, as brother David had a most successful business dealing in precious stones; his ship sailed all the way to the Far East, he himself often traveling along.

In those years, the reputation of Maimonides became established in all lands where Jews lived; he spent much time on community affairs, re-claiming the primary position in Judaism for the Rabbanites, wrestling it away from the Karaite branch. He wrote much, spent time in preparing his works for publication (that meant duplication, hand-copying over and over again). These works were generally well-received, although there were many who objected to some of his writings. Samuel ben Ali ha-Levi, the Gaon in Baghdad, for one, was not a devoted follower; he may have felt threatened by the new sage.

Maimonides completed his "Mishnah Commentary" in 1168, and was preparing for his major work, the "Mishneh Torah" when tragedy struck: his brother David perished at sea, along with all the treasure of the family and of many other people, entrusted to him. The loss of the beloved brother hit Maimonides painfully; and the requirement to look after both families, David's and his own, suddenly fell upon him. For a year, he could not cope with the changed circumstances; he lay prostrate, could not bring himself even to move.

Eventually, he had to earn a living, somehow. There were those who did so from the Torah, teaching at a salary by the direct permission of the Exilarch or Gaon; Maimonides refused that approach. Rather, he decided to make a living as a physician.

Those were difficult years, but he was an excellent healer, one who preferred moderation and healthy diets to drugs. His fame gradually spread, and eventually he became court physician, looking after the son of the ruler Saladin and also his vizier. By 1185 he was famous in all Muslim lands. In another few years, King Richard the Lion-hearted, in the Middle-East leading the third Crusade, invited Maimonides to join him, become his personal physician, presumably following him back to England. Maimonides refused; he was getting old.

By 1177 he was recognized as the leader of Egyptian Jewry, the Nagid. He worked very hard, yet found time to write his "Mishneh Torah", a summarization of the Talmud, so that it was now possible to understand the whole Law, by reading the Bible and this volume alone. Certain Rabbis in Provence and elsewhere in Europe considered this presumptuous.

Still, he proceeded to write his other major work, the philosophical treatise "Guide for the Perplexed", which he completed in 1190, perhaps a little earlier. In that work, he tried to resolve the conflict between reason and religion. He followed Aristotle and the Neo-Platonists in many of their opinions, even to the point of a willingness to re-interpret the Torah if reason so dictated. He pointed out that the Bible can be read in two ways: literally, for the simple people, and metaphorically, for the educated.

Maimonides did not believe in making the mysteries of philosophy available to all, for that would only confuse the uneducated. He insisted on revealing the deepest secrets only to the few who had attained high levels of understanding. So he did not write his "Guide for the Perplexed" for general publication; rather, he sent it, chapter-by-chapter, to his favourite disciple, ostensibly having written it expressly for him. The name of that disciple: Yosef ben Yehudah ibn Sham'un (often mistaken for another young philosopher, Yosef ben Yehudah ibn Aknin, with whom Maimonides had only a passing acquaintance).

In addition to his major works, Maimonides wrote many letters, medical monographs, "responsa" to queries from all over the world (in one, addressed to the Yemeni Jewish community, he directed them towards a life path that made their sufferings bearable, and also used his influence in the ruling circles on their behalf). One important treatise: "On Resurrection", written after having been criticised by the Gaon and other Rabbis, and also by the Islamic theocracy, who accused him of believing in the survival of the soul, or acquired intelligence, but not in the physical resurrection of the body. Maimonides stated that while the latter is not a scientifically conceivable phenomenon, nevertheless it must be accepted by every Jew as an article of faith.

Maimonides' first wife died childless. He married again in Egypt, and had just one child, a son Abraham, from the marriage. He looked after the education of the boy, who became a respected scholar on his own right.

Moshe ben Maimon died in December, 1204, and was mourned by all Jews everywhere in the world. Indeed, public mourning services were ordered for him in all communities. His remains were taken to Palestine and buried at Tiberias; his grave is venerated to this day.

2. *Yosef ben Yehudah ibn Sham`un (or Shim`on)*

This Joseph was the Rambam's favourite disciple. Indeed, as mentioned before, Maimonides wrote his monumental work, the "Guide for the Perplexed", expressly for Joseph. This may have only been a necessary device, pre-empting his potential accusers who might claim that he was revealing the deepest secrets to just about anybody, while warning against just such revelation, stating that only those who had achieved the highest levels of understanding should be allowed to read the great secrets. If so, that would nevertheless prove for us how highly the Rambam thought of this disciple, as the only one deserving to be given those new revelations, the only one perhaps capable of receiving shocking information about the world, information that may perhaps appear to be in conflict with the words of the Torah, and being able to resolve those conflicts in his own mind.

We do not know so much about his life story; this is what we have discovered:

He was born in Morocco, and studied under Muslim as well as Jewish teachers. The subject of his studies was the same as those of any learned man: philosophy. That included mathematics, medicine, astronomy and logic, and everything else that we would now classify as science. Indeed, he made a name for himself as a scientist, then called 'philosopher', and was noticed for his skills in mathematics and medicine at an early age.

Yet Joseph was not the typical scholar. For one thing, he indulged in poetry, as did Yehudah Halevy earlier, and as Maimonides would never have done, not wishing to 'waste his time'. Also, as we shall see, he was impatient, wanted new information, new discoveries, was hungry for advancement. In this, surprisingly, he differed again from his master the Rambam.

How did Joseph become a disciple of the great man? When persecution became unbearable in Morocco, he escaped to Egypt; there, as we have seen, Jews were permitted to practice their faith without subterfuge and pro-forma conversions. We don't know when that move took place, but it appears that from Alexandria, where he first stayed, he already wrote letters to Moshe ben Maimon, who must already have been famous; so if we assumed the year 1170, we are not likely to be off by more than five years. He soon moved to Fostat, to study directly under Maimonides, and became the favourite pupil of the sage. He learned astronomy and philosophy; the latter, as shown before, could have included everything then known to man, and probably did. Yet we can assume that religion, Bible and Talmud study was never distant from the centre of their attention.

He must have considered his education complete at one point, for in 1185 he left Egypt and moved to Syria. There, he established a business of commercial nature, travelled near and far and became quite well-to-do. Subsequently, he accepted a position as court physician to one son of Saladin who was the king of Aleppo.

But Joseph did not severe his close relations with Maimonides. Indeed, he demanded from his master new knowledge. It may be that such insistence was responsible for Maimonides' producing his final work of genius, the 'Guide for the Perplexed', addressed to Joseph. At the same time, he fulfilled an essential role in Syria and Babylonia: defending Maimonides. He was aware of the enmity between his master and the Gaon Samuel ben Ali, and he visited Baghdad and attempted to bring the two men closer; presumably, he was of sufficient stature as to allow him the undertaking of such an initiative without fear of rebuke (although we have no information about the success of the venture). He also demanded, in Babylonia, the excommunication of a scholar who attacked the teaching of Maimonides.

Joseph wrote several treatises himself, one on the creation of the world, and another, a philosophical work, on the 'Necessary Existence'. It is worth mentioning that in these writings he emphatically rejected the then prevalent notion of 'sphere spirits', celestial beings personally responsible for moving a particular sphere to which a planet, the sun or moon were supposed to be attached. Maimonides firmly believed in these spirits; but Joseph pointed out that those must be imaginary or allegorical things.

We know that he was still working as a most respected physician in the early 13th century, and was recognized by the poet al-Harizi, who visited Aleppo in 1218, as a 'mighty rabbi in the West who was anointed by God as a prophet in the East'. Prophesy was, apparently, one honour that Joseph craved and, to some extent, may have considered to have achieved.

We have no information as to when, where and how Joseph ben Yehudah died. So perhaps the admittedly outrageous premise of the present book, that he did not die in the 13th century but was somehow transported to the 20th, will not be invalidated on the basis of such historical data.

3.   *Thrust and Parry*

While Joseph ben Yehudah was the Rambam's favourite disciple, the master was surely annoyed at times by the rash, demanding demeanour of his pupil. Joseph wanted to be introduced to the "secrets"; yet was quite willing to reject those secrets gradually revealed to him as the nonsense many of them were. Maimonides was more than likely to resent that; he could easily have developed second thoughts regarding the promised revelation of all secrets to Joseph. It seems that this was exactly what happened, at least for a while: Joseph waited for the promised secrets, and the Rambam hesitated. Joseph was growing desperate. He was an unusually curious and extremely impatient man. He could not just sit there and wait. He was expecting the secrets, and they did not come. He feared betrayal. Finally, he decided to pen a letter to his master, in a humorous, allegorical mode, hoping that he can get his point across without insulting the older man and, indeed, with perhaps cheering him up a little. This is what he wrote:

"You can see that we have the same language and mind, no stranger has come between the two of us, still you behave this way, towards a friend who came to rest if the shadow of your love, who submitted to your intellect without shyness and bared his mind to your faith and fidelity. Yes, I, I am speaking now, and you must speak, too, for I want to do you justice. If you have arguments, refute me! Recently, Kima[1], your favourite daughter, has won my heart. She is a lovely girl, delight to my eyes. I courted her according to the Law of our Faith and according to the Halacha of Mount Sinai, in three ways: I brought for her an expensive gift, as the price of the suite; I wrote a love letter to her; and engaged her as her bridegroom. Thus she became mine. I invited her into the tent of friendship. I did not force her, did not hurry her. It was my love that won her love, my soul embraced her soul. And all this took place in front of two sound witnesses: Ibn Obeid-Allah[2] and Ibn Roshd[3], the associates. But then, under the firmament of marriage, she became an adulteress, turned her deepest feelings towards other friends. As ancient poets wrote: 'That bride is insolent, who breaks her vow under the canopy.' She has found no fault with me, yet she left me, sneaked out of my tent and will not me show her face, the beautiful, nor let me hear her voice full of beautiful tones. And you did not reprimand your daughter for her arrogance, did not rebuke her for her negligence, even encouraged her. This was wrong! Now, therefore, restore the man's wife; for he is a prophet (or will be one), and he shall pray for thee, and thou shalt live (and will also pray for her, so she will stand on her feet without staggering). And if thou restore her not, thou will get confused by the

---

[1] Kima: a mythological character, possibly the symbol of wisdom.

[2] Maimonides

[3] Averroës

end of the verse.[4] So turn towards peace, offer your hand in agreement. So that you shall be in good health and your days be numerous, listen to the Rabbis: 'Blessed is he, who returns lost things'. What if the lost thing is a bejewelled woman, crown of her husband? So I stand here, waiting for her return. I ask about her from each nation, each kingdom; because of her, there is no day that I don't pour out my soul. And among these nations shalt she have no repose. Happy is he who hopes and achieves."

"The truest of your devoted servants, his desire is to see the face of your dignity and to embrace your feet in the dust."

Well, Maimonides understood the allegory and the humour. He was not a man without some wit himself. Joseph was complaining about what he considered broken promises. The answer would be clothed in similarly fanciful terms (which, like the original letter, included Biblical and Talmudic expressions, as well as word plays, alliterations, poetic devices that, unfortunately, get lost in the translation). The response, while warm, was not, perhaps, as friendly as one would expect; clearly, the Rambam resented Joseph's claim of being already (or almost) a prophet; and his equating Maimonides with Averröes. So there was some sharpness in addition to much humour in the reply.

"Listen, Wise ones, to my words! Lend me your ears and step forward Adjudicate and argument between me and my opponent; if I am at fault, bear witness against me. I gave the hand of my child, Kima, in marriage to Kh'sil[5]. But he did not favour her, viewed the girl, who was raised in the environment of faith, as if she were touched by sin, for she had covered her face. Since her feet became entangled in his trap, and to his shame, stood before him naked, he was seized by the spirit of jealousy, and hate flamed in him towards his wife. He

---

[4] A take-off on Genesis 20:7, God's words to Abimelech. The second part of the verse does not fit.

[5] Kh'sil: another mythological character, probably the husband of Kima.

provided her with no food, clothes and lodging, lied about her, spread words about her. Having trapped her and bound her, he treacherously questioned her honour, added the flame of jealousy to her bridal trousseau. His witnesses were bastards, which is illegal, thus increasing the number of his sins. His purpose was to ruin her reputation in my eyes, so this man turned to me with these words: 'Your daughter became an adulteress under the firmament of marriage; oh, look at her shame, revenge her sin and her breaking of honour, force her to return to her husband, for he is a prophet, and will pray to the Lord for her and for you. He will help her welfare, make her steps steady and will forgive her sins, for he does not wish for her death; and God will also forgive her, for she was protected by the prayer of her father'."

"Well, you know the man and his phrase-making, as he reveals his thinking–he that trusteth in his own heart is a fool[6]–as he expounds the Halacha in the presence of his teacher. And he, the inventor of light chatter, believes that he is a prophet among prophets. Like a blind man holding onto a grating, he is always searching for opportunity to make grandiose statements and to bring reputations into question. He is known for his dirty mouth, while she is immaculate, having never been touched by any hand. It is impossiby far for her to do such thing as breaking her vows to her husband, or for Israel to be embarrassed on her behalf, or for her to follow any path other than those of Saul and Samuel."

"And so, form a circle, so I can mete out the penalty. But do not permit anger to enter your breasts, and keep sadness away from you. Like a loving father chastising his son, I will rebuke him with these words: 'Since you contended with me and spoke to me with a harsh voice and shouted loudly into my ears; since you took me to task on account of your wife; since you offered up, flagrantly, two witnesses, one a Jew, the other an Arab, and made no distinction between the holy and the profane; since you placed yourself among the prophets,

---

[6] Proverbs 28:26. The word *fool* is "Khsil" in the Hebrew, a word-play on Kima's mythological husband's name.

occupying the haughtiest place; well, were it not for my honour and the honour of my dear, faithful Kima, I would deal with your audacity and disgrace you with a single word'."

"Oh, my son, your thoughts are like confused people, none of them is capable of retrospection. The Lord let them be planted in such a ground that can bring no fruit. You are their master, so note and behold: it is inadvisable to bring suspicion of immorality to any wife, least of all your own. A clever poet could wave his allegory towards you, with such words as 'A fool's mouth is his ruin'. Or 'His horns grew from his own hands'."

"Listen to me, my son: here is your wife, take her and go. Trust in God always, whatever happens to you. Know that He is with you in all your works, while we walk on separate paths. He will assure that your paths and thoughts will always be straight, shall not stray. Listen to the admonishing of your teacher, do not permit your tongue to lead your body to the way of sin. Only the truth proceeds from my mouth; you can look and search, you will not find there anything which is false or untrue. Do not claim in pride to be at the level of the prophets. This is not because their ways tower above yours; rather, because their time had already arrived. Do not say 'Because Samuel could predict the future correctly, I, the giant of wisdom, will be able to do the same'. If you are wise, you are wise to yourself, to understand and to teach. Do nor concern yourself with the hidden things. Do not quote the Talmud to prove that a a wise man is even superior to a prophet. Consider: not everyone, who wears a sword, need to kill, just as not everyone, who desires fame, will be famous. Even if Samuel prophesied, and made miracles, need therefore Saul also be a prophet? So do not brag of wisdom; eliminate your pride, and reflect upon the modesty of our fathers; for he that is now called a prophet was beforetime called a seer. Give up all pride; do just as I instruct you. I will lead you in the ways of wisdom. Keep arrogance away from you till the end of your life; honour intelligence like a father and wisdom, like a sister. Until then, may the number of people like you increase in Israel."

BOOK I.

**From the 12th century to the 20th:
A historical review**

YUSUF BEN YEHUDAH IBN SHAM`UN'S
LETTER TO RAMBAM

22 Tammuz 5748 / July 7, 1988

To the immeasurably honoured Rabbi Moshe (may God be his guardian), son of Rabbi Maimon (may Paradise be his repose) the Spaniard; back in the year 4960; in Fostat, Egypt

So says Yusuf ben Yehudah (of blessed memory) ibn-Sham`un:

My dear Master, you will be surprised to receive this letter; that is, if you receive it at all. Strange things have happened to me, strange understandings have come to me. And since you, the Head of Teaching, have called me your favourite disciple, I am sure that you would want to know where I live now, what I do and especially, what I have learned since we last wrote to each other.

When I talk about strange things, you will be skeptical at first: I know that you have always found me unduly excitable and once, I know, I may have annoyed you by calling myself a prophet, or almost one. Do excuse me for that impertinence. But what I shall tell you now is an experience entirely different from anything that you have ever heard.

Before I explain where I live now, and that won't be easy, I have to tell you *when* I live. I last wrote to you from Aleppo. Later, I moved to Baghdad, there to defend your fame from attacks by the followers of the Gaon Samuel ben Ali. Meanwhile, I continued my studies of astronomy, mathematics, medicine and especially metaphysics. I have found, I think, many answers to the mysteries that we have discussed so many times. But not everything could be determined through study; and I must admit that I hoped for the gift of prophesy. Beginning in the year of 4976, (just as you predicted,) I was visited, I think, a number of times by the Holy Spirit, and that helped me understand many things about the future; but I did not become a prophet like our great men of the past.

(I think the Holy Spirit has also visited many other men from then on: for understanding, a re-birth of human society and spirit, began at various parts of the earth; indeed, the era that they later called the "dark ages" was drawing to a close. In science, medicine and especially the arts, insight was suddenly granted to Man, and he has begun to create wonderful things.)

Then, in the year 4986, suddenly, by an inexplicable act of the Holy One, blessed is He, I became transported forward to the year 5744. Yes, I know, that is seven hundred and fifty-eight years into the future. How it happened, I don't know. The people in this age can do wonderful things, I shall tell you about those, but even they could not call their ancestors up from the past. So I just have to accept the fact that the Lord did it, praised be He. And if He could move me forward in time, He may also want to move my letter to you backward. Who knows, perhaps His objective is that I should inform you about the strange happenings in the world of our future. Is this not what you have been hoping for? With the help of God, He is granting you a miracle through me.

Rabbi, if you believe me, the first thing you will want to know is, has Messiah come to help our people? For you thought that the strength of Islam and Christianity, and the persecution of the Jews by those heretics and idolaters, signalled the birth pangs of the Messiah. I am sure that you could not have been wrong; but those birth pangs were not on a human scale, for I am sorry to say that the Messiah has not come yet. But it may be soon now, perhaps another few hundred years.

Yet, meanwhile, the Jews are still here, strong, despite (or perhaps because of) many persecutions, most of which were far worse than anything we have seen in our days and before. For our people have been murdered, systematically, by the millions. And we also had to cope with a number of false messiahs.

But, Rabbi, now our people have their own country! Yes, in the Land of Israel! The land is returned to us, and Jerusalem is its capital! I shall tell you about it, later. Oh, how much I shall have to tell you!

My Master, what a difference between the world you and I have known and this one! I don't know where to begin telling you about it. I do not understand it fully, even though, I admit, I have been living in this world of my future for over four years now. Yes, I know, I should have written to you sooner, perhaps as soon as I found myself here; but it would not have made any sense to you at all. What if I told you that people sit in small boxes which run away at tremendous speed? That they talk into a tool the size of a hammer which talks back to them? That they can have daylight in their houses at night, if they want, without lighting candles? That tiny people, the size of your finger, move around and sing and dance in little boxes, appear and disappear? It was horribly confusing at first, still is, but it is beginning to make a little sense now. Oh, and the way they live! The way they look! The things they wear! How little things they wear!

I have been studying them. I have been trying to learn all I could about this world of the future—how it got to be like this, what is going on here, what happened during the last 762 years and, especially, what kind of people these are. I did not know if they were God-fearing, law-abiding people, *tzaddikim*, people who accept the commandments and uphold the words of the Torah, or were they perhaps heathens, pagans, people who deserved to be destroyed in this world and could expect no parts of the World-to-Come.

Rabbi, at first, in my confusion, I even wondered if this may be the World-to-Come. It is not that, this I know for sure. But, as I have told you. Eretz Yisrael, our ancestral home, our covenantal land, lives again, a Jewish state in Palestine, with Yerusholayim as the seat of its own government. So, perhaps, you shall say that the Messiah must have been here. I don't think so, at least not to stay; for the dead have not yet been resurrected. You be the judge of that; for you are gifted with the most perfect judgement, the most excellent knowledge, correct thinking, the surest insight, the worthiest qualities, the noblest senses, the most penetrating perspicacity.

So, in many pages, many letters to come, I shall attempt to tell you what I have learned about the last 762 years and about the present.

Master, forgive me if I use *their* way of denoting dates. We Jews still use our calendar, but only for religious purposes; and the rest of the world uses a system of dates that is, I am afraid, based on the birth of Yehoshua ha-Notzri in whose name, you will recall, the Christian faith was established. That dating system is used even in most countries that don't respect the Nazarene. In that system, this is the year 1988. Yes, almost two thousand years have gone by since those turbulent days, more than nineteen hundred years since the destruction of the Temple. No, Rabbi, it has not yet been re-built.

With the greatest respect and admiration, and wishing you good health and long life,

The truest of your devoted servants, his desire is to look upon your honour's countenance and to embrace your feet in the dust.

Yusuf ben Yehudah ibn-Sham`un

A DIFFERENT WORLD

6 Av 5748 / July 20, 1988

To the Honoured and Holy Master and Teacher B'Rabbi Moshe ben Maimon the Spaniard, in Fostat, Egypt

In the name of God, Lord of the Universe

My dear Rabbi,

I shall attempt to tell you, in this letter, all the things that Man has found out about nature in the last eight centuries. No, I could not tell you about all, for there have been too many such new things. Then, in this letter, I shall try to tell you about a few of the most important things, those that really changed the history of the world. Later, with the help of the Holy One, blessed is He, I shall write to you about many of the new sciences and inventions, what they do for Man today, how they change his everyday life.

My Master, this is a different world. But before I tell you how different, you should know that our world, yours and mine, was also different from earlier ones, only we did not know it. Things have changed since the days of the Temple, but we were slow to notice. Our understanding of metaphysics, mathematics, geometry, physics, astronomy and other branches of philosophy grew very much in the last few hundred years before our time. And in our days, some people may already have discovered America.

America? (you ask). This takes us right into geography. What did we know of the lands of earth? Since the days of Ptolemy, many minor discoveries have been made, but our view of the world had not changed very much. We knew of three connected continents, nothing more.

We were familiar with Africa, at least the northern part. We knew something about Europe, the continent of Castille and Aragon, Gaul, the lands of the Greeks, the Holy Roman Empire, and many other lands. That Empire included the lands of the Germans. Oh, Rabbi, how much Germany mattered to the Jews in this "20th century", how much suffering came from that land! I shall tell you about it, but you are not yet ready to hear about those troubles.

My Master, Europe became very important in the last millennium; for much of that time, it has been the leader of civilization. Jewish culture, indeed most of Jewish life, has also shifted to Europe. Africa and the Arab world, once proud and triumphant, have dismally deteriorated, became insignificant factors in the history of the world until recently.

We knew, of course, of Asia, the land of the eastern Arabs; and east of them, north of them, the Ottomans, Persians, Afghans, Indians, Slavs and still further east, the Mongols, Chinese, Japanese—your brother David, of blessed memory did, I think, travelled to many of those lands, trading with the Indians, Malays and perhaps even with the Chinese; yet later, somehow, people forgot about China, thought that India was at the eastern edge of the continent. That is what Columbus thought, that is what he was trying to find by sailing westward across the Atlantic Ocean.

Who was this man? Perhaps a countryman of yours, a Spanish (though originally Genoese) Jew from a forcibly converted family in the year 1492 (the year Jews were expelled from Spain by the Christians), he received the financial support of the King and primarily the Queen, monarchs for Castille and Aragon (who married and united those lands along with Granada and Navarra) for his proposal to expand the Spanish empire by colonizing the east via west, based on Aristotle's theory of the earth being a globe. He assembled a flotilla, an expedition to India. He found a distant land, he found primitive people there whom he called Indians. But that land was less than halfway from Europe to Asia; really, two huge continents reaching from the North Pole of the earth almost to the South Pole, connected by a narrow isthmus in the middle.

But recent evidence indicates that hundreds of years before Columbus, even before our times, other Europeans—northerners, even southerners—have travelled west through the sea, perhaps without a theory of a global earth, but desperate for new lands, or driven by God knows what spirit of adventure. Many have arrived to America—that is the name of those continents now—but apparently never could return to tell Europe about their discovery.

America is heavily populated today, mainly by descendants of European immigrants. So is Australia, another land discovered further west, further south. The entire earth is heavily populated. I tell you how many people live on earth today. There are five billion, or five thousand million people on earth!

Master, you taught me to honour intelligence as a father, wisdom as a sister; and I think I have done so. But what is wisdom? So many of the things I knew or thought I knew, so many of the things that you taught me are superseded today. Master, I am sorry to tell you this, but many of the things that you and I accepted as facts, as proven, turned out to be totally incorrect. Take Ptolemaic astronomy, for example.

We thought that all the stars revolved around earth—planets such as Mercury, Venus, Mars, Jupiter, Saturn did so with retrograde motion. The Sun and the Moon were also supposed to revolve around the earth. How wrong we were! Only the Moon revolves around the earth; the others move around the Sun! They are planets of the Sun; and so is the earth! It moves around the Sun in an elliptic orbit along with Venus, Mars and the other planets, nine in all.

(The worst part, my Master, is that while Plato and Aristotle confused us with their silly earth-based ideas, their contemporaries knew the truth: Herakleides and especially Aristarchus of Samos understood the heliocentric arrangement of the planets well. Their work was suppressed by the followers of your friend, the Chief of the Philosophers and, later, by the Christian Church.)

What about the stars? Do they also revolve around the Sun? Of course not. The Sun is simply a star, like those billions of others. Some of the large, distant lights of the night sky are more than one star, they are groups of billions of stars themselves, galaxies. The earth is part of the Solar system along with the other eight planets; the Sun is part of one galaxy, our Milky Way (that is where the term "galaxy" comes from in Hebrew and most other languages).

And, finally, there are billions of such galaxies, they form the Universe that God, praised be He, created. When did He do that? About seventeen billion years ago!

I am really sorry, Master, to have caused you such a shock, such upset of all of your cherished ideas. But I must tell you one more fact (although you may already have deduced this from the preceding): do you recall our discussions about the heavenly spheres? Each sphere surrounding the earth, each with one of the planets? The outermost with all the stars? The innermost with the Moon? Do you remember how we discussed whether or not they were animated? You thought, along with Aristotle, that they were; and that the outermost was moved by God, the Prime Mover. But, Rabbi, there are no such heavenly spheres! And nowhere, in Scripture, does God talk of such spheres. We tried to interpret the T'nach, force it to tell us about those things, animated spheres more or less at par with angels. Are there angels? Well, perhaps. I think there may be; but even when I lived in Aleppo, I concluded that spheres' spirits were entirely imaginary, allegoric inventions. (I know that you were annoyed by some of the things I said, at times even called me the "inventor of light chatter"; please, Master, grant me that in at least this one thing, I was right.

There were one or two other things, I shall bring those to your attention, if I can gather the courage.)

Master, these things are not important. What does matter is that God
did create the Universe; so, you see, Aristotle, the Chief of the
Philosophers, was wrong and you were right in maintaining that a
temporal creation is both according to Scripture and a logical
necessity. What did he create it out of? Was there a primordial matter?
Some say that there was: something which could be called cosmic
dust, or original chaos. The Hebrew words were *tohu vaBohu*. They
think that there was that, and then, suddenly, from one minute to the
next, the Lord, His name be exalted, created the world. But others say,
and I think that they may be right, that the Creator brought the
Universe about out of nothing, absolute nothing! *Tohu vaBohu* was
only the first step in the creation.

In my next letters, I shall tell you about many branches of philosophy
—really, science—and major discoveries since our days. I am afraid
I shall have to shock you more about some things, about the invalidity
of some of our favourite ideas in many fields, for example in
medicine. But first, I shall want to write to you about what science
really is.

The truest of your devoted servants

Yusuf ben Yehudah ibn-Sham un

HOW SCIENTISTS CHANGED THE WORLD:

MAJOR DISCOVERIES SINCE THE 12TH CENTURY

24 Av 5748 / August 8, 1988

To B'Rabbi Moshe ben Rabbi ha-Dayyan Maimon ha-Sfaradi,
Fostat, Egypt

My honoured Master:

I am ready to tell you about the great discoveries of science in the last eight centuries and how those have changed the life of Man on earth. This will be a long letter.

What is science? Superficially, it is a new name for what we used to call "philosophy", or "natural philosophy". Knowledge. But knowledge of facts, hard facts. There are many branches of science, old and new; all—or I should say most—deal with facts, not opinions. Without implying criticism, a scientist in this new age could not make a firm statement about animated spheres, not without offering solid proof for the statement, non-scriptural proof.

If the great philosophers of our age were working and teaching in this age, they would be either theologians or scientists. The main difference? Scientists will generally stand corrected, accept new discoveries, give up old theories when finally proven wrong. Theologians will never do that. Which would we be, Rabbi?

Aristotle approached science (at least biology) correctly: he observed things closely and repeatedly. He was willing to stand corrected by anybody with more facts, more up-to-date information, new proofs. He made many mistakes, misunderstood many facts. But then, he had no access to modern scientific instruments. Neither did we fifteen hundred years later. And so I do not call Aristotle, from the objective of this world, a poor scientist (although he turned out to be a poor physicists and disastrous astronomer, not because of lack of inst-ruments, but because he did not apply his own prescribed methods to these sciences; he imagined a scheme of things, and would not permit reality to interfere with his ideas); nor do I call ourselves that, nobody does. Yet science is now based on measurement and statistical analy-sis. Our science was comparable to a blind man making pronounce-ments on the appearance of natural beauty.

It is so much easier to perform scientific experiments today. Thousands, tens of thousands of diverse instruments, research tools are available. Everything can be measured accurately—temperature, pressure, physical dimensions, time, speed, chemical characteristics of a liquid or gaseous ambience, electrical and magnetic charges. (Some of these concepts are strange to you; I shall try to elucidate the important ones later.) All measurements can be performed with a high degree of precision. For example, the temperature scale is divided into 100 degrees between the freezing and boiling points of water; but measurement is possible to the one-thousandth of each such degree, or finer when necessary. (Of course, the scale extends far below the freezing point and very far above, really into infinity.) Such accurate measurement then permits a thorough analysis of any object or situation; reduction of the findings to a hypothesis; and then, testing of the hypothesis under exacting circumstances until a law can be confidently stated.

More important, those conditions can not only be measured but artificially created for the purposes of research. This provides for repeatable experiments. A scientist publishes his findings; other scientists, at other parts of the world receive the publication, with very detailed documentation, in days or hours! They are then in a position to verify the experiment. Depending on their success or failure, they will eventually confirm or reject the original thesis.

Of course, not every branch of science is based on precise measurements; but most are. Astronomy, for example; physics; medicine. Not
philosophy (what used to be called metaphysics); not sociology; not
law. There is still room for opinion in those branches.

In the rest of this letter, I shall try to summarize what Man has
learned. Bear with me, my Master.

Mathematics is the basis of all hard sciences; it has always been. But
Master, you would not recognize mathematics. What you taught me
is taught today, I am afraid, in elementary schools. True, not one in
a thousand people ever learn more, and most people never even learn
what is taught to them in school; but I must admit that we did not
have the mathematics to calculate, for instance, the relative motions
of all planets on their elliptical course around the Sun, as they may
appear to a hypothetical resident of a particular planet, say Jupiter. Let
alone the behaviour of the smallest sub-atomic particles.

But at least you would recognize it as mathematics. Physics, now, is
something very different from what it was in our days. True, it is still
the science that studies the behaviour of inanimate objects such as
solids, liquids and gases (we knew nothing about gases).

But those studies are based on precise measurements. For example,
when an object falls, physics will tell you why it falls, how it falls, at
what speed or, rather, what rate of acceleration, depending on what
circumstances. Master, the speed and acceleration depends on where
on earth the object falls! Yet it does not depend on what the object is:
a piece of iron or a feather fall at the same rate, at least under ideal
circumstances (when we pump all air out of the test chamber, air that
would slow the fall of some objects).

But physics now includes studies that are far beyond our imagination
of old. Take chemistry, for example (really, no longer part of physics,
but we did not have a separate discipline for the study of the
composition of elements). We knew, or thought we knew, that the

smallest elementary particle was the atom. How many types of atoms did we envision? How many elements were there in our world? Exactly four: earth, water, air, fire. Yet today's scientists have identified, at the latest count, 108 individual elements.

Let me tell you about some elements: iron, copper, lead, gold, silver, carbon (coal), phosphorus, sulphur. We knew those materials, but had no idea that they were distinct elements.

Three very important elements are gases. Oxygen, it readily combines with other elements, mainly carbon, when burning—in a sense, life is burning, for we breathe in oxygen and breathe out carbon dioxide which is the product of carbon from our body and oxygen. Without oxygen, we would suffocate. Then, there is hydrogen, when that gas burns, combines with oxygen, we get water. And nitrogen, a gas that combines less readily with others, but is an essential part of all living bodies. Nitrogen constitutes eight out of ten parts of the air, oxygen two out of ten; but the air is only a mixture of these gases (and a few others in trace quantities), not a compound.

And so, you can see how wrong we were about the four elements. Air is a mixture of several gases. Water is a chemical compound of two gases, as I have shown. Fire is not an element at all, but a chemical process.

Chemistry grew out of the work of the alchemists, medieval philosophers who were searching for a magical catalyst, something they called "philosophers' stone" that would help them turn lead into gold. They never found that, for such transformation is not possible within the confines of chemistry. But they have learned to make tens of thousands of different chemical compounds. These compounds can be based on any combination of the 108 elements—for example, ordinary salt is a compound of one atom of sodium, a common metal (though found only in combination with other elements) and one atom of chlorine, a gas. These two atoms form the molecule which is the smallest unit of sodium chloride, or salt.

Yet the vast majority of chemical compounds are "organic" ones: made out of carbon, oxygen and hydrogen, and most of the time nitrogen; along with a variety of other elements sometimes included in small quantities. For every element plays a part in life; this is a well-designed world, and we must praise the Lord for that.

And so we face a world where everything is made out of the same elements, the same 108, but most of the time really the same dozen or so. That leads us directly back to Plato, who formulated the theory of forms. Everything is made out of matter, but forms are what determine what the object will be. With regard to living beings, he was right; the forms are determined by something called genes, very small chemical compounds, really codes embedded in every cell of every living being. These genes regulate the reproduction and qualities of individuals and species. I shall tell you a lot more about that later. In inanimate objects, of course, the concept of forms is trivial: we make a piece of iron or gold into whatever object we want to.

Let me talk about a different science: nuclear physics. This branch is less than hundred years old now. What happened is that scientists eventually tired of the atom being the smallest elementary particle. They started to look within the atom and found the nucleus, consisting of several protons and neutrons, the numbers determining what kind of element it is; and the nucleus is circled by another number of much smaller particles, electrons, arranged in several shells or spheres (but with no animation). The electrons have negative charges, the protons positive: the two are attracting each other, but the centrifugal force—the spinning action—of the electrons would tend to throw them out, so they remain in balance. (The actual relation of the forces involved is much more complicated than that, but this should do for an initial explanation.)

By studying these three sub-atomic particles and several others, scientists could not only develop an understanding of why elements behave the way they do, but eventually learned to manipulate those particles to dramatic effect. Tremendous power binds some of those particles together, power that can be released and harnessed. And they learned that matter and energy are different forms of the same basic substance—does it sound familiar to you?

Energy is similar to what we called "motion". But there are other forms of energy, including heat; gravity, which is the attraction of two bodies (a large body, such as the earth, attracts all nearby small bodies; for example, the Moon, which would fall onto the earth if not kept out by the centrifugal force, while an apple will actually fall onto the earth, given a chance). Then there is electrical energy; nuclear energy; chemical energy; and several other types. When the apple falls, heat is generated. Energy is never created out of nothing and is never lost, only transformed into another form. That is the basis of the steam engine that I shall write to you about in my next letter.

Scientists also discovered, really confirmed, that matter cannot be created out of nothing, nor is it ever lost. But in the 20th century they learned that matter is really a condensed form of energy, that even a handful of matter, if converted into energy, could heat a city for years, or could destroy a city in seconds. They also found out about radiation that results from their manipulating those smallest particles; sometimes, radiation is a natural property of certain rare elements. This radiation, which is similar to our concept of "emanation", is an invisible stream of sub-atomic particles that can penetrate most bodies, certainly all life-forms, and can do immense harm or good there, depending on the type and strength of the stream used.

Then, there is electricity. It is created when the outermost electron shell of an atom gives up one electron to the next atom, which gives one of its own to the next one, and so on. Imagine a thin string made of metal, a wire. Electric energy can travel through that wire at nearly the same speed light travels, which is 186,000 miles per second! (Not even the 2000 ammot mile; closer to 3000 ammot.) And the energy travelling through such wires can be powerful enough to do almost anything—I shall tell you, in my next letter, about some of the things for which people here use electricity.

Meanwhile, in astronomy, scientists have learned about many secrets of the Universe—but not in a metaphysical sense, and certainly not in a religious, or theological one. In that respect, most of them are still ignoramuses. Yet they did learn that the Universe is seventeen billion years old, that it may have been born out of the "unexplained" gathering together of all the cosmic dust (or, more likely, out of nothing at all), whereby a sudden burst, a so-called "big bang" brought about all energy and all matter now in the Universe. The stars and galaxies have ever since been rushing away from each other, but scientists think that the speed is slowing, and they foresee the time when the process may stop and reverse, ending finally in the collapse of the Universe. Astronomers have telescopes—giant mirrors and lenses, finely polished to precise measurements that allow them to observe the farthest reaches of the Universe, see remote objects that cannot even be detected by bare eyes. Lately, even more can be learned about the Universe through radio-telescopes, devices that detect the faint invisible radiation emitted by the most distant stars.

Let me tell you a little about another branch of the new science where you (and perhaps myself, your humble disciple) have thought of yourselves as somewhat of an expert. I am referring to anatomy and medicine.

You and I were wrong. Well, not quite wrong; we knew much, but we did not know many simple, basic things.

The "Chief of Philosophers" discovered much anatomy through the simple expedient of observing nature. But his followers, for nearly two thousand years, did not observe nature: they observed books instead.

Aristotle was willing to be flexible, to learn new things, to replace obsolete theories when new research proved them incorrect. His followers were not willing to do so. Their theories, to them, were carved in stone.

Aristotle thought that the center of intelligence was the heart. He did not know that the heart is just a pump, moving blood around the veins, to and from all parts of the body, to supply those parts with needed oxygen. He did not know that the seat of intelligence is the brain. Neither did we; yet Herophilus knew that some thirty years after the death of Aristotle.

The culprit was, of course, Galen. He ignored all of the great discoveries of Herophilus, all his findings about the brain and heart and blood circulation. Galen based his anatomy on strange metaphysical concepts; one thing that science has learned in the last 200 years is that your ideology should not influence your dealing with facts. (There are always exceptions, Master. I have discovered that even in the 20th century, a huge country's agriculture was almost destroyed by the scientific theories of one man which went against the observable facts, but in line with another strange ideology fashionable at the time.)

Galen understood that Man is the object of creation; but he took shortcuts. He established his anatomy on the principle that certain spirits, or pneuma, control the function of the organs. Among many mistakes, he described canals that pierce through certain parts of the heart, through which blood passes between the chambers. He had no idea of blood circulation. That was bad enough; but what was worse is that his theories were accepted as scripture for fourteen centuries. Dissection for research was forbidden in our time, as you recall, and even for centuries afterwards. Later, when dissection was finally permitted in certain cases, university professors lectured on Galen's anatomy, while their assistants had to illustrate the lecture on cadavers, pointing to features that were not there!

Finally, in the 16th century, risking their reputation and indeed their lives, some physicians dared to return to reality, re-establishing anatomy through the observation of nature. Rabbi, I am not very proud of our age, of our accomplishment. (Yet, when comparing our life to those of today's peoples, I wonder. But more on that later.)

Let me try to summarize for you what we know about anatomy. Thinking takes place in the brain. The brain requires nutrients and oxygen: these are supplied by the blood which is pumped by the heart. Arteries carry fresh red blood not only to the brain, but to all parts of the body, blood enriched with oxygen in the lung; veins return the used blood, bluish in colour, oxygen-poor, to the lung again, for oxygen re-enrichment.

The circulating blood is purified in the liver. The kidney eliminates excess water and impurities from the body. Meanwhile, nutrients are ground up in the stomach and absorbed in the intestines, circulated from there to wherever they are needed, by the bloodstream.

There are many other important parts of the body including, of course, the reproductive organs and process; numerous specialized glands manufacturing chemicals required by parts of the body at different times; not to mention the limbs, the bone structure, sensing organs and nerves, and hundreds of other parts observable by anyone willing to look. But I only wanted to bring you up-to-date on the most basic concepts, to tell you what anatomy really is; how close we were to understanding it, yet how far.

Today, the inside of a living person can be observed without dissecting, through machines that generate one type of radiation, "X-rays", weak streams of particles or waves that enter a body and exit on the other side. The more dense parts cast a shadow. The bone, especially, blocks much of the rays; so do, in certain circumstances, malignant growths. The exiting radiation is captured by another machine that translates the rays into pictures that can be observed or recorded permanently and studied later.

Decisions are then made, based on such pictures; decisions on whether or not to operate, to remove a cancer, for example.

Surgery is so advanced! Not only do they remove cancerous growths, but can repair many other deformations and diseases, and usually without much pain to the patient. People are simply put to sleep with chemicals—a process called anesthesia—and when they wake, the operation has already been completed. Even heart disease, which used to be fatal, can now be treated surgically. And when repair is no longer possible, then replacement is done: the damaged part is replaced by either a healthy one of of an accident victim; or by an artificial organ—these have become increasingly successful lately.

Of course, surgery is not always necessary. Medications are available by the tens of thousands: synthetic organic substances specifically created to perform a certain function at a certain part of the body. These are delivered to the part usually by simply injecting it, through a very thin needle, into the bloodstream; sometimes, they can be simply swallowed.

Most illnesses are caused by very small living beings, "microorganisms" that invade the body and proliferate there. These things, called bacteria and the still smaller viruses, are so small that you could not see a million of them together. But today there are tools, called microscopes, that allow scientists to observe the villains fully. The body mobilizes its defenses and eventually, most of the time, conquers the invader. But some are persistent; some are strong; some can eventually vanquish the body if left untreated. These are the cases where chemical therapy is useful; such therapy is very common these days, for major disease and minor ones, even the common cold (although, strangely enough, that one is not cured faster with drugs than without; but at least people don't die from complications, such as pneumonia).

One effect of all of these advances in the field of medicine is that human life has been extended greatly. The average person lives to about seventy-five years; 90 or more is quite common, while dying at 50 is considered a tragedy. Women don't die in childbirth and children very seldom die. Yet, no human can reach the biblically significant 120 yet. But scientists are working on it.

My Master, there are many other branches of science—economy, law (which has almost nothing to do with religion today), archeology (the study of old civilization through unearthing their ruins), paleontology (the study of life-forms millions of years old through fossilized remains discovered), sociology and anthropology (the study of the behaviour of individuals and societies) and of especial interest to us, philosophy (our metaphysics) and theology. Those two last disciplines are far from identical, although, necessarily, they do relate to each other. I shall not discuss them in this letter, for I expect to write about those things to you in the future.

Man's knowledge has increased so much that it is no longer possible for one man to know everything. Not even a thousand men can know everything, perhaps not even a million. In a science such as physics, the most respected teachers know one small portion thoroughly, while his colleague would know another portion perhaps only distantly related to the first. In medicine, there are physicians who treat the heart, others for the foot or the eye, there are surgeons who only operate on the brain, others specialize in removing lumps from the stomach, still others treat women's problems. Even in theology, there are hundreds, no, thousands of areas of thought, specialization like in other sciences; but these specialists don't agree with each other, for, as I have said, in theology opinions still rule. That, at least, is not new to you; for when did a Jewish theologian agree with a Muslim one? Or with a Nazarene? Or even with another Jewish one?

Rabbi, I hope all is well with you and you are accepting these startling revelations in good spirit. In my next letter I shall offer you still more shocking facts about how Man has made use—for good and for bad—of all of these newly discovered facts.

The truest of your devoted servants

Yusuf ben Yehudah ibn-Sham`un

GREAT INVENTIONS OF MAN

9 Elul 5748 / August 22, 1988

To B'Rabbi Moshe ben Rabbi Maimon ha-Sfaradi,
Fostat, Egypt

My honoured Master:

Let me tell you what Man has done with his new-found knowledge in
the last eight centuries. Actually, most of the development is very
recent, the most exciting new things are not more than fifty or 100
years old; but Man has been laying the foundation for these advances
through a greatly changed social, economic and educational structure,
a change process that started soon after our time.

Master, this will be another long letter, and it will take you lots of
time to understand it and believe it, even though your mind was
undoubtedly superior to anyone else's in the 12th century.

This letter, then, is about practical science, also called technology. Let
me start, perhaps at random, by talking about books. In the 15th
century Germany a certain man created a new process where he
assembled little carved letters, reverse image letters, in channels on a
board to make up a page. He inked that board and pressed it against
a blank paper. He could produce hundreds of identical pages in an
hour. Later, a machine improved the process still further, so tens of
thousands of copies could be produced in little time, and it permitted
a large variety of letter types and pictures as well.

Other machines soon bound the pages into books. By the 18th century there were millions of books around. Today, thousands of different books are produced every year, each in tens of thousands of copies.

Now, let me tell you about a different kind of machine. In the 18th century England, a man thought about pots of boiling water, covered by lids. He found that he could not keep the lid in place, the power of steam was too strong. Based on that principle, he created a machine in which water was constantly boiled. The steam forced a piston in a cylinder to move up and then (through switching the steam, by the machine itself, to the other end of the cylinder), move down again. The motion was then converted so that a wheel was turning around without cease, at high speed; that machine could then be utilized to do hundreds of functions previously requiring heavy human or animal power, or at best windmills, waterwheels.

The steam engine was soon installed on board of ships, there turning powerful propellers and replacing the need to row, or to depend on the vagaries of the wind. Bigger and bigger ships were built, ships that could cross the Atlantic Ocean in little over a week; the Mediterranean, from Spain to Palestine, in four days.

Also, iron roads were built across the lands; really, not roads but two thin strips of iron, mounted in a parallel mode on wooden slats. On those rails, huge iron steam engines were pulling coaches full of people and goods at very high speed. The Cairo-to-Jerusalem trip took about five hours. (Today, the trip can be made even faster, by other means; I'll tell you about that later.)

Soon, Man found a great need for good roads and bridges, for horseless carriages begun to proliferate. Man built small carriages, little boxes seating four or five people, and large coaches for fifty or more. At first, these were driven by steam engines, but that was found a clumsy mechanism, because of the need to shovel coal. But in the late 19th century, a different engine was invented, one that used a liquid fuel, something like oil or petroleum, only lighter. These vehicles can travel as fast as a hundred miles per hour, if the road is smooth, which it usually is. A gallon of this fuel is sufficient to drive the vehicle from Alexandria to Cairo; drive it fast, smoothly, quietly. A man or woman is needed to control it, to turn a steering wheel and to adjust the speed according to need; almost every person on earth has learned how to drive such an "automobile" or "car".

There are wide, smooth roads connecting all cities and towns, and also within towns the streets are wide, allowing a number of cars to go side-by-side. Broad bridges cross rivers, some are several miles long and allow cars in six or eight parallel lanes to cross side-by-side; so there may be hundreds of cars on the bridge at once, rushing across at tremendous speed. England will soon be connected to the continent through an underground tunnel, thousands of cars cross from Europe to Asia and back every hour through bridges at Constantinople, and before long, Europe may be linked to Africa by a long bridge at Gibraltar.

Yes, Man can build wondrous things. The tallest house I remember . seeing, in our days, was four stories high. Now Man builds some to 120 stories! (And the Lord does not confuse their tongues.) In these buildings, people get into small boxes that move them up and down very fast; they can reach the top in one minute.

Why would Man want to build tall houses like that? Well, there are so many people on earth, and very little space in the cities. People need those big buildings for living space, for working space. In a 120-story building, if its purpose was to provide lodging for people, about ten thousand families could live, each having several rooms, a fully equipped kitchen, a bathroom with hot and cold water running into a washbasin from pipes coming out of a wall, on demand; as well, a bathtub, also with hot and cold water; and a flush toilet that cleans itself. Actually, the usual purpose of those very tall buildings is not residential but commercial: people work there in offices.

But how to feed so many people? Especially, since there is a need for so large cities, taking away farmland? Well, there have been advances in agriculture as well—another science that I have not yet mentioned. Food is still produced on the fields, grain and fruit are harvested, animals fed and then slaughtered. But there are many machines that make such farm work easier, more productive. And increasingly, though still slowly, food production is moving inside, into buildings where artificial light and heat are utilized; it is a more expensive method, but one that does not depend on the vagaries of the weather, an important factor, especially in northern climate. All the work, of course, is done by machines.

Does the food taste as good as it did in our time? No, Master, it does not; and in the future of this world, in another hundred years, I think it will have even less taste. But people's expectation adjust. The important thing is, there is plenty of food; not too many of the world's over five billion people starve now, and soon, nobody will.

But talking about machinery, as I have just been: all the work that man had to do, but did not like, is now done by machines: all the heavy work, such as digging ditches, loading vehicles, carrying things up and down; all the repetitive work, such as making rope or thread, sewing cloth, adding up numbers, copying writing or pictures, milking cows, cleaning cloth and thousands of others. There are machines for cooking, cleaning rooms, writing, talking into, making music, treating the ill, even for making other machines.

What is the force that makes these machines work? Well, some very large machines are still driven by steam engines, or heavier versions of the internal combustion engine that drives the automobiles. Yet most of today's machines are driven by electricity.

Rabbi, I have already tried to tell you what electricity is, but it is very hard to grasp the concept, I think even for you. Yet it is an essential one, for the wonderful world of this 20th century would not have been possible without electricity.

So let us have another look at the idea. You are familiar with lightning. A thunderbolt strikes the ground from the clouds. It has terrible power, it can strike a man, or five, dead; it can set a house, or tree on fire. It is pure energy, electrical energy. Man has learned to capture this kind of energy, store it and use it again, slowly, under controlled circumstances.

Really, I don't want to mislead you; electricity does not actually come from captured lightning. Man can make it other ways, without having to depend on the weather. He makes it out of burning coal, wood, oil. He also makes it out of rapid rivers, waterfalls. These watermills turn something called "generators", things that have large magnets in them, electrical magnets, for electricity can generate magnetism as well. These generators create vast amounts of electricity which travel through thick wires at first, to distant cities, and from there, through thinner and thinner wires (it's a little like the blood circulatory system) to people's houses and work-places. On every wall of every room, there are some small holes. If you want to use electricity, want to "turn on" some machine, you put the wires of the machine into those holes, push a button, and it begins to work. And so, machines in a house will keep food cold until needed, then cook it, stir it while cooking, clean the house, heat it or cool it, keep it light at night, if desired, cut a person's hair, wash his teeth, keep his house secure from burglars (yes, those are still around).

Yes, electricity is a very useful, very powerful thing. It is also dangerous; if you don't use it carefully, it can hurt you or kill you just as a thunderbolt can. But not one out of a million people suffer such a fate, for people learn how to use electricity.

Let me tell you about still more things that electricity does for people. You see, most of what I have written so far about electricity had to do with harnessing its immense power. But it can also be used, in very weak versions, to carry messages.

We can send a letter to the other end of the world; riding on electricity, it will get there almost at the same time it was sent.

We can, using electricity, talk with a person in another country, or the next house, if we don't want to dress up and go there. The machine that does this is called "telephone".

We can see people and things happening at various parts of the world, on the front of boxes in our houses. These are called "television". I don't need to explain to you how these names have come about.

We can capture people's action and voices, pictures and sounds, watch and hear them later; watch and hear them again and again, whenever we want to.

We can watch stories—real ones and fictitious ones—told by story-tellers, we can see those stories about people, watch those peoples' lives as they happen, whether real or not (actors are playing the roles of real people). Sometimes millions of people watch the same stories, listen to the same real or fictitious events.

We can also use electricity to do complex calculations for us, or simple ones: add up columns of numbers, multiply by other number, divide, as well as perform higher level mathematical operations, instantaneously. These kinds of machines require so little electricity that there is no need for wires: they run on tiny packages of stored electricity, or sometimes simply by capturing the natural light and converting it to electricity. And these calculators are small, they fit into your palm; and they are cheap, every schoolchild has one.

Now, Master, I shall talk to you about something even more difficult to understand, but as important in the 21st century as electricity was in the 20th: "computers".

Computers are machines that operate on low-powered electricity, for no heavy work is involved; in fact, nothing physically moves, only information in the form of tiny electrical pulses.

The computer can do mathematical calculations; but it can do a lot more than that. It can store letters, a whole book even, in an area smaller than my fingernail. I can change anything in such a book, add pages, rearrange chapters; and when I am ready, it will print out the book on paper: if it is a very long book, it may take five or ten minutes. If I am not fully satisfied, I can change some things and ask the computer to print it again.

The computer can compare two sets of information, each containing millions of numbers or letters, and warn me if they differ anywhere. It can compare a plan with the actions taken and warn if there was a deviation.

The computer can help me evaluate several alternative courses of action and recommend the best decision. What kind of decision? Business matters, for example—what to buy, what to sell, for how much; travel decisions—what route to take, what vehicles to use; agricultural decisions—what to plant, where and when; architectural decisions—what materials to use for building the 120-story house; and thousands of others. It can tell us what to do in so many situations; in other cases, it will actually take direct action. How? It does not have arms and legs, it is not going anywhere; but it is connected to many other machines through electrical wires; it can send messages anywhere in the world, it can make things happen.

A computer thinks. Well, perhaps not the way humans think; but it does have a brain and—almost—a mind.

The brain is the machine itself: it can hold *information* in its memory and it can hold *instructions* in its memory as well. What kind of instructions? Well, whatever its master, Man, orders it to do. At the right time, it will carry out the instructions, typically doing something with the data it stores and with other data freshly received, producing new data, information for its master and perhaps direct instructions for other machines.

These machines, the computers, are sometimes called "hardware". The mind of the computer, if we can call it that, is the set of its instructions, which is called "software".

The computer, "animated" by its software, does not really think like a man or woman. It cannot feel (although it can be made to sense physical conditions); it has no emotions. It cannot get angry or happy. It cannot love.

But what it can do, it can do millions of times faster than man can.

Some computers are very large and expensive; others are small and cheap enough for almost anybody to be able to afford one. There are even smaller ones, with limited capabilities, these are parts of other machines, such as those that cook our food, cut our lawns, present us with moving pictures and sound in our homes.

Imagine, Master, we can travel in cars, while the computer tells us which is the best route, the least congested at this moment, how much fuel we'll need and have. Sitting there, we can be talking with somebody in another country on the telephone (for those electric signals used to carry information can travel though the air, taking advantage of some radiation, at the speed of light, without the need for wires). The car is heated or cooled, as necessary. Meanwhile, we can listen to music coming from somewhere in the world, music made by musicians right then, or, in other cases, recorded years earlier.

Now, Master, you are perhaps beginning to understand—no, not understand, but have a general idea, a concept—what kind of world is the world of the 20th century. Let me mention only a few more things.

People can travel from one place to another by still faster means: through the air. They sit in a big machine, "airplane", dozens or hundreds of people sit there. It has wings, but those don't move; it is powered by huge engines with their internal parts spinning strongly enough to keep the machine moving in the air (after all, a man would sink in the water, but rapid movement keeps him afloat; and, of course, birds are strong enough, relative to their weight, to stay up in the air). With a loud roar, it starts running forward on the ground, its speed increases, and when it is fast enough, it lifts into the air, and rises higher and higher, while moving forward faster and faster. It flies, eventually, at six or seven miles high. It can get from Cairo to Jerusalem in an hour; from Cairo to Cordoba, two hours are needed. To America, ten hours. Around the world, a 26,000-mile trip, we can fly in less than a day.

And that is not all. People are beginning, just now, to learn how to travel outside the earth, to its sister planets. One day, they will even reach other stars.

Rabbi! Man has travelled to the Moon! Man has walked on the Moon! There is no air there, so they had to wear special clothes with its own oxygen supply and heating, for it is unimaginably cold there. They walked around for days, then came back to earth!

Master, is all this good? I would so much value your opinion. I think it really is good; Man has been progressing steadily, moving ahead. Perhaps he is not happier than he was in our days. But much of the worst suffering is now eliminated.

Yet not all. There have been situations of horror and torment in the 20th century; man-made situations. I shall tell you about those, later.

And, before you make up your mind about the merits of all of these technological advances (I do hope that you'll approve), still, you should consider some other things.

Having understood the genes that regulate the reproduction of life, Man has now invented "genetic engineering". He can make new kinds of life-forms. For instance, a fruit that is half peach, half plum. An animal that is half lamb, half goat. Well, he could do some of these things even in our time. But now, soon, he will be able to manipulate human genes, so to be able to decide, first of all, to have a boy or a girl, according to choice; then, what kind of child to have, how tall, what colour eyes and hair, what disposition.

Master, is this a good thing?

Back in the 15th century, Man invented the "gun". That was a device somewhat like the bow, made out of iron and wood. It included an iron tube in which a hard metal projectile was placed; and behind it, a special powder which, when hit by a spark, exploded, driving the projectile through the tube at tremendous speed, fast enough to penetrate the body of a man some great distance away.

The gun was slowly improved. By the 19th century, it was small enough to fit in the palm of a man's—or woman's—hand. It did not need any spark: you just squeezed a lever, and the projectile flew.

Well, in the 20th century, there are many ways of using electricity to kill people. But they also have something else here. Nuclear energy—I have already mentioned it to you briefly.

Man can use nuclear energy peacefully, building dams, roads, letting a few ounces of matter do the work of millions of men. He can also use nuclear physics to generate useful radiation, for example, a type that heals certain types of cancer.

But then, there is the hostile use of nuclear energy. A few ounces of certain matter can be dropped onto a city from an airplane, or sent over by a large gun, perhaps from the opposite end of the earth; that handful of matter, upon hitting the ground, converts into energy, enough to make a city of any size burn up in a few seconds, disappear without a trace. The radiation that is created as a by-product kills many more people in the surrounding areas and even far away.

It has happened, twice. Since that time, now forty-three years ago, Man has been very careful with these nuclear weapons. But the largest countries have thousands of them, all ready to hit their enemy; they don't use them because of fear of retaliation.

Some people think that inevitably, one of these weapons will be used, perhaps by accident. Then the other country will retaliate, starting a chain of vengeance that will, in a matter of a few hours or days, kill all people on earth, through nuclear explosions or radiation.

I do not think so, Master. I think that God, praised be He, watches over the people; He has plans for Man and will not permit such a horrible thing to happen, But I would so much like to know your opinion.

The truest of your devoted servants

Yusuf ben Yehudah ibn-Sham`un

SCIENCE: YOUR ENEMY OR FRIEND?

SCIENCE AND RELIGION: DIVERGENCE AND CONVERGENCE

26 Elul 5748 / September 8, 1988

To B'Rabbi Moshe ben Rabbi Maimon ha-Sfaradi,
Fostat, Egypt

My honoured Rabbi:

I realize that I must have placed a grave burden upon you, not only by the confusing and probably shocking information in my last two letters, but also by their sheer volume. I know how hard you work treating patients in the Sultan's court, and then, late in the evening, when you finally get home, with the private patients waiting there —you hardly have time eating your only meal of the day. At the end of that work, you are dead tired; yet that is the only time to read by candlelight. Thank the Lord that He chose to maintain your eyesight in reasonable condition. And so I am concerned about how you would find the time to read my long letters, let alone to think about these new things?

So, from now on, I shall attempt to write shorter letters, dealing only with one topic. Yet I may not always succeed: some of the topics are necessarily extensive; I'll try to break them in two halves, if possible. The next two letters will be really two halves of one topic. Today, I would like to write to you about some more of my thoughts on science; really, science and religion. Or, if you prefer, the age-old question of reason and faith.

As you may have gathered, science (philosophy to your thinking) has progressed greatly since our age. I have told you about a number of great discoveries and also inventions. But I think that these things, while individually they may do a lot to improve Man's life, don't come close to the ideal function of science, if they don't add up to something, a new understanding of the basic questions about Man, about God, about the Universe, about metaphysics, if you like.

Well, scientists have learned many facts about those basic questions, especially about the origins of the Universe and the creation of Man. Let me try to summarize what they think they know today. I shall repeat myself a little, but it may be necessary, for I am now trying to bring the relevant events together. (Actually, Master, I shall probably do so several more times in the course of these letters, as I'll be trying to develop, with you, a new and rational understanding of those all-important, basic questions.)

It seems that space itself did not exist before the Universe was created. Space, and perhaps even time, may have been created together with matter and energy. So even saying something about "before" the creation may be meaningless in our mind, and on our terms if time, as we conceive of it, did not exist "before". (What this world needs is more metaphysicians, to answer these questions.) About seventeen billion years ago, for undetermined reason, matter suddenly appeared in a tremendous explosion. In the first second, most of that material changed into "photons", sub-atomic units that form the basis of light, and could be considered half-way between matter and energy.

In the next few seconds, much of this huge amount of photons condensed into the lightest elements—hydrogen and some helium —which were, at the same time, hurled out into space at very high speed.

During the next interval, matter condensed further from swirling nebulae, gases of protons which are the nuclei of hydrogen atoms. Protogalaxies emerged and, eventually, nuclear furnaces—stars

—became ignited, generating heat and light in the process, as well as heavier elements. While earlier, energy became matter, now some of the matter changed back to energy. Some of these suns captured smaller, inert bodies as satellites on circular or elliptical courses spinning around them, planets; thus solar systems appeared. Millions of such suns were ordered into galaxies, in the shape of flat disks, with these suns spiralling around a centre that is not yet well-understood.

Our Sun did not appear until much later, after many-many other stars were born and died, generating much-needed heavy elements in the process; otherwise, there could have been no life on earth.

On the third planet of our Sun, certain elements came together in specific combinations, perhaps as a result of lightning and other weather conditions. Certain scientists (but not all; nor the best ones, I think) believe that this has also happened on millions of other planets, of other suns, of other galaxies. What was created was a combination of carbon, nitrogen, oxygen and hydrogen to form a group of chemicals called "amino acids". Having a good supply of those, they assembled in chains called "proteins", of different length and order. These, in turn formed tiny globules called "cells". Those became the basic building materials of all living beings. A cell can split into two identical cells, so soon you'll have four, eight, sixteen; before you notice, there are billions of cells that comprise a man or a tree.

You will ask, why? Why would the elements behave that way, why would amino acids form, and then proteins and later cells? Don't ask the scientists, they will shrug their shoulders and claim that this is the way it works, that is the law of nature. I shall have more to say about those scientists, about that law later on.

The first living beings were very simple things, small, transparent microorganisms swimming in the sea. After millions of years, these developed into increasingly complex organizations. That is a most important discovery of science. Aristotle came to the conclusion that all life forms are different versions, different levels of development of the same principle. But his teaching was conveniently forgotten, denied, mainly by the religious authorities of our days and later.

Finally, in the 19th century, an Englishman, a disciple of Aristotle, determined that a species of plants or animals can develop into another one, a different species. This is his theory: the driving force behind such transformation is the environment: under nearly impossible circumstances, only those individuals which are the fittest for those specific conditions will survive and regenerate. If such conditions persist over many generations, the species (at least at that location) will either perish or change into a different one. He called this process "natural selection".

For example, a fish cannot exist on dry land. But there are minute differences between the makeup of every individual fish, just as every individual human is different; this is due to very small changes in the coded material in every cell that determines the characteristics of individuals; these changes are called "random mutations", alterations of the genetic code that occur all the time. Most of these changes result in inferior beings, unfit for the environment; these will soon die out. Yet some others thrive in difficult environments; these are reenforced and become major hereditary variations of the species. And so, some fish may have a certain type of gill that is similar to a lung, permitting it to stay on dry land for longer time. Also, some fish may have strong fins which it can use to propel itself on land. There are such fish today. And were circumstances forcing fish out of the sea, those best equipped with the appropriate gills and fins would survive for a long time. Given a chance to procreate, their offspring, when exposed to similar (perhaps seasonal) peril, would be better equipped to cope; more of them would survive, easier, for longer time on land. In perhaps a hundred generations, or ten thousand, who knows, a land animal, some kind of a reptile, would emerge.

More sudden changes can also happen, through cataclysmic changes in the environment, say a sudden increase of the nuclear radiation of the Sun; but let us not discuss that now; enough to note that this kind of change often causes the extinction not only of a species of animals or plants, but that of a whole family of species.

So, according to the Englishman and his followers, species gradually or rapidly change into others, reaching the point where common offsprings are no longer possible. First, there were sea creatures of a single cell. From there, larger and larger, increasingly complex animals and plants developed; at a certain point, the fish became the highest level of all animals in the sea. Climbing to the ground, we don't know for what reason, the reptiles emerged; and from there, various invertebrates and vertebrates, including some who found survival through flapping leathery "arms" and staying in the air for a long time. The time came when the best chance for survival of the species involved protection of the eggs to the point of carrying the fertilized eggs in the mother's body: mammals. (Strangely, some of these mammals found their way back to the sea.)

The highest non-conscious mammals are the large apes—gibbons, gorillas, chimpanzees, orangutans. These are the most intelligent animals, they can be taught to read simple sign language and even to express themselves through similar means.

Eventually, one form of ape learned how to make a tool, how to light a fire, how to talk to another in meaningful sounds—Homo Sapiens was born.

That is not how we learned the creation of Man, Rabbi. But is it true? Well, yes and no. Species do develop from other species, though not the way Mr. Darwin imagined, nor yet according to the ideas of his followers, the "Neo-Darwinians". I may offer a variation to the story later.

Please, Master, do not reject the entire notion for now, if only for Aristotle's sake; I shall attempt to convince you later. Please keep an open mind while I tell you about scientists and theologians.

There has been this battle of words going on for the last hundred years. On the one side are the scientists and other rational people, many of them atheists. On the other side are all men of religion —Jews, Christians, Muslims and others—who hate each other fiercely. But these latter people agree that in any conflict between scripture and science, the former must be correct.

Specifically, these men of religion claim that God created the first man, Adam, and then the first woman, Eve, as stated explicitly (if redundantly and conflictingly) in Genesis. Many would insist that this happened 5748 years ago.

But scientists say that Man appeared on earth as a group, ascending from an ape-like creature millions of years ago.

There are two groups of religious thinkers. The pragmatists teach Scriptures, yet will not oppose those proclaiming the scientific theory. Somehow, they pretend that those are two different way of looking at things, both valid; the two should be kept separate, with no attempt of integration. Some of the greatest philosophers of the last few centuries have supported this view. Religious thinkers of this persuasion accept the findings of science, yet preach the words of God, as written. I believe that, deep down, these "men of God" don't believe, not only in Scripture but in God Himself. If He does not exist, then why worry about the rationality of His words? But they strongly believe in tradition, a way of life that has been governed—albeit with an ever weakening reign—by the written law and, in the case of Judaism, oral one as well.

The other group of religious thinkers, or leaders, are the funda-mentalists. They insist that God's words are true, every single one of them, that Scripture is inerrant, cannot be questioned. There is no room for interpretation. If God said He created the world in six days, then it was six days, 144 hours, not less, not more.

When scientists discovered in the early 16th century that the earth was moving around the Sun, the Christian church rejected the concept, considering it a contradiction to Scripture. A leading exponent of the new idea was actually forced to recant. Later, of course, they had to admit that they were wrong. Master, they have admitted such errors so many times, but always hundreds of years too late, always after causing untold misery by their shortsightedness.

Yes, priests and rabbis and mullahs have been obtuse, but so have been scientists. They thought that by proving specific words in the Bible incorrect, they can repudiate scripture and through that, prove the non-existence of God.

Many scientists have gone as far as trying to create life artificially, to prove that it could have appeared on earth by accident; of course, with no success. Others insist that, since evolution of life out of inorganic material is simply a natural phenomenon, there must be life on billions of planets in the universe, and have been spending time, effort and public funds in finding such life outside earth.

Were you to conclude, Rabbi, that despite all his new knowledge, discoveries and inventions, today's man is every bit as stupid as he was in our days, I would not disagree.

But back to ourselves. How did we handle an apparent contradiction between reason and revelation? Very sensibly, I think. You insisted that Scripture should be read in its intent, not in its words. You said, many times, that the Torah speaks the language of Man. The Lord, blessed be His name, tells us things beyond our understanding, in allegorical language that we can grasp.

The six days of creation, for example: some of those days may have taken a fraction of a second—how do you explain it to primitive man?

Other days may have taken millions of years, or billions; again, early man did not understand those numbers.

The Lord could have talked about eras, epochs, instead of days. But the words "era", "epoch" may not have been known in that early age. The only time units that man was familiar with were the day, the Sun's cycle; the month, the Moon's cycle, a little less well-defined; and the year, not as important for people living in the south, before the days of agriculture, than to modern- day northerners. And so the clearest, most obvious unit, the day, was the time-unit He decided to use.

Adam, then, was not one person, but many. The story about Eve, the apple and the serpent was, as we have recognized all along, just that, a story, Aggadah. A legend. Undoubtedly, there was a reason for it; the concept of the original sin, a cornerstone of Christian guilt, was based on that; without it, Christianity would not have been possible either in theory or in practice. And we can reasonably assume that the spread of Christianity was something that the Lord desired, or it would not have happened.

Meanwhile, though, while arguing about how many days it took the Lord to create the Universe, scientists completely miss the fact that obviously He did create it; created the earth, life on the earth, Man.

How did He do it? Very much as the scientists understand it, or would understand it if they would choose to open their eyes. And very much as it is described in Scripture, as men of religion would understand it if they were not afraid to do so. I will show you, later, a brief history of the Universe that, apart from a few minor exception of wording and order, describes what is in the first chapter of Genesis; yet one that today's scientists would have some trouble opposing.

Just one aspect, as an example: God created animals first (we don't know in what order, from the book, but we do know from science) and then Man. Obviously, lower forms were created before higher ones. How did He move from one animal to the other, from ape to Man? Clearly, through evolution, directed by Him, using the methods of "random mutation" and "natural selection".

Man has been able to manipulate plant and animal species, create new forms, ones better suited for a particular need, certain environments. Do men of religion not think that God could have done the same? That He could have done it on a much higher scale?

The trouble is, my Master, sometimes it seems that not only scientists don't believe in God, but clergymen, people of religion don't, either. I think that any minister, priest or rabbi who insists on Scripture's verbatim validity, yet knows the truth of the science of creation, effectively denies not only the Words of God, but His very existence.

Rabbi, you always wanted to reconcile faith and reason. I think one must: anyone not trying to do so can believe only in one, or more likely, neither.

The truest of your devoted servants

Yusuf ben Yehudah ibn-Sham`un

HAS SCIENCE PROVEN GOD'S EXISTENCE?

29 Tishri 5749 / October 10, 1988

To B'Rabbi Moshe ben Rabbi Maimon ha-Sfaradi,
Fostat, Egypt

My honoured Master:

In my last letter to you, I wrote about the short-sightedness of certain type of people, men of science and of religion. I wanted to tell you, now, about a few who do have vision, who can not only reconcile God's words with Man's knowledge, but actually use that knowledge to confirm God's words.

There are two ways of proving God's existence scientifically. One of the arguments is based on a law of physics that was established in the 19th century. The other is a late 20th century discovery.

The former is called the second law of thermodynamics, that branch of physics that deal with the behaviour of objects when heated. It states that the level of usable energy, in any closed system, constantly decreases, while entropy, or the state of disorder, constantly increases.

In the words of the layman, it is easy to understand, I think, that the total usable energy (that is, energy that is capable of flowing from higher to lower level, while producing work in the process) in the Universe becomes less and less, until it will all dissipate; what we'll have, instead, is absolute entropy or chaos. That was the state of the world right after its creation, and that is where it will return.

Put still more simply, the law says that complicated things tend to fall apart. To create something highly complex requires a high level of energy or effort. Eventually, for one reason or another, that complex thing returns to its most simple components, even to the level where each elementary component is on its own, with no power left to bind it to other components.

There is an old English nursery rhyme, dealing with a fabled character named Humpty Dumpty. This character—in illustrations usually depicted as an egg—fell off a wall, got smashed, and hosts of people could not put him together again. Really, Rabbi, all you need to do is think of an egg. It is easy to break, but no matter how you shake the broken egg, it will never re-assemble itself, even by accident, into a whole egg.

No, the natural tendency of the world is to fall apart, to decay. So how did complex things—galaxies, solar systems, proteins, genes, cells, plants, animals, Man—how did they come about? The fascinating thing is that we have learned about this by the very scientists who, earlier, tried to disprove God's existence through science. They would have said, that while they had no idea about galaxies and solar systems, with regard to aspects of life, "those evolved according to the law of random mutation and natural selection", that is, by the survival of the fittest. And they were almost right. Only, those mutations were not so random; and the selection process was not quite "natural". For the trend has been to move from simple to complex, and that goes directly against the law of entropy—at least in a closed system. (I shall have more to say about that in another letter, much later, with the help of the Lord, blessed be his name.)

Further, the law of random mutation and natural selection, as formally stated, makes no sense at all when talking about the appearance of the first living being, first cell, first gene. Such a complex organization simply cannot evolve, cannot emerge naturally, because that is forbidden by second law of thermodynamics.

There have been many scientists who wanted to disprove God's work and therefore His existence. Large amount of scientific experimental work has taken place, to create artificial conditions under which life could (it was hoped) emerge naturally.

Needless to say, scientists have not succeeded in this. But were they even to succeed, that would only prove that with the injection of vast amount of external energy into a closed system, and especially with the use of human intelligence, which is the highest level of complexity that we know, a set of circumstances could be established suitable for bringing about relatively simple life, complex but not nearly as complex as the minds that created it. Well, we already knew that! That is what the Holy One, blessed is He, has done here on earth. But that is not a natural phenomenon! It is the opposite, a totally artificial process.

This is what I mean, my Master, by saying that scientists, the very ones that wanted to disprove God's existence, showed us how He created life and intelligence on earth.

The second proof, the 20th century discovery, has to do with the ever increasing understanding of how the world was created. It is now generally accepted that this happened in the so-called "big bang", some seventeen billion years ago. But what scientists have recently discovered is that no big bang could have produced a stable universe, unless its original conditions were "fine-tuned", set to very precise accuracy, in the first instance. Even were that done so, the universe could not possibly support life, unless that precision was increased still further, much further—when having created, say, two specific sub-atomic particles, it was essential that for every one billion of one there should be exactly one-billion-and-one of the other. Hundreds, thousands of other such fine setting were required, things adjusted down to billionth of billionth of degrees for the universe alone, and much finer for life and finer still for intelligence.

So do you see, my Master, what has happened? Science has proved that God exists, with a higher certainty than most accepted scientific dogma. But, can you imagine what happened next? They, at least the majority of the scientists, hid this fact, hoped that the average person will not notice it until they can undo the proof by more science. Of course, they cannot! The more they search for ways the universe and life in it and intelligence could have come about "by itself", the more they prove that only God could have done it.

Yet, they have succeeded in hiding the truth from the average person. A the end of the 20th century, probably not one out of a million people knows that God's existence has been demonstrated scientifically. Indeed, most people seriously believe that science and theology are at loggerheads, that you can only believe in God if you pretend that science does not exist, yet we all know that science is right, so all this "religion-thing" is just pretense, make-believe, at best tradition, but it is not to be taken seriously.

How sad! Why is that so? Why are so many scientists, supposedly intelligent people, so short-sighted, so misguided?

Perhaps what I said earlier about scientists being willing to reject obsolete theories, adopt new ones when proved superior—perhaps I was too optimistic about them. They may be, after all, not that much more flexible than men of religion.

The truest of your devoted servants

Yusuf ben Yehudah ibn-Sham`un

THE NEW WORLD:

HISTORY AND GEOGRAPHY

9 Heshvan 5749 / October 20, 1988

To B'Rabbi Moshe ben Rabbi Maimon ha-Sfaradi,
Fostat, Egypt

My honoured Master:

With due respect for your distaste for history (for I think you considered it a waste of time), I believe that I must deal with it now, when trying to explain to you how we got where we are. Believe me, Rabbi, history is very important; more than any nation on earth, we can call ourselves the people of history.

I shall try to make sense of what has happened on earth between the late 12th century that we knew a little (the early 13th was not really different, in retrospect) and the late 20th century where I now find myself. Can I squeeze the history of the human race, and also geography, for the former makes no sense without the latter, into one letter? A very long one, I am afraid; I shall try to break in into two, if I can.

I shall have to be quite specific about geography. I shall describe each continent as they are today; so that when I talk to you, later, about what happened, say, in Switzerland in the 13th century, you shall understand what part of the world I am talking about.

There are the following continents: Europe, Asia, Africa, North America, South America and Australia (there is still another continent, under the permanent snow of the South Pole of the earth; nobody lives there except a few explorers).

Europe has been, for most of the past eight centuries, the centre of the civilized world. Here is an outline of the continent:

Currently, the most important countries in Europe are England, France, Germany and the Soviet Union (formerly, and maybe soon again, Russia). Italy and lately Spain also wield considerable influence.

Asia is the most populous of all continents. Much of Asia is also the poorest.

This continent includes two huge countries: the Soviet Union (yes, also in Europe) and China. India, while not so large in size, has the second largest population of the world.

And then, this continent includes a very small, but for us, very important country: Israel, the land of our fathers and of our sons. Eretz Yisrael is re-established after 1900 years, praised be the Lord.

Africa was once important because of the advanced civilization on its
northern extreme. Over the last eight centuries, "our" continent has
declined into poverty and insignificance.

While no country here carries a world-wide influence, South Africa is
often in the news as a land of white settlers in conflict with a hostile
black population, by now the majority. The northern third of the continent is still occupied by Arab lands.

North America is connected to its southern sister through an isthmus (which holds six countries itself). The continent consists of only three very large lands:

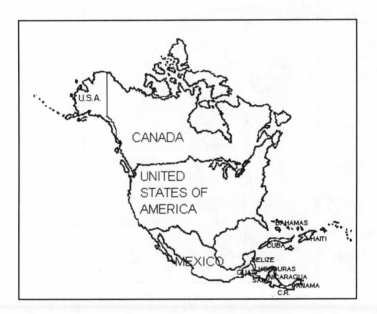

The United States of America, or U.S.A., is the most important country of the world. The language there is English, as is in Canada, where French is spoken is some areas. Mexico is a Spanish-speaking country, as are six of the seven smaller ones on the isthmus.

South America, along with its northern counterpart, was discovered in
the early 16th century.

The largest and perhaps most important country is Brazil, a Por-
tuguese-speaking land. All of the other countries are Spanish-speaking.

Australia and *New Zealand* were discovered more recently and settled only for two centuries.

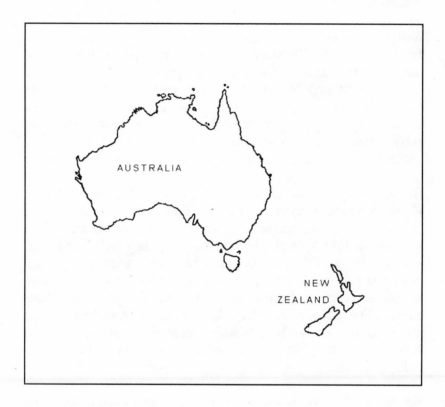

Both of these lands are populated by English-speaking people. Australia is a country of medium importance in the world today. It is located directly south-east of the Asian continent, at a not too great distance.

Now, my Master, that you know the geography of the earth (at least the political geography, as they call it today, for I have said nothing about the physical or natural geography), I shall attempt to tell you about a few of the most important events that have shaped human destiny over the last eight centuries.

Well, let us start with Spain. The recovery of its various parts from the Arab rulers by Christian kings started during our lifetime, and lasted over two centuries. Andalusia suffered very heavily from the re-conquest; it was beaten into poverty and its situation has not improved much to this day. The importance of the re-conquest movement became secondary to unification as Arab power faded; and today, Spain is actually proud of its Arabic heritage (and also of its Jewish heritage, after centuries of systematic murder of the Jews).

The weakening of Arab role in Spain coincided with the decline of the Muslim thinking everywhere. I like to think that there, as in most places in the world, people made outstanding political as well as economic and intellectual achievements while they had a significant Jewish segment of their population. Once they started to persecute, expel and kill the Jews, the country inevitably begun to decline, collapse and lose significance on the world scale. That certainly happened in Spain, twice, under the Muslims and, later, under Christian rule. And you know about Islamic persecutions that we suffered through in North Africa; by the 14th century, and right though the 20th, North Africa became, and remained, a poor and backward land.

Yes, the Jewish population re-established itself in Spain under the various Christian kings during the 13th and 14th centuries. But in the 14th and 15th, persecutions started again, or shall I say continued? 1492 was a fateful year. That year saw the formal end of the Moorish occupation of Spain, yes, after 800 years of Islamic rule all of Spain became Christian. Also in that year the Ferdinand and Isabella, the so-called "Catholic Kings", who married and united Castille with Aragon (as well as Granada and Navarra) financed a naval expedition for the reaching of Asia, sailing westwards, a venture undertaken, as

I've already told you, by the Jewish explorer, Christobal Colon. And in that same year the Jews were expelled from Spain—at least those Jews who did not convert to Christianity. The ones that did could stay, but if they were caught practicing their Jewish religion—which most did—they were tortured and then executed by burning at the stake by a Christian institution called "Inquisition".

Meanwhile, Columbus' expedition was successful beyond expectation, even though he died without realizing that he discovered a new continent (really, two) and not reached Asia. During the next two centuries, the Spanish occupied much of South and Central America (the isthmus), killing most of the natives, plundering their wealth and becoming weaker, not stronger, in the process. (You remember, it had no Jews by that time.) Other European countries decided to try their luck on the American continents: Portugal, England, France, Holland.

Eventually, Spain lost some important wars against England, while its American colonies liberated themselves, and Spain declined into a small and unimportant country. After centuries, it may overcome that sorry state in the near future.

Spain's small European colonies, Flanders and the "low lands", on the seashore north of France, freed themselves—only to be oppressed by a series of other foreign occupiers; Belgium became independent only in the 19th century, along with its northern neighbour, Holland. These small countries have always been important on the world scene, perhaps because of their sizable Jewish population. They established strong naval forces and numerous colonies around the world. Even after those were freed in the 20th century—there are no more colonies today, at least not formal ones, I'll tell you about oppressed countries nominally independent—Holland and Belgium remained strong industrial and commercial lands.

England (really, Great Britain, including Scotland to the north and parts of Ireland) gained strength steadily over the centuries; by the 19th, it was the most important, strongest, richest country in the world

with a large naval force, powerful industry, innovative entrepreneur-
ship, excellent finance and high level of civilization. For a while,
most of North America was an English colony. They fought there,
successfully, against the Spanish in the south (what is now Mexico)
and against the French in the north (eastern Canada). They also
colonized Australia and New Zealand.

Gaul also grew in strength: the former land of the Franks, united with
Provence, Savoy, Lorraine and Aquitaine, now called France, became
a power to reckon with. During the 15th to 18th century, it was the
world centre of civilization and might. The end of that era was
spectacular: it ended in a great, bloody revolution of the common
people, with royalty and aristocrats slaughtered without mercy, along
with anybody suspected or denounced. A republic was established
that, with periods of notable exception, has lasted to these days.
France also managed to acquire some important colonies in America,
Africa and elsewhere, which it lost recently.

The Holy Roman Empire shrank and eventually fell apart. Its northern
lands are now Germany. Its middle became another German-speaking
land, Austria. It lost its western provinces to France, as I've shown.
Its eastern territories are now semi-independent Slavic states; while the
south is now part of the united land of Italy.

Germany was not a fully unified country in our days, and while strong
central power did evolve soon after that, over the centuries German
history was mainly a succession of joining and seceding forces. The
principalities did not unite until the 19th century. At that time,
Germany became important due to three characteristics of its people:
their diligence and industriousness, striving for excellence; their
outstanding abilities in the arts, especially music and literature; and
their bloodthirsty cruelty. Even in our time, the Germans were famous
for their inhumanity; and while it was hoped that civilization would
tame those brutal tendencies over the centuries, they erupted in the
20th century like a volcano. I shall tell you more about that in my
next letter.

Italy is another land that was created by the association of various principalities, the earlier territories of the Papal States, Naples, Sicily and the southern flank of the Holy Roman Empire. It is also a land of art and beauty; its people are also known of their industriousness; they blissfully lack the brutality of the Germans. The great power of ancient Rome is, of course, long gone. In the 19th and 20th centuries Italy did accumulate a small collection of colonies, but was itself occupied over the centuries.

In the capital city of Italy, Rome, there is a small enclave, the same now as in our time: the Vatican. It is the spiritual headquarter of the Christian world. Well, not exactly. Like all major religions, the Christian creed has split up, again and again. The creed that is ruled from the Vatican is the Roman Catholic church. It is the largest, most powerful in the world, with some 800 million adherents.

In the 16th century, in Germany and Switzerland a movement arose that objected to the worldly power, wealth and corruption of the church fathers. In their own cities, and soon countries, including also England, they overthrew the power of the Vatican and established Protestantism, itself a collection of several distinct creeds by now probably a hundred. Ideologically, they accept most of the tenets of Christianity, such as the divinity of Jesus Christ and the concept of the Trinity. They also accept the Immaculate Conception, but do not revere Mary, the Mother of Jesus, as a demi-god in her own right. Their liturgy tends to be more simple; and they have less complex church hierarchy and less central control.

Today, and for the last several centuries, practically all of Europe, the Americas and Australia are Christian lands, as are numerous countries in Africa and Asia.

Yet the strength of religion, on the whole, has waned over the last 200 years, in Christian lands as well as among Muslims, Hindus, Buddhists and certainly Jews. I shall write many letters to you about the attitude of the Jews of this age towards the commandments, towards Torah.

The vast land spanning Europe and Asia on the maps is the Soviet Union. People think of it as Russia, even though it includes some fourteen other countries, held together (against their wish) by a force based on a strange ideology called "Communism". That force seems to be disintegrating just about now, as I am writing these letters.

Most of the European countries were important at one time or another; their power grew, and then melted away. Portugal had many colonies, I have mentioned Brazil, the largest one; now they are all independent, leaving Portugal one of the poorest, least significant countries of Europe. (Mind you, poverty in Europe would still be viewed as an extravagance of richness from a typical African or Asian country.) Hungary ruled half of Europe in the 14th century; now it is an unimportant, small country. Turkey, the land of the Ottoman and Seljuk Turks, and what remained of Byzantium, sent its troops, in a second wave of Islamic expansion, into the Balkan peninsula, into Hungary, threatening Austria and much of central Europe form the 15th to the 17th century; now Turkey is also small, carrying no international weight. It has the potential to rise again.

Switzerland overthrew the Austrian occupying force in the 13th century and established a republic, one that has worked admirably well ever since. It is a tiny but exceedingly wealthy country today. In the north, the Scandinavian lands of Norway, Sweden and Denmark, after centuries of minor warfare (in the case of Sweden, sometimes reaching deep into Russia), are now peaceful, rich countries, as is neighbouring Finland.

Poland, which had a very large Jewish population from our time until the mid-20th century, but nearly zero today, is one of the countries recently freed from Communist occupation. Others are Bohemia and Moravia, with Slovakia now joint as Czechoslovakia; Hungary; Yugoslavia; Romania (you may recall the Wallachs) and Bulgaria. Other then Poland and Hungary (and in a cultural sense, the land of the Czechs), these countries have never been influential in world history.

Greece! What does it mean to us? Mathematics, medicine, astronomy and so many other sciences. Philosophy, metaphysics. Experimentation with forms of civic rule including democracy, which is the only acceptable form of government in the world today; some countries practice it earnestly, others pay lip service to it. And then, Homer, Aristophanes; poetry, drama. Music. It was the seed of civilization for the world, reason came from Greece just as faith came from our land of Israel. Then a little later, Byzantium was very important as a bastion of the eastern Christian empire up to our age; Constantinople was the last gathering place for Crusaders before attacking the Muslim-occupied Holy Land in eight or nine waves, (you recall the first two; the last took place in the early 14th century). Today, Constantinople is part of Turkey; Greece is a not very important part of the Balkan peninsula.

Master, there is so much more to tell you, even at this superficial level. I have not yet said much about Russia; what happened there may have paved the way for the German horrors of the 20th century. Let me relate those things to you in my next letter.

The truest of your devoted servants

Yusuf ben Yehudah ibn-Sham`un

HISTORY AND GEOGRAPHY (cont.)

16 Heshvan 5749 / October 27, 1988

To B'Rabbi Moshe ben Rabbi Maimon ha-Sfaradi,
Fostat, Egypt

My honoured Master:

This is the second half of the letter telling you about what happened
to the world in the last eight centuries. You will be interested, I think,
in hearing about Russia and Germany, and some of the horrors they
have perpetrated in the 20th century. I also owe you some more
details about other parts of the world.

For centuries, Russia—the term was sometimes used to include the
Ukraine and White Russia—was a large land consisting of several
relatively weak, quasi-independent nations that constantly threatened
but seldom seriously hurt others, except our people, the Jews. (The
grateful population of Ukraine has erected their leaders statues for
killing Jews.) But, over time, Russia grew in importance until in the
19th century its rulers even wanted to adapt to western ways, but with
minimum success.

So how did that land become, for a while, the second most important
power in the world? I'll tell you, Rabbi. The story starts in 19th
century Germany.

Why the Germans hated our people so much, I am not sure. We have
been persecuted almost everywhere in the world, at one time or
another, and as one result, we have got used to it. So when agitators

blamed Jews for every ill in the world, typically to deflect attention from their own shortcomings, we just shrugged our shoulders, saying, let them talk, it won't make any difference. But it did. Earlier, in the 14th century, when bubonic plague, a terrible pestilence, killed a third of Europe's population, we were blamed and slaughtered as a "punishment". And the Russians themselves used us as the scapegoats for all of their problems; in the 17th century, they rode through much of eastern Europe, killing a large part of the Jewish population of the Slavic lands. Still, we have never learnt.

Even before the emergence of monstrous antisemitic leaders of Germany, a self-hating half-Jew, by the name of Marx, came to fame. He listened to the worst things said about the Jews and he believed those things without questioning. For the worst things had to do with money.

In those days, Jews were getting wealthy. An entirely new economic structure came into being, centered not so much on agriculture anymore, but commerce and, especially, industry. They called this structure "capitalism". Goods were made in large buildings, so-called factories, by workers and machines. These workers lived under miserable conditions, the sons of peasants in the first generation, then they evolved into a new class, the "proletariat". Their lives were pitiable: hard work, long hours, little pay. Yet they were not slaves; they were free men and women.

As things turned out (and I am jumping ahead to a 20th century vantage point now, for a moment) their lot, while hard, improved constantly over the last 200 years. Without fail, the poor has been getting richer, while the rich has been getting poorer, with the re-sulting erosion of financial differentiation between classes; indeed, erosion of any class structure. The working class today, to the extent that it can be distinguished from the middle class (not very well known in our age, this class constitutes over 90 percent of the population in all western countries) is really rich. Most have their own houses, furniture and all kinds of goods, with their children attending schools, even universities—few people in our age lived as well.

This development should have been foreseen in the 19th century, for that is what has made capitalism into the great success that it has become: greatly enlarged customer base. Rather than, say, a thousand customers, today millions, sometimes hundreds of millions participate in the economic life of a country; in the "Western world", these "ex-proletarians", workers in factories, manufacture the goods being sold to the self-same million or hundreds of millions. And little physical work is involved (for that is done by heavy machinery); the typical man or woman works seven and a half hours a day, five days a week, 48 weeks a year.

However, none of this has been understood in the 19th century. The agitator Marx saw the facts to be exactly the opposite to the reality: he believed that the rich were getting richer, the poor poorer. On that basis, he started to spread his hate-messages around: hate towards the capitalists, owners of the industry and commerce, hate towards the Jews.

His ideas spread and festered; and erupted their poisonous infection in two major trends in the 20th century: Communism and Nazism.

Communism was born in Russia, in 1917. Circumstances were right: a major war, with Russia, England and France on the one side, Germany, Austria and Hungary on the other, had been dragging on for three years; people were suffering and disenchanted. (This was called the "World War", later re-labelled "First World War", for there was a second.) Marx predicted that popular revolutions will overthrow the capitalistic systems in the rich, industrialized countries. But what happened instead, that under the leadership of his followers, such a revolution overthrew a feudalistic system in a poor, agricultural land, Russia.

As seems to happen in revolutions, it soon turned around and fed on itself. In a wave of violence, the revolutionary leaders were exiled or killed (or both) by a band of murderers, who then grabbed power to their clique, the Communist Party.

Communism became a brutal rule of terror, ostensibly performing atrocities "in the name of the proletariat". That class had little to do with the party, except to die in its name. But it was mainly the peasants who died, by the millions: they could not be won over, they had to perish.

Gaining strength, Russia occupied several neighbouring countries and created the Soviet Union, meaning union of the councils. In all, the Communist Party ruled with terror. Their idea was to extend that rule to all parts of the world, and they have been scheming towards the achievement of that objective, from the beginning until quite recently.

A term used in the 20th century for totalitarian, militaristic regimes with no respect for human values, not even for human life, is "fascism". The Soviet Union became a fascist state. But certainly not the only fascist state of this century; there have been others, foremost among them Germany.

For in this century, Germany became increasingly militaristic, reflecting perhaps some inherent character flaw of the people. The First World War ended in their defeat, but not destruction. Increasingly, the Jews were blamed for all of Germany's troubles. Around 1930 a murderer worse than Haman, worse than Antiochus, worse than Hadrian, (even worse than Chmielnitzki, the 17th century Ukrainian butcher) arose, by the name of Hitler; and managed to incite practically all of the Germans, some eighty million of them, to attack the Jews. This took the form of rounding up defenceless Jewish people, first in Germany and Austria and then, when it became obvious that this will not achieve the eradication of the Jewish nation, then in a dozen other countries attacked and conquered by Germany, apparently for the specific reason of finding and killing Jews there. The Second World War started, for the express reason of destroying world Jewry!

Men, women and children were collected by the hundreds, thousands and taken to camps in Germany, Austria, Poland, where they were systematically slaughtered. People by the thousands, by the hundreds of thousands, were processed like products in factories, from railroad freight cars to camps to gas chambers to furnaces and mass graves! The mind refuses to accept the reality of the monstrous concept; yet we must constantly tell ourselves, remind ourselves that it really happened. It happened, in the modern, civilized 20th century. All told, about six million European Jews perished over a six-year period.

But, you ask, who was on the other side of the war? Was it a war against the Jews only? If so, why would they call it a world war? No, there were others than the Jews against Germany. On the Germans' side were the Austrians, Hungarians, Romanians and Italians (the term "fascism" originated in Italy). The main opposing countries were England, France, the Soviet Union, the United States of America, Canada, Australia, New Zealand and others. But these countries joined the war not out of any sympathy for the Jews; no, they were worried—for good reason—that Hitler, in his increasing rage of madness, will attack and conquer their lands. Most of Europe was already under German rule. In Asia, the Germans acquired a powerful and almost equally fanatical ally in Japan, which threatened most countries in the area between Asia and America, the Pacific Ocean.

Indeed, many of the countries fighting the Germans would not make the smallest effort to save Jews in mortal danger. Ships full of escapees from Nazi lands, seeking refuge, were turned back, with its passengers ending up in the death camps. Apart from the population of a few small European nations, themselves under German rule, the Jews had no friends in the world.

Rabbi, do you remember a key tenet of the Nazarene faith? The Original Sin? They claim that Man is born sinful because of the sin of Adam and Eve. I have always considered that sin relatively minor, compared to others committed later on. Surely God will not hold Man responsible for the transgression of ancestors that many generations removed. But I would like to suggest to all Christians, those who murdered us and those who looked away in embarrassment, those who refused to help us—well over ninety-nine percent of Christianity—and to their children and grandchildren and descendants into many generations, that from now on they should assign a new meaning to the term "Original Sin". For all future generations, that Sin should be the persecution and murder of the Jews by the Christians: the Holocaust of the 20th century. You could argue that other brutal enemies of the Jewish people, from the Crusaders to Chmielnitzki, were just as bad as the 20th Century murderers, only lacking the means; perhaps you would be right, perhaps all of those atrocities should be included in the definition of the Original Sin. Perhaps. But it seems to me that jumping on horses, shouting "let's go get the Jews" and killing as many as they could, horrible as that was, still did not reach the evil of planned and organized processing of millions of people in "death factories".

This Original Sin shall really be the cause of shame and mortification for future generations, which shall beg the Lord for redemption.

Nobody wanted to help us. Nevertheless, when the "Allies" finally won the war, killing Hitler and his henchmen, the surviving Jews were liberated from the camps and hiding places all over Europe; so we have to thank America, the Soviet Union and other nations for eventually saving the remainder of the Jews, even if that was not their explicit intention in the war.

There were some other results. The Soviet Union came out of the war stronger than ever, having taken over a large part of the German empire, consisting of some eight eastern European countries where they imposed Communist rule—while maintaining the facade of inde-pendence—as well as outright annexing some others.

The other result was that Zionism, the movement of the Jews for the creation of a new Jewish homeland in Palestine, could no longer be stopped. In 1948, Israel was established as the land of the Jews after an absence of nearly two millennia. How did that come about? I shall tell you about the background that led to that movement in a letter dealing with the Jews of today, soon.

Do you agree, Rabbi, that these were momentous events, worth expounding in detail, even though they took up only a relatively short time in human history? Compared to them, many of the other highlights of history—wars, discoveries, famines, pestilences—became relatively insignificant.

I could tell you about other lands. About how the United States of America became the richest nation by striving for (even if not fully achieving) democracy, freedom and equality. About the impoverishment of South America. About the suffering of China and other Asian nations under Japanese occupation. About Japan finally joining the civilized world. About the continuing poverty of India. Oh, there were many remarkable events, occuring in strange lands. But perhaps I should try to limit this letter to those that have directly influenced our destiny more than the others.

Most important for us, let me tell you about the countries of southwestern Asia, especially the Arab lands.

I have told you about the decline of the Islamic thinking and Arab civilization. The Arab countries have gradually reverted to near barbarism, in some cases at a level of primitivity formerly identified with native tribes of black Africa. The only exception was the Islamic, though not Arab, country of Turkey, which played the role of successful conqueror in the 15th to 17th century.

Strangely enough, it was the establishment of Israel that seems finally to have awakened the Arabs. That and the finding of vast amounts of natural oil under their lands; oil that is essential as the source for making the fuel that drives automobiles, airplanes and all the other industry everywhere; even for the generation of most of the world's electricity. The Arabs became rich.

They joined forces to attack the new State of Israel right after its establishment, in 1948. Israel defended itself; over the next forty years, they kept attacking, again and again. Israel has less than 4 million people, the Arabs have 80 million. But we have repelled the attacks, wave after wave, and shall continue to do so.

The Arabs are using their richness not to better the lot of their people, but to buy arms against Israel.

On the whole, the Arabs are still uneducated, still primitive, still murderous, still fanatical, still misled by their leaders. But that is gradually changing, with today's inevitable exchange of ideas across borders, television, travel. It is hoped that with the help of the Lord, may He be exalted, the Arabs will learn enough over the next hundred years to realize that Israel is there because God wants it to be there, so there is no use fighting it.

The truest of your devoted servants

Yusuf ben Yehudah ibn-Sham un

ANTHROPOLOGY

28 Heshvan 5749 / November 8, 1988

To B'Rabbi Moshe ben Rabbi Maimon ha-Sfaradi,
Fostat, Egypt

My honoured Master:

I want to write to you now, I am afraid in another long letter, about
the people of today, at the end of the 20th century.

Of course, there are different people at different parts of the world;
but that difference, as I may already have told you, is disappearing
rapidly. People of North America, Europe, Japan, much of South
America, Australia, New Zealand, South Africa behave very much the
same, and do so even in a number of other Asian countries. Those
who don't would probably like to: they are being held back either by
tradition (say in the Arab countries) or by oppression (in several
"totalitarian" countries), sometimes by a combination of both of those
things (in Iran which used to be Persia; I have not yet told you much
about that land, but I will. Oh, I will say a lot about Iran yet, my
Master!) Poverty is another reason that keeps people from behaving
like those in the prosperous lands; and so, India, Haiti and some other
countries are still different; but it seems to me that they will share in
the good life in the not too distant future.

So, for now, I shall ignore those traditional, poor or oppressed lands
and talk to you about the behaviour of people in the prosperous, free
world. But before I do, a word about freedom. It is a beautiful
concept, one that we did not even dare to hope for in our life. But

freedom for everyone to do as he wishes does not necessarily result in the best possible behaviour. Sometimes, the opposite may be true. There are people who behave abominably because those of authority cannot stop bad behaviour, or will not, for fear of being accused of suppressing individual freedom. In the West (a general expression defining, vaguely, parts of the world that includes much of the south and even the east), democracy and freedom are almost holy concepts; so much so that most people take them to mean "good", "fair" or similar pleasant things. Few realize that these ideas, which drive human progress, behaviour and indeed history are, far from being identical, actually contradictory. Democracy requires that the majority shall decide all important matters, even if to the detriment of the minority's interest. Freedom, on the other hand, allows everybody to do whatever he or she pleases; at least, ultimate freedom does, and once freedom is limited, is it still freedom?

These days, freedom seems to be winning over democracy; to act against evil-doers or simple miscreants is to interfere with their basic freedom, and so, the wish of the majority takes second place to that of the minority. And so, everywhere in the West, minority rule is revered. (In South Africa, it is institutionalized, because of the white settlers are now in minority, and they are trying to preserve their way of life, to the strong disapproval of the vocal leaders of the western countries.)

I wanted to start with this warning, because I think that you may not approve of all human behaviour when I begin to present it for you, my Master. Well, fortunately, not all human behaviour is criminal or abominable. Let me tell you how people live, work, rest, travel, eat and drink, sleep, love, learn, read, sing, marry and divorce, raise their children. How they behave when they are healthy and when they are sick; yes, how they live and how they die.

At least, you will be comforted to learn that they are still born of women; they grow up, eat and drink, love, have children, grow old and die. This much has not changed—yet.

Why do people live? What for? Well, in our time, they lived for their families, for themselves, because life was, sometimes, sweet; and because that was what the Lord, blessed is He, demanded of them, the alternative, suicide, being forbidden. This has changed somewhat. People are generally less concerned about His commands; and, as one result, quite a few do kill themselves; I have no way of telling how many more now than in our days, although I think many more.

While most people still live for their families, many more now live for themselves. The idea of pleasure is glorified; and especially pleasures of the body in preference to the pleasures of the mind. Even when it is the mind that is served, the provision is usually less than appetizing to our views. I will tell you about this when I describe how people entertain themselves.

Very few really understand life, what its objective may be, how to make the best use of it so as to please God at least as much as themselves. The most intelligent people tend to pose the "big questions"—what is the purpose of life, why do we exist, is there any meaning in all of this—but few of them produce a good, solid answer. Yet the answer is there, has been there all along. It is interpolated differently today, in modern language, but it is the same answer as always.

Meanwhile, people work. I'll tell you exactly who works today: with a few exception, every adult. Children go to school until the age of at least eighteen, more often 22 or sometimes even 26 or more. In some countries, they then enter a regular, conscription-based army, spend two or three years there, defending their country, (sometimes attacking others, but aggression is on the wane). After that, they start working, and do so until the age of sixty-five; and then, they retire, usually with a pension, sometimes two: one from the state, provided to everyone, another from the organization where they worked.

However, let me explain, in this regard, the difference between men and women. Up to about thirty years ago, women only worked until they married; after that, they generally stayed at home with their families, had children, raised them, looked after the house, cooked, cleaned—really worked harder than in a job, but earned no salary.

Now, increasingly, that is changing. Women once earned much less than men. These days, in advanced countries, with the same experience and doing the same work, they are getting nearly the same pay as men. Yes, and they can do the same work, any work. (Remember, the heavy physical work is now done by machines.) So they don't give up their jobs when they marry; even when they have children, they usually go back to work, while someone else, perhaps a professional child-raiser, looks after the children during the day.

In countries where there are many children in a family, this is really not so. But in most modern nations, one or two, at most three children is the norm. It was no different in our days, well-to-do families had few children; only now, most families are well-to-do.

How do people work? Well, there is still some physical work in agriculture, mining, forestry, manufacturing; but the most difficult, most dangerous parts of the jobs are all mechanized. A huge machine cuts the wheat and ties it in sheaves; another machine separates the kernel from the chaff; another grinds the kernel into flour; another mixes the flour with water, cuts the loaves after rising, puts them into the oven and removes the baked loaves from there. (Does it taste as good as before? Not really; but nobody needs to break his back in providing for themselves and their families.)

In mining, whole underground labyrinths are dug out by powerful machines controlled by people; they descend to the tunnels by elevating machines and fresh air is pumped in to them by other machinery. Yet it is dangerous work still: the mine can collapse, sometimes does. There are explosions, suffocation. And the construction industry is also dangerous: even though the heavy lifting of material to the 10th, 50th or 100th floor is done by machines, a worker does sometimes fall down, despite every precaution.

There are not many women in the mining and construction industries, but they are there in manufacturing. This industry is typically centered in factories, buildings where small or large groups of people, with lots of machines, make things. What do they make? Oh, thousands of things, millions of things: furniture, cars, airplanes, clothes, clocks (for accurate measuring of time), paper and writing instruments, carpets, books, pots and pans, plates and glasses, forks and knives and spoons, lamps, radios, television, telephones—and innumerable other things, many of which even I don't understand.

Then, other people work in offices—places where papers are written, typically for commercial purposes; they are read by others, business decisions are made, numbers are added up—administrative offices, trading houses, government locations. Actually, most people in cities today work at such places.

Others work in services: restaurants and hotels (like inns; places where travelling people come in to eat and sleep); repair shops for cars; places for cleaning and laundering clothes; driving autobuses (which are automobiles for fifty or eighty people), or trains or airplanes; cleaning windows or houses or offices; and so on.

Many people work in stores, places you would at least recognize, where goods are sold. In a large city, there are tens of thousands of stores, all specializing in one type of ware: women's clothes, or jewellery, or hygienic material, or office supply, or entertainment machinery, or books, and of course food, specialty stores for many type of food, and I could go on. There are also stores that sell not just one type of goods, but almost everything at one location, and what a location! In a building five or ten story high, each floor specializing in a different type of merchandise.

Still other people work in schools, teaching small children and bigger ones too, up to age twenty-two or more. Then, there are the hospitals, still places to look after the sick, but these days that is where the physicians work about half their time (in the other half, they still have private practices, in their offices which is sometimes in their houses, but more often in large medical office buildings). In hospitals, they have assistants, women and sometimes men called nurses; and there are many other service persons there.

(Rabbi, you may be pleased to hear that in Israel, a famous hospital is named after you!)

There are thousands of types of employment. Almost everybody either has a job, or sometimes is looking for one; for people do lose their jobs. They may have been sent away from one, for any number of reasons—but this is not different from our age. Or he may have left on his own, again, for many possible reasons.

When people work, it is usually for seven or eight hours a day, five days a week. In western countries, where the prevailing religion is Christian, the holy day is Sunday; but people have two days off work every week, and these are normally Saturday and Sunday, so Jews have no problem observing the Shabbat, if they want to. In Muslim countries, as you know, the day off work is Friday. (In Israel, a young country that cannot afford two days off, people work from Sunday morning until Friday noon.) But there are always exceptions. For instance, the autobuses are still running on those days, the restaurants are still open, places where people entertain themselves are the most busy on those days; so workers who have to work get other days of the week in exchange. The only exception is in the very religious parts of Israel and the United States of America, where all kinds of work ceases for the Shabbat, except for emergency.

When people have jobs (which is most of the time), they are in a quasi-contractual situation. In exchange for fulfilling the work obligation, they receive pay and usually other things: two to seven weeks of paid vacation, (depending on the country and on the length of their service with the particular employer); payment for medical expenses, continuation of pay while sick, often a retirement pay plan, called pension; and other benefits. In some countries these things are regulated by the government; in others, workers sometimes get together and form groups to bargain with the employer for these benefits and especially for salary level.

Usually, people work from morning till afternoon, often with an hour off for lunch and two more quarter-hour breaks. But in some jobs, afternoon and night shifts are necessary.

Workers also get time off on major holidays; in Christian lands, those would be the days commemorating the birth, death and resurrection of Yehoshua haNotzri, and so on. There are also national holidays, celebrating important historical dates.

Enough about work. What do people do when they don't work, when they rest?

Well, of course, they sleep seven or eight hours. And, in a city of several million, it takes them sometimes an hour or more just to get to work, as much again to get home. But that still leaves plenty of time for other activities.

The concept of "entertainment", one that you, Rabbi, hated and considered a waste of time, has always been around. Kings were constantly and systematically entertained; but for the ordinary people, the term meant a special event when many of them got together, typically for singing and dancing, sometimes to see a travelling show. Of course, for those who read, books written for purposes other than education and illumination or spiritual uplifting have always been available, and became widely used soon after the invention of printing. Among the many kinds of books produced for entertainment purposes, the most common has been the "novel", typically describing the story of a fictional person, or family, sometimes an entire people in some specific situation. Often, while the protagonists are imaginary, the situation is quite real, perhaps validated historically, or more recently, actually experienced by the readers. The writer does not pretend to write a true story, nor does the reader expect it. Some novels are happy, some sad, others both of those things—so is human life. Many a pleasant hours can be spent with a good book.

Then, more recently, with the spread of radio, it has become possible for everybody to listen to music, discussions or whatever "program" may be on the radio at any time (and there are hundreds of programs on at the same time); or watch events on television—real people doing something that the majority considers interesting—singing and dancing, for instance—or there is a choice of drama, comedy and tragedy available, and other things, people talking, giving their opinions about various topics, current events and ideas. There is a wide choice of such programs at any time, so that people can have their entertainment every day.

Yet other forms of entertainment are widely available—yes, this is very important for the 20th century man and woman. The cinema is another form of drama; in this case, hundreds of people sit together in a large room (where they need to pay to get in) and watch the acting on a huge screen in front of them. The same program is shown again and again, several times a day, for weeks; but in another cinema, perhaps next door, another program is shown. In a large city, say one for three million people, there are about 300 such cinemas. Some very famous such "moving pictures" are seen, eventually, by millions in various cities and countries. There is not that much difference between cinema and television, but the latter is much smaller, and everybody has it in his house; people buy the machine and can watch whatever programs are provided, a choice of several dozen, usually without additional payment.

Then, there is live entertainment: singing, drama, dancing. In large cities, there are dozens of theatres to choose from on any day.

And a number of concert halls, where one listens to music. Master, why did you hate music so much? I wish I could send you some examples of today's music. I could, they are available in little boxes, but you could not play them back. Yet it is so beautiful, complex,

abstract, exciting, satisfying, fulfilling. Sometimes just a few musicians perform, other times an orchestra of some 100 men and women,
playing on dozens of different instruments, all precisely together, but
playing some six or ten or more different melodies that intertwine
according to the plan of the composer, giving out beautiful har-
monies—Rabbi, but this must be the entertainment of the Lord, may
He be exalted! For in the World-to- Come, if you are right in your
belief that we shall have minds only, no bodies, then we shall not sing
or act or dance, or paint pictures, but music shall be surely with us!

But I think I know what it was that you disliked so about music. You
were annoyed by the custom of singing that you had encountered in
synagogues. You thought that people were mistaking the pretty little
songs for real, deep devotion to the Lord. In that you may have been
right: ever since, in non-Orthodox congregations, just as in Christian
churches, people enthusiastically sing songs, thinking that they have
thereby fulfilled some duty, some obligation to God (forgetting the
original purpose of melody, a simple mnemonic device, to help all
remember the prayers: in our days, with no printing presses, not every
believer possessed a prayer book.)

On the other hand, there is beautiful church music today, to be
appreciated on its own right, not as an instrument of devotion. This
music compares to the music you knew, just as the palace of the
Sultan compares to the tent of a Bedouin. You cannot condemn all
buildings when you have seen nothing but that tent.

And, of course, there is good music and bad one; the large majority
of people listen to bad, cheap music. About thirty years ago, well-educated people complained that most of the population read bad books;
and some still do; but most people today don't read any books, just
watch television, where almost every program is bad. Well, this is
what the masses demand, bread and circuses, and that is what they
get. Yet it seems to be a pity that after literacy became almost
universal, it is in the process of disappearing again, due to television
and other technology (for example, I may be one of the last persons

to write a letter: normally, people just call each other on the tele-phone, and talk to each other, wherever they may be).

But there is still another form of entertainment, perhaps the most popular of all: watching sport events. Not since the days of ancient Athens have the competitive physical games been so all-pervasive. Athletics is practiced in schools; but what people really like is ball-games and related team events, with the rules well-defined. Every city seems to have at least one major team for every type of game; people attend the competitions; watch them on television; and discuss them afterwards, with apparently no end.

Let me talk about other things. What do these people do on their weeks of vacation? They usually go away somewhere. Go to a city or country they have never visited before; or one they like; perhaps their birth place, or where their relatives live. But most people go to special "vacation places", say in the mountains, or by the sea shore. They may take a ship cruise (you, of all people, will find it hard to understand why one would think of that as relaxation, but today's ships are equipped with stabilizing machinery, so people don't usually get seasick). And on vacation, people entertain themselves even more, doing things they don't normally do, eat and drink more than they should, enjoy themselves. It's only for a few weeks.

When talking about various jobs, I forgot to mention the thousands that are connected with the entertainment and vacation business, on beaches and mountains (where people go in the winter to "ski", slide down on the snowy slopes wearing long, narrow strips of wood on their shoes).

Enjoyment is really the driving force in this age. People think they must enjoy life; they must have "fun". In doing so, they sometimes lose sight of what is proper and what is not; what is good for them, what is good for others and what is not.

Today, people understand quite well what food and what drink is good for the body, and how much of it. They know that they should eat lots of fruit and vegetables; little meat, and then the meat of poultry, not cattle; little fat or oil; few sweet things. They should eat bread, drink milk; eat cheese, drink wine, but not much. Clear water is best to drink, or the juices of fruits.

They know these things, but don't necessarily observe the sensible rules. They will eat too much red meat, fatty substances, eggs; drink too much wine and stronger things. Then they become ill, often die at a relatively early age.

There is a plant called tobacco. Its leaves are dried, ground up and packaged into little sticks covered in very thin paper. People put fire to one end, so it smolders, and then suck the other end. It burns slowly, the man or woman inhales the smoke. There is a narcotic substance in that smoke, it provides a good feeling; it is addictive, very hard to stop using it. The smokers tend to die 10, 20 years too early, with their lungs and hearts destroyed.

And there are still more dangerous things around. We have known some of these substances, usually extracted from plants: drugs, narcotics. Now they are also being made artificially, synthetically. They are even more addictive than tobacco. People, trapped into using them, don't live long.

But I don't want to create the impression that all people eat too much, drink too much, use tobacco and harmful drugs. Actually, the majority have relatively healthy habits, they watch out for their bodies. Some even exercise, as they should: with the disappearance of physical work, exercise has become very important, so bodies won't atrophy, won't become soft and limp.

Also, many people entertain themselves intelligently, learn while enjoying themselves, while reading or watching television or attending a theater. They listen to good music, there are tens of thousands of recorded music available at any time, you just drop the little box into a player, at home or in the car. Well, perhaps not many people listen to good music, read good books; but at least some do. The better an "art form" is, the smaller its audience: that seems to be the nature of things.

People learn while entertaining themselves, intentionally or accidentally. But studying for its own sake and without any entertainment still exists. Not too many adults will spend time studying, proportionately less, I think, than in our time; but it is good that some, at least, still do.

How do people learn? Well, first, there is formal and compulsory education for children. It varies with the country, but normally there are two levels: elementary school, from ages six to ten or 14; and secondary schools (sometimes called middle or high schools) to age 18 or so. After that age, non-compulsory university or college education begins, three to five years; some university graduates take further courses, to achieve advanced designations, including the "doctor" title, usually given to physicians, but available in all disciplines.

Actually, a physician studies even longer than others, longer than, say, scientists (for I've told you that those are very different fields of knowledge today). He typically acquires his doctorate at the age of twenty-five, but his full licence to practice will only be earned after two or three more years of hospital work. Then, if he wants to specialize in one of the dozens of areas of the human body, say kidneys and urinary system, or throat, ear, nose problems, or the eye, or the skin, he has to study for several more years; even more if he selects the mind as his field of specialization. Many choose surgery (and there is specialization even within that), which requires, again, long years of study and practice under a senior surgeon.

Master, I have told you so many things already, and yet I have told you nothing. I don't believe that you could begin to understand today's people from what I have written. I must tell you about the family life of today's people; but my letter is already too long; so I shall leave that subject to my next letter to you.

The truest of your devoted servants

Yusuf ben Yehudah ibn-Sham`un

ANTHROPOLOGY (Cont.)

7 Kislev 5749 / November 17, 1988

To B'Rabbi Moshe ben Rabbi Maimon ha-Sfaradi,
Fostat, Egypt

My honoured Master:

There is so much more to tell you about these strange people of the
20th century. Some days I feel that I understand them fully, have even
learnt to live a little like them; and then, on other days, I am almost
ready to give up ever understanding them, disapprove of them strongly
and sometimes even despair. But the Lord must have had a reason for
sending me here, and so I must continue studying them. What else
could I do? I shall tell you about what they do when they love; about
marriage and children and families.

But this is difficult, because what people would like to do, should do
and actually do are different things. In no human endeavour is that
more true than in love, and has always been so. And if I were writing
about our own time, the 12th century, I would still have difficulties;
for who knows what people did and thought when it came to love?

Still, in our time the rules were relatively straightforward. Young men
and women got married, had children, brought them up. In our
religion, in our time, the reason for sexual activity was procreation
and, in your view, satisfaction of only the strongest, most persistent
desire of men. (Later, Jewish authorities came to believe that desires
of women are at least equally worthy of consideration: they have
made more frequent sexual activity compulsory for men.) In Chris-

tianity, also, procreation has been, until recently, the only justification for the sexual act; not so, I believe, in Islam.

Today, in most societies, the primary reason for sexual relations is the satisfaction of the biological urges of both men and women. Having children, while part of that urge, is a secondary consideration at best; in most situations, pregnancy is actually prevented by artificial means. Also, unwanted pregnancy is usually terminated medically through a process called abortion.

The most orthodox Christian church fathers, those belonging to the Roman Catholic mainline, controlled by the Vatican, strongly oppose abortion on the basis that the foetus, from the moment of inception, is a human being, a fact that makes abortion, in effect, murder. (A view that would carry stronger moral authority if that church also opposed the murder of those already born: the millions of Jews during the Nazi times.) Nevertheless, the view equating abortion with murder is supported by many Orthodox Jewish thinkers. Roman Catholicism also opposes artificial contraception of impregnation, because only God should be able to decide whether or not a conception should occur, humans should not make it impossible for God to do so; in that, they have little support from outside their faith.

In fact, sexual intercourse (in vulgar term, "sex"), is now a very common activity within and without wedlock. Young people do it from the age of sixteen or before. Again, it is the Roman Catholic church that forbids this; but its prohibition is not treated with general respect. Among Jews, only the most strictly observant are following the old moral code. But more about the Jews later.

So when people are in love, married or not, (worse: married, but not to the loved one!), they don't think twice before having sexual intercourse. Still worse: they do it even without being in love, "just for the fun". Because of contraception, pregnancy seldom results, except in the lowest social and economic classes, where contraception is barely understood; there, it is not uncommon for young unmarried girls to have a child every year.

Then, there are those who love their mates sufficiently to live together, but would not marry, because of fear of the enforced permanence of such arrangement (even though, people divorce easily enough). More often than not, they do marry once children are on the horizon; but not all care for such niceties. The term "bastard" has lost its significance.

Before telling you about raising children, about families (a concept that is now considered almost too traditional), let me comment on another facet of this so-called "sexual revolution" that has taken place only within the last thirty years: among those who consider "sex" just a form of entertainment, there are some who do it with members of their own gender. Of course, such behaviour was not totally unheard of in our times; but when caught, they were dealt very severe, generally with capital punishment. Today, such behaviour is condoned! It is considered simply a matter of choice.

It is hard to predict when and how the Holy One, blessed is He, metes out punishment; but he did strike sinners in Sodom and Gomorrah; and it seems to be happening again. A horrible sickness has appeared some years ago; it is spreading fast, mainly among homosexual men. It looks as though in another ten or twenty years, there will be few left openly practicing their depravity. The sickness has spread to the "normal" population: normal in the sense of some homosexual men also having relations with women, who become infected and pass the disease to several men who pass it to several other women and so on. Thank the Lord, it does not seem to affect those living in moral, traditional sexual relation with their spouses. Yet it is in His hands; He may decide to treat the entire human race as He treated the inhabitants of those two cities. Let us hope for His mercy.

Families, then. The word has acquired a pleasant sound, for it conveys a sense of comfort and stability, it sends out an unstated message that "everything is all right". Not that family life is smooth and uneventful everywhere; rather, in a world of increasingly rapid change, it is comforting to see an institution that has not really changed that much over the centuries. You would not think so, were you to spend some time with a typical family. Yet they are relatively stable. They tend to have two or three children. Those are born in hospitals, under excellent medical care. Few babies and few new mothers die.

More often than not, families are well-to-do, or at least not poor: their have their own house or apartment (a set of rooms in a large building). The children have at least one room to themselves, more typically each would have his or her own room, or at least one for the boys, another for the girls. There is enough food. There are enough clothes. The houses are well heated in the winter, cooled in the summer.

The children go to school; the parents go to work; in the summer, when school is suspended for two months, the family takes a vacation. They have one or two cars. They also have two or three televisions; several radios; a refrigerator in the kitchen, to keep enough food for a week or more cold and fresh; an electric stove and oven for cooking and baking; plenty of electric light in every room. They also have hundreds of other electrical appliances: clocks, sewing machines, razors, calculators, exercise machines, lawn mowers, entertainment machines of various kinds, telephones, electric toys for the children—I could go on and on, and would still not be able to tell you about what you would find in a typical family's home. A child, any child, would have at least two hundred toys of all kinds: balls, dolls, games, puzzles, miniature cars, airplanes, ships, animals, furniture, electric toys that I could not even start to explain to you.

Are families happy? I think so, even though, wrapped up in their day-to-day problems as they are, the would seldom consider themselves happy. Yet children do remember their early family life as one of great happiness, but only after they have grown middle-aged. They claim that it was a happy family, and it was: if it was.

For divorce, as I have said, is very common and very easy. Again, it is the Roman Catholic church that objects, strongly yet ineffectually. Impermanence has penetrated all aspects of life. People change houses often; they change their jobs every few years; so, they feel, why spend their entire life with one person? (In our days, people normally lost their spouses by early death, married several times because of that. People now tend to live to a ripe old age.) Of course, the more they change spouses, the less happy they are. Sure, there are those who married the wrong spouse and then correct the mistake by divorcing and re-marrying; the second time around, or even the third, the right mate may be found. But such broken families are surely not good for the children.

So perhaps, now, you begin to see what this world of today is all about. It is very different not only from our age: it is almost as different from the world of thirty or fifty years ago. Yet these people either prefer things this way, or shall change their ways back to the more traditional mode. Somehow, I think, that will happen soon.

I have talked to you about many aspects of life today; life, but not death; nor sickness. Yet that is an area that you understand so well; or did in our days.

People don't get seriously ill so often these days, for most illnesses are understood and prevented by medical science. There are the simple, trivial ills, such as the common cold, which come and go, an annoyance but no serious concern to anybody. There are childhood epidemics, minor diseases that most children get once and become immunized against it; artificial immunization is also available. Still, there are diseases that take longer to fight; the patient is sometimes moved to a hospital for full care, often involving specialized machinery. They also receive the full attention of physicians and nurses, are treated with a variety of synthetic chemical medications and receive other treatment, such as extra oxygen gas, if that is what they need, or transfusion of extra blood (of a type that matches their own! there are some six or eight major types).

Of course, there are the very serious cases, those from which the patient may or may not recover. Cancer of various parts of the body is still with us; it is removed by surgery (after its presence and location has been confirmed using X-rays), but may recur; it is treated with specific nuclear radiation and with chemicals. Heart attacks and strokes kill many people; again, a variety of therapy is available, from surgery to chemicals, if detected and treated in time. But people must die, after all; and so, if one disease is prevented or cured, another will crop up. There is, of course, dying of old age. Men die, on the average, at age seventy-two; women, at 79. Reaching 100 is still rare.

One major cause of serious illness or death is physical accidents. Cars and trains are moving at tremendous speeds, typically at 35 miles per hour in towns, 80 miles per hour in-between cities. A mistake is easily made; or the machine may malfunction. Accidents are a major cause of untimely death or permanent injury.

Death is not different from what it was in our days. The person dies, is buried and mourned. Some are easily forgotten, others leave a painful emptiness for a long time. Financially, the passing of the "main breadwinner" can sometimes cause very serious problems; people are urged to buy "life insurance", an arrangement where they pay a relatively small amount of money to a company every month of their life, and upon their death, their family receives a rather large sum of money. Almost everybody participates in such a scheme.

And that, Rabbi, should complete this letter. I know that there must be millions of things in today's life that I have not mentioned. But if you can even vaguely visualize today's people, then I have achieved my objective for the last two letters.

I would like to ask you, my Master, not to condemn the people of today too fast. They behave abominably, I know; but these are their standards. It is very difficult to live up to the highest moral plateau on your own, against the example set by everybody else: one is then considered a strange person, perhaps dangerous; one's neighbours may make his life miserable. There are upright people; there are also depraved ones; but do accept the great majority in-between as simply doing what everyone else does. For times do change. Perhaps.

The truest of your devoted servants

Yusuf ben Yehudah ibn-Sham`un

PROGRESS

19 Kislev 5749 / November 28, 1988

To B'Rabbi Moshe ben Rabbi Maimon ha-Sfaradi,
Fostat, Egypt

My honoured Master:

I would like to write to you about progress.

Having slowly come to an understanding of this 20th century world, I was struck by a thought: how blind we were in the 12th century, how we missed all the small but important signs of forward motion.

I shall have to use, for this letter, a device that has become quite common in this age for communication of ideas. It is the graphical chart. Change, increase and decrease of anything can be depicted analogously as a moving line; so one dimension represents time, the other, that which changes with time, say quantity of something. (There are other types of graphical charts as well, depicting things other than temporal change, for example, static situations; also, I am sure that it has already occurred to you that there could be three-dimensional charts, and there are; those are more difficult to construct.) And so, while the concept is new to you, I am sure that with your extraordinarily sharp mind, you will be able to absorb this device at once.

Let me give you a trivial example: The following chart depicts the Jewish population of Eretz Israel over a recent 60-year period (shown in thousands):

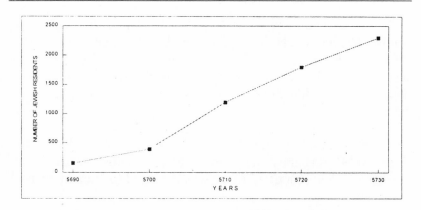

You do see that it is a simple concept. So I would like to show human progress on a chart, one not clearly as obvious as the above, for progress can be sensed, but not quantified like number of people.

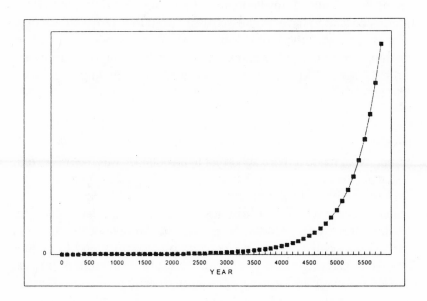

Well, human progress is obvious today, few people living in this age don't realize how life is changing day-by-day. But eight centuries ago, we were still on a part of the curve that sloped mildly, not in the shocking way that everybody must notice. So we did not notice. I hope that this justification is rational, that we cannot be accused of being blind.

But what is meant by human progress? Better people? More pious, more God-fearing men and women? More intelligent ones? More charitable? More beautiful? Taller ones? Longer life-spans? Or what?

That is very hard to answer. Perhaps one could say that human progress is a movement away from the animal and towards the spiritual or divine.

Having said that, one is then bound to be attacked by critics, foremost among them yourself, my honoured Master, saying "How can today's humans be said to have progressed away from the animal? They may have complicated machines. But the people have not improved; if anything, the opposite has happened. The 20th century brutalities are certainly worse, closer to animal behaviour than anything seen in the 12th century."

First, I am not sure that this is true. Certainly the treatment of the Jews by Germans and others during the Second World War was bestial; what made it more abhorrent to an outsider was the organized, systematic torture and murder of millions, as opposed to perhaps more random cruelties of the past, say those of the Almohades in the 12th century, or the Martinez Christians of Seville in the late 14th. But cruelties there were, Jews were persecuted throughout the ages (as were, occasionally, others, but none so persistently); and I am sure that those carrying out those deeds were just as merciless, just as sadistic (a new term for those who enjoy causing pain and suffering) than the Germans; only less well organized. Again, a possible difference: the leaders of past persecutions were, perhaps less evil than those in the 20th century. But is that certain? Torquemeda, of

Inquisition fame, Chmielnitzki of the Ukraine, the Crusaders—oh, I could name hundreds, thousands of murderers. Were Hitler and his cohorts worse? (Yes, I think they were, because of the cold-blooded execution of an organized plan for the annihilation of our nation.)

In any case, I think that progress is never quite level, and a smooth curve is deceptive, the line should probably be ragged, at least from a human vantage point; but it is moving upward irresistibly, nevertheless. And again, we cannot measure progress, but perhaps the Lord can; He sees things that we don't.

We could postulate, perhaps, that it is easier to understand human progress by viewing the approaching target rather than the receding origin; for surely we are past the mid-point; let us look at the future, not the past. Is that reasonable?

Rabbi, I am sure, quite sure, that we are well past the middle. It seems clear to me that we are now on the steepest upward arm of the curve. I think, I believe that we are getting less animal and more divine every day.

Do I also believe, then, that human bestiality is finally a thing of the past? No, I don't. I wish it were so. But I am afraid that bestiality will be with us almost to the very end of our progression. Yet, on the other hand, some minor aspects of divinity have been with us, well, if not from the beginning, then at least for a very long time. Certainly there have been instances of divine spark in the human mind (or heart, as used to be thought) in all recorded times; and there have been men and women who were not divine, but more than ordinary people. Think of Moses, our Teacher. Think of Aristotle. Think of the prophets. Think of Yehoshua ha-Notzri. Think of Muhammad. Think of Buddha (no, I don't think you know about him). And outside the world of religion, there were poets, painters, musicians whose creation could not, whatever your personal opinion of these things, have been the product of unaided human mind.

Humanity has progressed rapidly and by now, very far. This is evidenced not only by the current technology—airplanes, computers, nuclear energy, space exploration, or even "simple" electricity—no, of equal importance are all the achievement of human literature, art, architecture—oh, and medicine! And pure mathematics! And so many other things—we are not only advanced, but are rushing ahead at dizzying speed.

And the remnants of the past? The narrow-mindedness, the male-volence, the bestiality? We have them still, but surely in ever decreasing numbers. They are still here, they are always trying to stop God's work, but they can never succeed. And in the end, they always perish in infamy and humiliation.

Rabbi, I think that the one main advantage of living in the 20th century, rather than the 12th, is that it is so much easier to observe the Lord's work from this vantage point. He has His grand design; now He is moving into the final phase, and the design suddenly becomes clear to all but the blind. All the same, I am somewhat embarrassed for not having seen it in the 12th century, or at least in the 13th.

And what exactly is that design? Where is Shaddai taking us? Let me discuss my thoughts on that topic at length, but not yet. I'll do so in a future letter, if He shall aid me. Meanwhile, there are many things that I want to write to you about this world of the 20th century people.

The truest of your devoted servants

Yusuf ben Yehudah ibn-Sham`un

THE JEWS OF TODAY:

MODERN JEWISH PRACTICES

4 Tevet 5749 / December 12, 1988

To B'Rabbi Moshe ben Rabbi Maimon ha-Sfaradi,
Fostat, Egypt

My honoured Master:

I have told you, in my earlier letters, how modern people live. I am
sure that you were shocked by some of their behaviour. And you must
have wondered whether everybody lives that way, or if the Jews of
today are different. Some are, Rabbi; most are not. In this letter, I
would like to tell you about the Jews of today; in the next one, with
the help of the Holy One, blessed is He, I shall try to explain to you
what has brought all the change about, and how today's Jews are
different, not from Gentiles but from each other.

For there are many kinds of Jews today. Of course, there have always
been. In this letter, I don't want to detail the major divisions among
our people; let me just classify them into two groups: the large
majority, which range from the "secular Jew", one who not only does
not observe the law, the *Halakhah*, but wants nothing to do with God,
to the Orthodox, who not only fears God, but professes to observe the
commandments, the *mitzvot*, yet not always, not consistently. There
are many intermediate grades within this large group, and they would
be surprised to hear me classifying them in one group, yet from our
12th century vantage point, they are all the same.

And then, there is a small minority, just two or three out of a hundred, the "Ultra-orthodox", Jews who still observe the law as much as possible, in its form if not in its intent. We shall talk about them later (oh, if I could really talk with you!) For now, let us have a good look at the others, the not-so-observant majority.

The lifestyle of these Jews is hardly different from that of the Gentiles. They work in mostly identical jobs—but not quite, for there are very few Jews doing heavy menial work, except, of course, in Israel; even there, Arabs work on construction, although Jews have become proficient again at agriculture and industry. And there are jobs, professions with disproportionately heavy Jewish representation: small business ownership, commerce, accounting, education, medicine and entertainment tend to be good professions for young Jews to consider. And also law. You know, Rabbi, Jews have given up their jurisprudence system including all courts and rabbinical decision-making (except in purely religious matters) and have accepted the jurisdiction of the secular judicial system of the land they live in instead. But so many Jews are lawyers! (Of course, they were lawyers before, even during your youth in Spain.)

With the exception of teaching, the professions I've mentioned are the ones where the financial rewards are the greatest. Do Jews pick these jobs because of the money? Or have they simply managed to demand more and more payment for their services over the years? In either case, it is a fact that Jews tend to be, on the whole, better off financially than the entire population. Not much better, mind you: there are rich Gentiles and poor Gentiles; there are rich Jews and poor Jews. This situation also varies from country to country; nevertheless, I would think that in lands with significant Jewish population, the average Jew earns at least a third more than the average Gentile. In order to achieve such financial objectives (and not because of the love of books, love of studying), he also tends to be better educated.

When people have time off from work, as I've told you, they rest and they entertain themselves and each other. Jews are very active in most forms of entertainment. The studios that make cinema, the large-screen entertainment form for hundreds of people to see, I've told you about it, these studios were, at one time, all run by Jews. Live entertainment—theatre, music—are also very often run by Jewish business-people and artists, and are supported financially by Jews, not only by their disproportionately large attendance, but also by provision of grants. (Indeed, music has become a specially Jewish form of art; it is ironic that this should be the case, considering your strong stance against music as a "waste of time". I have already told you what I think: that music is more than that, it is elevated spiritual entertainment, the pleasure of the Lord, blessed be His name.)

There are special, predominantly Jewish vacation areas; but in other respects, the vacation habits of Jews are not different from those of anybody else's. Actually, I think that it were the Jews in the first place who taught the concept of vacation to the larger population. But there is an aspect of life where Jews and Gentiles do behave different-ly: during the holidays, days off work. These are usually religious occasions, Christian holidays in most western lands, commemorating the birth of Yehoshua haNotzri, his death and resurrection and other related events. For Gentiles, these days are sometimes for attending religious services in the church; more often, for relaxation, eating and drinking, "having a good time".

While for Jews the religious holidays are different, they don't normally work on the official rest days of the land. Because of that, it is difficult to have too many additional days off work to observe the Jewish holidays. What does the typical Jew do, then? Well, he takes off about three days every year from work, usually without pay, or using some of his vacation days: two days for Rosh Hashanah and one for Yom Kippur.

I know that you don't like this at all, and you are right. Well, there are many Jews who do celebrate the other most important days of the year. Many go to the synagogue on Pesach, Sukkoth and Shevuoth. But, in this group of the largest majority that I am describing, few would take time off work for these holidays. Yes, some do; but, on the other hand, there are many more who don't even observe Yom Kippur; quite a few Jews actually celebrate the Christian holidays, in form if not in substance, as they say, "for the children's sake, so they won't feel different"! I am sorry, Master, for having to say this.

But even the Jews who observe their own holidays do so, again, in form, rather than substance. For example, a typical Rosh Hashanah would involve going to the synagogue in the evening and perhaps briefly during the day; and a nice family dinner, with head covering worn as a generous concession to tradition.

Indeed, tradition rather than deep faith defines religious practices. People like performing the rituals—just a few, easy ones—that they remember having seen performed by their parents, grandparents. And they get sentimental thinking about life in small, poor Jewish villages in Eastern Europe, a hundred years before this time. But if you were looking for observance of the rules in this large group, observance simply because *that is the law*, that you would not find. They would be surprised at the suggestion.

Let me talk to you about the dietary laws, *kashrut*. Eight or nine out of every ten in this large group will eat anything, anywhere, anytime. The remainder will observe the law regarding prohibited foodstuff; but how? Selectively. They will not, perhaps, cook pork or shellfish, but they won't worry about how the animal was slaughtered; and they will mix meat and milk freely. And even if they are a little stricter in their observance of the rules, that is done only in their home; once outside, they will visit restaurants of every nation, eating their "exciting" dishes of pork, shellfish and who knows what other horror.

When you ask these people why they are going to the trouble of observing the law (to the extent they do) at home, but not outside it, they will tell you that Grandmother would not eat in their house otherwise; I think the true reason is that they realize that formal observance conveys some distinction on the house, the family. Yet they will not be consistent about this.

On Shabbat, the Jew seldom works (he does if the extra workload demands it); seldom goes to the synagogue, but often plays with his children, goes to sport events, drives his family in the car to a nearby vacation house for the 2-day week-end.

So, as I've said, the life of the Jew is not really different from that of the Gentile. You will find the same family pattern, same type of marriage and divorce, pre- and extra-marital sexual activity, natural and unnatural practices—well, perhaps statistics would show the Jews a little more family-oriented, and therefore less promiscuous, but I am not so sure of this. There is less homosexuality among them, I hope.

In time of need, the Jew does find his religion. There are many rabbis who will perform the needed services: brith milahs, bar mitzvahs (and also bat mitzvahs!), weddings, funerals. After the funeral, the close relatives often do sit for seven days, as required: they truly mourn the departed. They also truly love their children, their husbands and wives most of the time, their parents and, usually, their brothers and sisters. Jews are people, human beings, rather nice human beings.

They are not Jews as you and I used to know Jews. Of the 613 commandments, they observe perhaps 150. And they are proud of that, proud of being Jewish.

Now, what about the minority, the Ultra-orthodox? Well, they try to be like the Jews that we used to know: they observe most rules, attend synagogue regularly, live a life very close to correct: that is, commit no more sins than people in our days did. Perhaps less.

Yet the "ordinary" Orthodox would be upset to hear my excluding him from sharing the life of the righteous. This is a man (or woman) who lives the life of a 20th century person; he tries to observe the Jewish law, *kashrut* and as many *mitzvot* as possible, as conveniently as possible. He calls himself a religious person, knows most of the prayers by heart; but there is always "personal" variation, individual-ization of the rules. Indeed, the Jews increasingly consider it proper that they create their own set of rituals, own permissions and prohibitions, based on what they saw at home, based on what they see elsewhere, based on convenience, sometimes on fear of the Lord, respect for the Torah, other times on "enlightened reason" and who knows what other manners of rationalization.

Only the Ultra-orthodox won't do this. Even among them, I have come to know a few who will also bend the rules, if they feel they must, but will find a semi-legal way of doing so, a technique that appears to conform to the letter of the law, if not to its spirit.

Again, my dear Master, I am sorry if I have caused you disappoint-ment and distress in relating these things about the 20th century Jews. In my next letter, I shall try to explain to you the background of these changes; and then, perhaps later, with the help of the Holy One, blessed is He, consider a little whether these developments are all for the worse or, God knows, in some ways better.

The truest of your devoted servants

Yusuf ben Yehudah ibn-Sham`un

BACKGROUND OF MODERN JUDAISM; DIVERGENCE OF PRINCIPLES, VIEWS, PRACTICES

14 Tevet 5749 / December 22, 1988

To B'Rabbi Moshe ben Rabbi Maimon ha-Sfaradi,
Fostat, Egypt

My honoured Master:

There are numerous groups within Judaism today, and I have studied them for a while now, so I can explain to you about these and how they came about. I should not be surprised about this plurality, and neither should you: there have always been groupings and differences of opinion in our faith (and in everyone else's).

As a matter of fact, leaders offering people new directions have never lacked for followers. These new ways were sometimes well within the permissible scope of Judaism, other times clearly without. You will recall the three most famous schisms: the Samaritan one (we still argue if it was a schism, or were they different people) of some 2500 years before this date; the Christian one of 2000 years ago; and the Karaite schism, now some 1200 years in the past. (Incidentally, both Samaritanism and Karaism have largely withered away; there are traces of both in Israel, very small number of people practicing their faith there. But Christianity, as I have told you, has succeeded beyond expectation.)

In the 17th century a false Messiah arose, one Shabbetai Zevi who, before his downfall and apostasy to Islam, brought much shame and suffering to Jews. Many of his followers moved away from Judaism.

An offshoot of the Shabbatean movement in the 18th century, Frankism, created a serious threat to Jews and the most important schism since Karaism. Thank the Lord, this Frankist schism has now completely disappeared.

But there have been many non-schismatic differences in the past. The Sadducees and Pharisees; then, the schools of Hillel and Shammai—they disagreed violently on occasion, even with murderous attacks—and right down to our own age. (Why, even you, my Master, have had your disagreement with other religious leaders; remember, for example, that Gaon in Babylonia.) And your work, while undoubtedly inspired by the Holy Spirit, has not achieved universal acceptance in Judaism. Certainly in this age, and for several centuries now, you are revered as the greatest sage since Moses our Teacher; and so, perhaps, you will not be too upset to learn that in the 13th century, some rabbis hated you so much (ostensibly because of your affinity to Aristotle, but perhaps because of simple jealousy) that they actually excommunicated your work.

The 14th century brought a re-birth of intellectual advancement to Europe, and this movement, 400 years later, blossomed into something called enlightenment in central Europe. People started to think for themselves, accepted fewer prescribed formulas, religious or otherwise; craved truth, liberty, equality. These trends brought about the French Revolution of 1789; and that, in turn, shook up people everywhere, forcing them to think, to reject the old, to insist on new and free modes of social interaction. This trend, inevitably, reached our people.

Three great men arose in the early 18th century. In Lithuania, a new "Gaon of Vilna" was proclaimed, one Elijah ben Salomon, greatly learned in all matters spiritual and secular, one who wanted nothing less than the preservation of traditional Jewish values even while bringing them into the new age. Meanwhile, in the south of Poland, Hasidism was established by one Israel ben Eliezer, the "Baal Shem Tov".

You have been familiar with the ancient mystical movements. In Judaism, that movement gathered strength in Provence, beginning just about in our days, and eventually spread all over Europe. It was called "Kabbalah". Originally, the movement concerned itself with deeper understanding of the T'nach, and of the Holy One, blessed is He. This they hoped to achieve through finding the hidden meaning of His words, using such devices as gematria and notrikon. Then, under the leadership of the Baal Shem Tov, this originally ascetic movement became transformed into a joyous way of life, complete with miracle-making rabbis, singing, dancing, extasy. While all command-ments were unquestionably and enthusiastically observed (and still are; indeed, today's Hasidim are among the Ultra-orthodox, as are the followers of the Gaon of Vilna), Hasidism was excommunicated twice by the Orthodox, especially by Elijah ben Salomon.

The third great man of 18th century Judaism was a German Jew, one Moses Mendelssohn. His work may have had the most lasting, most pronounced effect on our people in the last two centuries. He brought enlightenment to the Jews. This movement was called the Haskalah, an internal effort to bring light and understanding to the mind of the Jews. The most important tool for this was the innovative idea that Jews should study the sciences as well as Torah. The idea goes back to a certain Moshe ben Maimon, sage living in Fostat; and let me tell you, it was not enthusiastically accepted in your days or in the centuries following our time. I think that you were right, such studies are important, but if you ever wondered what the result may be, it is now demonstrated in the 20th century.

Haskalah led to young Jews forming bonds of friendship with Gentiles involved in similar studies; eventually, these young people began to demand full rights, equality for Jews; and in several countries, they actually achieved that objective. This was the "emancipation" of the European Jews.

(As an aside: Moses Mendelssohn had six children. Two of them became Catholics. Two were Protestants, while two remained Jewish—last generation Jewish.)

Emancipation necessitated for Jews to give up their self-government, their judicial system and with it, the entire rabbinical Judaism of the last two millennia. With no central rabbinical authority, pluralism was born. A most important concept emerged: that of Judaism being simply a religion (as opposed to a people living temporarily in exile with their own ways of life, religion as well as jurisprudence).

As a result of these radical concepts, and also to traditionalist reaction against them, several major new movements developed in the 19th and 20th centuries: Reform, or Liberal Judaism, based on the idea of hala-khic progress, "newly revealed insights of reason"; Orthodoxy, steadfastly traditional, but encompassing three or more levels of strictness in observing the laws, in some cases accepted fully without questioning, while in others re-interpreted slightly; and Conserva-tivism, an intermediate philosophy, at first closer to Orthodoxy, but pushed further to the "left", to liberalism as a result of the more recent Reconstructionist split. The latter has stated that Judaism has been in constant development, renewal; and that a major renewal was now called for. There is even a Secular branch of Judaism. I shall tell you more about the various branches soon. But first, another movement needs to be mentioned: Zionism.

This movement, the one that has, with the help of the Lord, blessed be His name, succeeded in re-establishing the State of Israel, emerged in the 19th century as a result of frustration, of the apparent failure of the emancipation, especially in Eastern Europe. In Russia and Ukraine pogroms, organized attacks on Jews became increasingly frequent, a heritage of the Chmielnitzki massacres of the 17th century. Jews, now equipped to think freely, began to ask the question: Why do we have to live under constant oppression? Why could we not have our own land?

Zionism was greatly opposed by most Jewish leaders, especially those of Reform who thought of Jews as Germans, Frenchmen, Englishmen, Americans of Jewish faith. Nevertheless, the Zionist movement has constantly gained strength; the eventual agreement of the major nations of the world to the establishment of the Jewish state, while important, was perhaps simply recognition of inevitable facts: Jews were returning to the land of their forebears. Of course, the main reason of Jewish return to Israel was the Nazi Holocaust of Germany in the mid-20th century.

But Zionism has never been a religious movement—far from it. To the contrary, it has been extremely secular, even if it has always encompassed some religious branches, groups within it; so perhaps we should not consider that movement when discussing the branches of Judaism. In a sense, every Jew today is a Zionist, regardless of religious affiliation; with the notable exception of several groups of Hasids and other Ultra-orthodox; these people question the legitimacy of the State of Israel, since it was not created by the Messiah. (But how can they know?)

And so, let me try to explain to you about the main branches of Judaism that I have already mentioned briefly above.

Let me start with Reform. The movement rejected the three main pillars of Judaism: the Halakhah; the concept of national deliverance (indeed, the movement was strongly anti-Zionist until the creation of the State of Israel, but that stance has changed radically since); and the Hebrew language (again, now considered an acceptable "alternative to the vernacular" in the service; now respectable, of course, as the living language of Israel).

At first, Reform advocated the observance of the Shabbat on Sunday, because of convenience; now, they have long retreated from that position. Indeed, Reform has moved steadily closer to Conservativism. Yet it still rejects Halakhah and Jewish tradition as authoritative guides to daily living: considers them, rather, a resource to be selectively mined for its mission. Politically, too, Reform tends to be on the "left", that is, supporting the most liberal causes.

Synagogue service, in Reform, has been "cleaned up", simplified; it resembles a Christian service, with the leader reading passages in the vernacular, and the congregation dutifully responding with alternate passages. Head coverings are seldom worn. Men and women sit together; the proceedings are extremely decorous.

Yet Reform is not rejected by most other branches. The reason, I think, is a realization, by all, that Jews must "stick together" remain parts of the same large group, regardless of services and observances. The Holocaust made this point obvious; and years later, when Israel was in deadly peril by its Arab enemies, all came to its aid, and all cheered its victory.

The mainline branch of Judaism is Conservatism. In its early days, it strived to restore the halakhah to the modern world. In that, it differed little from the more liberal branches of Orthodoxy. The Reconstructionist split was a major shock, and resulted in the movement's willingness to "re-study" Halakhah, consider changes for "better" observance of the law. A Committee on Jewish Law and Standards has been established. Also, as in Reform, women are accepted as equals (or nearly so) in synagogue service and all aspects of Jewish life.

A Conservative service is also very decorous, not noisy and apparently disorganized, as it used to be in the old days. The synagogue is considered a smaller form of the Temple (and the size and pomp of some may approach that of the original). Conservative Jews are seldom observant outside the services; nevertheless, they consider themselves good Jews; and some ways, they are. They tend to be solid family men and women, do not hesitate to provide for charity, and have deep respect for those whose Jewish knowledge and observance exceeds their own.

Orthodox congregations follow all of the traditional rules; their adherents are supposed to be God-fearing and observant. In most Orthodox congregations, that latter expectation is not fulfilled. Indeed, it is safe to say that the vast majority of Orthodoxy of this age would have been excommunicated in our days, or punished with stripes. I am not condemning them; an argument can be made that times have changed, standards have changed. Another argument can also be made, that the Lord's words are for all times. Ah, but the interpretations! Can't every age re-interpret those words?

But then, there are the Ultra-orthodox, the "Haredim". (The word, means, as you know, those who *tremble* in fear of the Lord.) They do observe the Law. The letter of the Law. I mentioned that some of them bend it, find ways to conform to the Law, but not, perhaps, to its spirit. Just one example: money lent by a Jew to another should carry no interest. Yet paying or receiving interest on borrowed money is a standard way of doing business today. The Ultra-orthodox will make side-agreements, trying to make the interest appear as something else. They would not consider lending money without interest; will pay interest without undue argument; but consider those side-agreements very important, for they make the transaction appear legal according to Jewish law. Yet, if interest is truly abhorrent in the eye of the Lord, then no amount of hiding will make the transaction acceptable to Him; while if He agrees that times have changed, interest is a necessary component of today's business life, then why pretend it is something else? I suppose that they feel that if they demonstrate to the Lord that they have made the effort, He might find that sufficient.

You would find the appearance of the Ultra-Orthodox very strange. Their lifestyle is conspicuously traditional, the tradition in this case being one of 17th and 18th century Poland and Ukraine. Theirs is a devout and family-oriented life; in today's permissive world, they manage to keep the evils of drug abuse, sexual aberration and immorality at bay. They are fully aware that their dress is out of date by several hundred years; they consider that flagrancy an absolute necessity for maintaining their way of life: this makes straying by a member very difficult, if not impossible. (It is interesting that similar anachronistic mode of dress and, indeed, behaviour, is to be found among several isolated Christian sects).

The Hasidic movement is part of Ultra-orthodoxy, but quite distinct. (The difference is seldom understood even by the secular Jews.) They stress piety and spirituality, somewhat to the detriment of scholarship, as the highest desirable objective. They are, as I have mentioned, very religious; they are observant and they do wear old-fashioned garb; but they are, on religious occasions, joyous, extatic, they sing and dance and express their adoration for their "rebbe", the rabbi, teacher, leader who is, at best, reputed to be a miracle-maker. In some respects they, too, have their parallel among the very religious Christians: those are called "charismatics", groups that believe in common miracles, especially invoked through extasy, song, dance, laying on hands, speaking in tongues and other strange practices. Also, despite the joy expressed in their services, Hasidim, like those Christian groups, conduct a nearly ascetic lifestyle—private joys and enjoyment are considered sinful.

At the other extreme, there is also a branch (although it is hard to accept it as such) called Secular Judaism. They are atheistic or, at best, agnostics; but want to maintain their Jewish identity. Can a Jew be a Jew without believing in God? I think not. Perhaps they remember the comfort of the Jewish religious ceremonies at their parents', grandparents' house and try to bring some of that warm feeling back without the demands inherent in serving a Supreme Being; but their children, grandchildren won't have those same memories. Would you not expect that "branch" to die out? Yet, perhaps, remembering nothing but the fact that they are Jewish will be enough for those children and grandchildren to awaken their sense, their desire of belonging, fully, to the group; and that, in turn, may lead them to re-adopt Jewish practices and eventually begin searching for God. Something like that has actually happened in the Soviet Union, where seventy years of Communist suppression, indeed eradication of religion has not succeeded in killing off Jewish identity; where a Jewish re-awakening is a miracle of the 20th century.

Somewhat more serious are the Reconstructionists. They want to renew Jewish religion; they seek to define what it is in Judaism that makes it particular and they try to preserve that particularity, without God, perhaps, but with rich spirituality. They leave the decision regarding personal belief to the conscience of their individual members; but they value Jewish tradition. They hope for spiritual fulfillment, salvation in this world, rather than the next. In maintaining tradition with many of the rituals, yet eliminating the necessity of venerating, adoring and fearing God, they seem to create a religion that is, in my humble opinion, Jewish in form but not in substance. Each member makes his or her choice about what to accept, what to reject. It is true that most Jews, members of all movements except perhaps the Ultra-orthodox, tend to pick and choose anyway; but they are not encouraged in such selection process; so you could either say that Reconstruction makes a travesty out of the Law; or that this is the only honest group that does not pretend to adhere to a Law which is blatantly ignored by its membership.

These major groups, or branches, are typical of North America and, with some variation, to other "western" countries. There are Jews in other lands, but they can hardly afford the luxury of choosing their classification within Judaism.

And most important, in Israel there is no religious formal pluralism. There are no Conservative, Reform or Reconstructionist congregations (although there are representatives of the major American organizations there). There, every Jew is considered simply a Jew; every congregation is considered Orthodox. In customs and ritual, there are vast differences: first of all, the Sephardic, or southern Jewish customs have diverged from the Ashkenazi, or northern ones over the centuries; and then, obviously, there are congregations that are less strict in their services, observances, customs than others. But all are Orthodox in name, so the problem of factionalism does not exist.

Or would that it were so! For the Ultra-orthodox *are* different. They are relatively few in numbers, but they are trying to impose their ways on the whole country. I am not criticising them for that; after all, it may be necessary, it may be the Lord's will that the majority of Jews be brought back to the fold of Orthodoxy, acceptance and full observation of the Law; but then, it may also be that by their inflexible attitude they shall alienate the large number of Jews who like the religion for its comfortable traditions, but have no intention of living the life of the devout. There has actually been some violence, even quite recently, between the Haredim and the non-observant.

There is also one big problem; I wish I knew how you would solve it. In the countries of the diaspora, there are many mixed marriages. As many as one out of two Jews marry Gentiles, and many of them will be lost to Judaism. Fortunately, a large number of these mixed marriages, perhaps half, result in the non-Jewish partner converting to our faith. The Rabbis usually convert them with a wink, as it were; for obviously, only those should be allowed to convert who come to that decision out of deep personal conviction for the validity of Judaism, not as a convenience towards marriage.

However, the conversion itself should not be an easy matter; usually, it is not. Normally, it includes long periods of study, immersion into our customs and practices; typically, the converted party becomes a better Jew than his or her Jewish partner. But why are there many diaspora (though not Israeli) rabbis willing to convert anybody, quite easily, almost as a formality? They do this with the best of intentions: it is always better for a Gentile to convert than to loose a Jew. They don't want to make the process difficult; they don't want to scare a potential convert away.

Unfortunately, conversions by Conservative and Reform rabbis are not considered acceptable by the Ultra-orthodox in Israel, and you cannot blame them for that view. Every diaspora Jew has a right to become an Israeli citizen at any time; but the Haredim want to take that right away from those converted by a non-Orthodox rabbi; also, from the children of women so converted. Such a move would go far to maintain the purity of the Jewish stock. Some claim that it would also, increasingly, make us inbred, diminish our stock. It would certainly alienate many important supporters of Israel in the western world, supporters whose assistance and involvement is desperately needed. How would you, Rabbi, solve that dilemma? I wish you were here to help us.

The truest of your devoted servants

Yusuf ben Yehudah ibn-Sham`un

HOW ARE THE JEWS OF TODAY WORSE THAN IN THE PAST

28 Tevet 5749 / January 5, 1989

To B'Rabbi Moshe ben Rabbi Maimon ha-Sfaradi,
Fostat, Egypt

My honoured Master:

I am sure that you received a great shock when reading my letter
about the Jews of today—how they live, how they behave, how they
ignore the Law. I am sorry to have saddened you so. In this letter I
would like to commiserate with you and give you my views on how
today's Jews are worse than those of our own age: what they have
lost. Yet in my next letter to you, with the help of the Merciful, I
shall also give you arguments on how today's Jews could be considered better than those of, say, eight centuries ago. I think that there
are good arguments for that case, too.

Yes, today's Jew has lost a lot. He has lost his knowledge of Torah,
first of all—nay, most important of all! Apart from a few simple
stories, familiar to all in most parts of the world, he has no idea what
is in the various parts of T'nach. Nor does he know what it means to
be a Jew; at least, not in a legalistic sense. Of the commandments,
while he may actually observe about 150, he could not name more
than, perhaps, twenty.

Well, would that matter if, nevertheless, he loved his God and was
willing to stand up for Him and for his faith? But that is exactly the
problem: the average modern Jew has lost his dedication to God. We
cannot say that he loves God, except in a vague sense, based on
something he may remember from childhood, his mother may have

told him that God was good and, therefore, is to be loved. More often than not, even that much is missing: parents bring up their children without instilling in them any religious feeling at all, with the comment: "he'll make up his own mind about these things when he grows up".

Master, the modern Jew, along with the modern Gentile, does not believe in God!

Or, at best, God is a mystical being to him, one that may be out there somewhere, but has little to do with daily life. Also, to the intelligent modern Jew, to all modern people who are willing to think, God is somebody who simply represents ethics and morality; either an allegorical embodiment of ethics or, in the unlikely case that He really exists, somebody who is good and is sad to see that man is bad; somebody who would like man to be good, but is powerless to interfere; somebody who sees the earth being destroyed by man, sees life being eradicated on earth, but cannot stop the destruction process. In other words, a useless God, an observer.

If you asked an honest, average Jew today about God, he would tell you that it would be so nice to believe in God, but how can he, after what happened in this century. Yes, the Holocaust has left a horrible wound on the psyche of the modern Jew. Very few recognize that it was a necessary evil; that God, far from powerless, was the one who willed it; and that it was for the benefit of Jewry!

You cannot blame people for not seeing this, when they have lost some of those closest to them, dearest to them. It takes a very great man to accept God's will without complaining, when it is so painful. If one cannot accept the fact that God sees things differently, from a higher level, then one is forced to choose between denying His existence, and calling Him "bad". In that case, the best choice seems to be the former, with the added proviso that "or, if He exists, then He is powerless".

But is today's Jew still a Jew? Despite his disregard for the Law, or much of it, he would answer this question with a resounding "yes", based on the few traditions that he still follows, or if he has none left, then on the fact that he has been born into Jewry, the group, the race.

Yet, I am afraid, that is where today's Jew has lost most. He may belong technically; he may have Jewish relatives, Jewish friends; but he is really like everybody else. The strength of his identification with Jewry has weakened, while his affinity with the surrounding nations has reached the point where there is little difference between a Jewish house and a Gentile one.

While people will still point at him, call him by derisive names behind his back, hiss "Jew" at him, the term means very little. (In Eastern European countries, for instance, people, influenced by their priests and often by state leaders, keep making antisemitic remarks while admitting that they have never seen a Jew or know what one is like.)

What has happened is that the uniqueness of Jewry, its moral leadership, its heavy ethical standards, even intellectual attainments have eroded.

Of course, it is possible to look at that fact positively: that we have carried those high standards through the centuries and millennia, unfailingly and in the face of the strongest opposition and persecution, until the world has become tired of fighting it and has gradually come around to accepting our standards. On ethical, moral and legal levels, at least in the western democracies, today's norms do indeed approach (and in some respects even surpass) the demands placed upon a Jew by his Law. So we have won even as having lost our identity to the vanquished.

Yes, we could say that; but then, there are the Haredim who are still separate, still different, still God-fearing, still law-abiding in the Jewish sense. And while the modern Jew points fingers at them the same way Gentiles point at the modern Jew, and is quite a bit embarrassed by the Ultra-orthodox, yet deep down he wonders if he should not be with them, should not wear their ridiculous garb, openly inviting derision and forcing himself to be different, removing any other option, cutting off assimilation at the root.

For the Reform, Judaism is just another religion. For Reconstruction, it is a way of life without the necessary subservience to God. For the Conservative, it is a little of both, along with bowing to God, but not necessarily believing in Him. For the Orthodox, it is observing more laws, without much thinking about the existence of God. Only the Ultra-orthodox is willing to be a real Jew, observing all the commandments, again without speculating on the Prime Mover; according to them, such speculation is not an intrinsic part of being a Jew, and I think they are right, notwithstanding the fact that you, who are the Head of Teaching, and I, your devoted servant, could not have existed without such speculation. The Haredim are the real Jews even if, occasionally, I question their sincerity, too. The others, really, are not Jews as we used to know them. But, nevertheless, they still are Jews, let us remember that.

As I mentioned in my last letter, after seventy years of religious oppression in the Soviet Union, after forcing Jewish parents not even to mention the fact of their Jewish identity to their children for fear of state-encouraged denunciation by the youngsters, after three generations of official atheism reaching the inside of every home, pride of Jewishness suddenly erupts; anybody who can prove Jewish origin does so, in the face of still further persecution. Certainly it may provide some with the opportunity of leaving their country; but that process takes years, years of suffering. No, let us allow it: a Jew is a Jew, regardless of what laws he observes, what commandments he fulfills. He has lost a lot, but he has also gained something. I shall try to give you my opinion on that in my next letter.

The truest of your devoted servants

Yusuf ben Yehudah ibn-Sham`un

HOW ARE THE JEWS OF TODAY BETTER THAN IN THE PAST

6 Shevat 5749 / January 12, 1989

To B'Rabbi Moshe ben Rabbi Maimon ha-Sfaradi,
Fostat, Egypt

My honoured Master:

I would like to suggest to you some positive aspects of today's Jew; show you how he has gained something over the last eight centuries, especially the last one; how he has become, some ways, a better person, better Jew than we were.

First of all, the average Jew—perhaps even the average Gentile—is a more moral person than ever before. All the basic rules that needed to be hammered into his head over the millennia are now quite natural to him: prohibition against murder, against theft, against unnatural acts (with the unfortunate exception of homosexuality), certainly against creating and worshipping idols; and against exploiting the labour of fellow human beings.

Today's Jew—like most Gentiles—is knowledgable about things we could not even conceive of eight centuries ago. He knows much more than even you did, my honoured Master, in areas of advanced mathematics, arts and music, economics, geography, ecology, archeology, anthropology, electricity and electronics, nuclear physics and various other aspects of physics, chemistry—why, the most simple chemical reaction that any ten- year old knows would have been a great revelation in our age! Most people today understand the automotive forces including the internal combustion engine; millions of people are capable of performing simple repairs to cars. Hundreds of millions know how to install electric lights, how to tame the deadly forces involved. Most people can perform reasonably complex arithmetics and administrative functions and everybody can use calculating machines and duplicating machines and I could go on and on and on.

I could not prove to you, or to myself, that the Jew of today is more intelligent than eight centuries ago. But I could prove that his understanding of the world, all aspects of it (except understanding the Highest) is far more advanced than anybody's in our age, including yours or mine.

I would go as far as saying that today's individual is well ahead of one in the 12th century, much advanced in God's grand design, His plans towards—well, let us speculate about that later on.

Secondly, forgetting about the individual, there is Jewry as a whole. Is it better today? Actually, many ways it is. It has firmly established itself as a moral leader among other groups in all western lands. There are few intelligent people in the world who do not realize that all of the modern ethical, moral, egalitarian, labour relational, jurisprudential and familial concepts have been adopted from Judaism. Jews may be disliked everywhere, but it is a dislike based on envy, not only envy of wealth (for Jews tend to be excellent businesspeople) but envy of moral and intellectual achievement.

Nonetheless, Jews have assimilated in most countries into the social and economical structure of the nation. This assimilation has mixed benefits: it allows Jews to stay at the forefront of all modern development, be it scientific, economical, cultural or other; but it gradually attenuates the ties binding the individual to the group. Every once in a while the Lord, blessed is His name, needs to do something for the individual Jew to be pulled back into the group; in every generation there are those who rise up against us.

Jewry, the community, is highly visible as builders of hospitals and schools, as contributors to worthy causes, as protesters against injustice. For their relatively small numbers, Jews are everywhere, conspicuous where people educate, heal, write, perform, plan national economies or lead in almost any walk of life. No, you cannot say that Jewry has deteriorated. It is strong, active, vigorous, but in areas vastly different from in our days.

And thirdly, there is another way of looking at today's Jew: one may consider that what matters most is not the individual; not various groups of Jews, not even Jewry as a whole; but the State of Israel. According to this view, what has mattered all along the last three and a half millennia has been a strong state that the Lord has used as the focal point of His development plans, and in that sense the State of Israel has always been there. But, in order for it to become very strong and be able to defend itself from the tremendous forces of the modern world, it was necessary for the Lord to disperse the people, to let them live among the various nations for 1900 years, to let them learn all kinds of things from those nations, and then to let them to return stronger than ever.

If so, the plan was extremely dangerous; any critic would have rejected it on the basis that the Jews could not possibly survive two millennia among the nations of the world. They would be either killed or assimilated; would disappear one way or another. Indeed, there never was an instance of such a diaspora, with the possible exception of what may have been the Lord's experiments, involving our own people in Egypt, perhaps Assyria, certainly Babylonia. Clearly, the plan was impossible; to this day people are trying to understand how it could have worked, why it did work; but it was God's plan, blessed is He, and so it *has* succeeded, miraculously if painfully. (It is not easy to be part of the chosen people.)

And, as part of the plan, God made one major change in the nature of the Jew: through forcing the natural selection process, the concept of the survival of the fittest, He has bred a Jew who is a natural survivor.

Greater and greater disasters have been visited upon us; many perished, some survived: those with the best instincts combined with the soundest judgment on how to avoid deadly danger.

So now we have a state, one that is the most advanced in terms of knowledge, law, social structure and, especially, defense. Israel is a country that is able, again, to lead the world in the next stages of the Lord's plan: stages that are, obviously, going to be as difficult as earlier ones, or more so, stages that require a stout and intrepid leader, not an individual but a whole nation, small but strong, resistant, permanent.

The good Lord has not abandoned His people; to the contrary, He has brought them along on a difficult and painful road to new heights of glory. Praised be the Lord who keeps His covenant with His people forever, Amen.

Master, this is the last of my first series of letters. Blessed be the Merciful who has aided us.

The truest of your devoted servants

Yusuf ben Yehudah ibn-Sham'un

BOOK II.

Rambam, we don't agree with everything you said.

YOSEF BEN YEHUDAH IBN-SHIM'ON'S LETTER TO RAMBAM

7 Elul 5749 / September 7, 1989

To B'Rabbi Moshe ben Rabbi Maimon ha-Sfaradi,
Fostat, Egypt

My beloved Master, the Head of the Teaching:

I have done a lot of thinking lately. How could I help doing so? The fact that everything is so different in this age forces one to think new thoughts; all things are presented in the extra dimension of a new age. I think that even a moron, when transported backward or forward in time, would become somewhat of a sage, through being forced to re-consider all that he, along with the best minds of his own age, has taken for granted.

When you think deeply, you develop new views, new convictions. I have done so. I have no doubt that you will accuse me of having simply accepted the views, the standards of the current age, which you may call a godless age. Be assured, Rabbi, that is far from the case. I don't accept their views; I may deplore many of their thoughts and practices; but I try to understand them. Yet more important, I am afraid that by now I disapprove of many of the thoughts and practices of our own earlier age, the 12th century; and perhaps by explaining these current thoughts of mine, I can convince you to adopt some, if not all, of these thoughts.

You see, it is my secret desire that by being able to see the world from two vantage points, those of the 12th and 20th centuries, I may be able to extrapolate the progress of the last eight centuries into the future, many centuries or millennia into the future; and having done so, look back from there at the primitive early ages, both yours and my current one!

For primitive, indeed, was our twelfth century; and no doubt so will the twentieth be viewed from the vantage point of, say, the thirtieth. Primitive, narrow-minded, dark, oppressive, intolerant, smug. At least, in the 20th century, the better minds realize how little we know, how the store of accumulated knowledge changes as it grows, how views and standards alter rapidly over the centuries, even over decades. But in the 12th century, we did not know that. We were not, perhaps, in a position to know that.

Nevertheless, you are bound to ask if I am equating the average thinking of the 11th and 12th century with that of the minds of that age, people such as ibn Rushd (they call him Averroes now), Abelard, Halevy, ibn Daud and the greatest of all, Moshe ibn Maimon, the man they now call Maimonides?

No, of course, I am not. But I shall point out that yourself, and other sages of that age, may have attempted, could have tried, to see the world in motion, rather than frozen in one moment of history; if so, you could have developed different views, paid less attention to the temporary, the fleeting, less respect for that which applied to one particular age alone.

You may very well respond, my Master, with the comment that I was always partial to "light chatter". It would pain me, but I should not be surprised if you said that; or if you made a biting comment about my pretension to prophecy. Yet may I remind you, Rabbi, that some of my ideas have withstood the test of time quite well: I rejected the doctrine of emanation when it was the rage of all thinkers, yourself first among them; look where that doctrine is today: nowhere; it is dead. And do you recall that I endeavoured to prove the creation of the world from purposeful functionality? That is one thing I am still trying to do, and modern science seems to be on my side. And, again,

I rejected the concept of the heavenly spheres and their spirits, I called them allegoric inventions. I did; some people did not do so.

I hope you don't mind these words, Rabbi. They may be harsh, but I know that you always wanted to learn new things, and you can only learn from someone who has things to tell you that are new to you. I would not dream of pretending to have anything even approaching your intelligence; but I have learned new things in the 20th century. Accepting new things is often painful. I would like to cause you just a little pain by writing about intolerance; and following that, about various aspects of the law and modes of living, aspects that will force you, I hope, to reconsider some of your views.

Do I dare to criticize the great Rambam (the name we Jews have used for you over these centuries, an acronym from *R*abbi *M*oshe *b*en *M*aimon)? No, how could I? But were that Rambam to come to the 20th century, were he to live there for some time and were he, then, still to maintain his original views stubbornly, then yes, I *would* criticize him. And Master, you *were* criticized by many eminent Jewish thinkers throughout the ages, even as they revered you as the greatest of our sages for the last two millennia.

What I would like to do, Rabbi, is to write you a number of letters —oh, perhaps a dozen or more—on these topics, all familiar to you, but put in the light of this different age, so you can share my views on how things have changed. At least, I hope that you will come to such sharing; that you will not reject those views, those letters out of hand.

Your devoted disciple

Yosef ben Yehudah ibn-Shim`on

INTOLERANCE:

CHRISTIANITY, ISLAM AND OTHER FAITHS

14 Elul 5749 / September 14, 1989

To B'Rabbi Moshe ben Rabbi Maimon ha-Sfaradi,
Fostat, Egypt

My beloved Master:

Let me write to you about various religions. Other than our own, you
were most familiar with Islam, slightly with Christianity. (Oh, but how
they have changed!)

There are other important religions in the world, especially in the Far
Eastern countries of Asia: Hinduism, mainly in India; Buddhism, there
and in all other lands to the east, especially in Japan and, to the extent
permitted by the totalitarian Communist regime, in China; the same
comments apply to Taoism and Confucianism in China; and then, a
large number of local variations of these faiths; also, Shintoism, again,
in Japan; Jainism and Sikhism in India, and Zoroastrianism, too; and
yet many others. Lots of religions in Asia. But then, were we to count
the varieties of the Christian creed, we may very well find just as
many in America alone; even Islam has numerous branches.

Having enumerated these religions, I must admit, Master, to having
also exhausted the store of my knowledge accumulated so far on them.
So why talk about something unfamiliar? I better stick to Christianity
and Islam about which I know at least enough for one or two letters
to you.

Christianity, in its various versions, is the primary faith of all of Europe, with the exceptions of Turkey, Albania and parts of Yugoslavia. In addition, it has a similarly dominant position in all of North America, South Africa, Australia and New Zealand. In South and Central America, it is more than dominant: it is almost exclusive. And then, there are significant pockets of Christianity among Asian people, including many of the Koreans; and even in Lebanon, there are many Christians busy killing Muslims, and being killed by Muslims.

Islam, then, is prevalent in northern Africa (indeed, you will find heavy Islamic presence all over Africa, except in the extreme south), in western Asia including all Arab lands and such countries as Iran (Persia), Afghanistan, Pakistan (two large countries in-between Persia and India), even some parts of India itself. In the south of the Soviet Union, the religion that was oppressed for seventy years is not Christianity or Judaism but Islam. (The oppression is now easing.) In Europe, Turkey, parts of Yugoslavia—a land rapidly falling apart to its constituent parts—and Albania are the only Islamic countries; elsewhere, that faith is almost unknown, even vestiges are not to be found. As far as I can determine, there are no Muslims, other than visiting foreigners, in countries like Spain and Hungary, despite centuries of Moorish or Ottoman occupation. Bulgaria and Greece may be exceptions.

Now, to understand the attitude of those who follow these two major creeds, you must remember that during the last eight centuries Christian civilization has greatly advanced, while the Islamic one has regressed. By the beginning of this century, with very few exceptions Islamic countries were backward, primitive nations, with populations that were generally considered ignorant and crude; and so far, the consideration was largely correct. Unfortunately, some westerners went further and described Arabs as genetically inferior; that view must be rejected; for the past indicates that under different circumstances, under extended periods of enlightened leadership, Arabs are capable of achievements in no way less remarkable than people of most western lands. The decline of those nations must, I think, be

attributed to Islam; perhaps the innate fatalism of the currently
dominant Ash`ariyan theology has worked its deterministic way
through its logical conclusion, engendering a deep-seated hopelessness
while removing all incentive and ambition from the mind of those
people.

It must be difficult for you to accept these facts, for you were so
familiar with Islam at its peak, with all of its glorious philosophers,
mathematicians, poets, physicians, astronomers. Nevertheless, it is
true, the decline was real. Worse, from our standpoint: to some extent
the Jews who were living in those lands have suffered similar
deterioration: while there have been a number of great men among the
Sephardic Jews, more recently almost all of the outstanding Jewish
leaders, as well as men of science, philosophy, medicine and art have
come from the Ashkenazi branch of the family.

Christianity, on the other hand, has produced great cultures, im-
pressive civilizations. Christians, especially in those lands where the
help of Jews was more often then not accepted, at least in the critical
age of enlightenment, have succeeded in building modern, efficient
countries with advanced economies based on sound infrastructure of
agriculture, mining and industry; excellent educational systems;
constantly improving standards of living, at least in recent times;
culture at levels we could not dream about; along with instances of
religious intolerance, proud bestiality reaching from the Crusades to
the Nazi holocaust. Yes, I know, it does not make sense. Muslims
have always hated Jews, but only infrequently massacred them; also,
they often offered the alternative of conversion. Many did convert, as
you well know, for appearance's sake; but conversion did not impress
Hitler, the Nazi; he killed anyone even with only one Jewish grandparent.

How did all this intolerance come about? What really has happened
to Christianity? For that matter, what has happened to Islam, which
seems to have inherited Christian intolerance? I don't think that I can
explain it all; what I can do is tell you about their recent histories,

first; and then, in my next letter, show you how cruel, how intolerant they all are, or were. I don't think the history will justify the intolerance; you may be able to show cause and effect if I fail to do so. Let me review Islam first.

You knew Islam in its golden age in the 12th century. Perhaps you were also familiar with its early days: its history includes more shameful periods than proud, up-lifting ones. It started with an astonishing burst of energy and became established over a very short period, less than half a century, in a very large part of the world. After the death of Muhammad, Islam became a ruthless regime, perhaps a necessity for a new, growing revolutionary movement; murdering those whose opinion was only slightly different from those in power, so- called heretics, became routine. There were many-many heretics, as the ideology twisted its way through pragmatic expediency.

But later, in our time and before, the religion became more civilized, more tolerant of diverse views, with some notable exceptions, such as the Almohades whom we knew so well. Still, from the 10th to the 13th century, it was not generally unpleasant for an outsider to live under Islamic rule. (It was not exactly a delight, either. I recall others, including my namesake Yosef ben Yehudah ibn Aknin expecting the Messiah soon, because he thought that we were living through the worst possible times.)

You were familiar with the rationalist Mu`tazilite theology that eventually was discredited by the Ash`arite orthodoxy. In a sense, Islamic theological philosophy (but "philosophy" became a detested word after al-Ghazzali) is still based on Ash`ariyanism, at least in the principal branch of Islam, which is the Sunni sect. There was, it is true, a mystical, spiritual movement from the 12th to the 18th century, Sufism, in some ways surviving even to this day; yet even it has always considered itself (with the exception of a few sects) to be part of the Sunni mainstream.

Relatively minor movements or branches flourished and sometimes shrivelled: the Isma'ilis, with various sub-sects, very much in evidence today; the Assassins and the Druze sects which are also still around in the 20th century; the Fatimids under whose rule you actually lived for a while; the Kharijites, only traces of whom now survive; the Ahmadyans, a 20th century movement from India and Pakistan; an offshoot called Baha'i, now based in Israel, which also incorporates aspects of Christianity, Buddhism and other religions.

But I have not yet mentioned the second most important branch of Islam: the Shi`a, followers of `Ali. They are parts of Islam, but oppose most of the main practices. In earlier days, the Shi`ites were known for more flexibility than the Sunnis, accepted outside influences from Christianity and Zoroastrianism. But in the 20th century, Shi`a has become the most inflexible core of Islam; and as such, the sect lays claim to the role of the truest follower of the Prophet. They have established their own version of the Hadith, even expanded the basic creed, which now includes reference not only to Muhammad but to `Ali ("There is no God but God and Muhammad is his prophet *and* `Ali is his friend*")!

What happened in the 20th century is that in most Islamic countries, the original concept of the Shari'a became obsolete: religious tenets notwithstanding, separation of the state and religion became necessary. The Shari'a calls for the Qur'an and later works to be the state law; that has proved impossible in the modern world. Reformers have attempted to change the religion formally; that also proved impossible. Religion has gradually become less important in Islamic countries; in Turkey, it was formally abolished as an integral part of state government; in most other countries, informally ignored.

But in some Islamic lands, the power of the mullahs was too strong; they have managed to exert sufficient influence over the populace to effect a coup d'etat, taking over the government and establishing something called "Islamic republics". There are a number of those around now: in Pakistan, in the Sudan, in Lybia and, especially, in the stronghold of the Shi`a, in Persia, now called Iran. And that appears to be the start of an entirely new chapter in the story of Islam, a chapter that you may find appalling when I recount some of its aspects in my next letter to you.

But let's leave Islam for a moment and talk about Christianity, with some 1000 Million adherents (versus 400 Million for Islam). In our days, it appeared a somewhat barbarous religion, good only for the ignorant masses of the north. But how times have changed! Now the knowledgeable, the advanced in science, philosophy, arts, technology and most other disciplines are the people of the north and the west. It is worth speculating what has caused the change; it is hard to escape the thought that just as religion may have stifled all creativity in Islam, it may have awakened it in Christendom. I don't know if it is so; there are backward Christian countries, even in Europe and certainly in South America; but there are no truly advanced Muslim countries anywhere. There are rich ones: many are sitting on a buried sea of fuel oil; cultural advancement could stem from those riches in another hundred years or more; a few Muslim scholars are now beginning to show evidence of high-level scientific and literary activities. Yet, meanwhile, even the backward Christian lands are catching up with their more advanced brethren, fast.

But the term "Christian" does not always mean the same thing. It does cover a wide range of creeds, branches and sects. Schisms in the Christian religion have been quite common since the days of Paul, the law-giver and law-taker. As the strength of the religion grew, heretics, some with truly insignificant doctrinal differences, were not only excommunicated but murdered as a matter of routine. And that methodology for keeping the Christian dogma pure had persisted into the 18th century. Spain was an especially fertile land for dogmatic murder.

You may recall the early heretics of Christianity: the Montanists, the Marcionists, Manicheans and other varieties of Gnostics, all in the first century. None of those heresies have survived: murder worked. But a more important schism evolved gradually between the western Church of Rome, having a Latin-Germanic culture, and the eastern variety based on Greek culture and centered in Byzantium. The two churches became increasingly unwilling to submit to the orthodoxy of the other, and by our age were part of the same faith only nominally. Soon after that, even that pretense disappeared; so now, there are eastern, or Byzantine and western or Roman churches. The process of schism was probably expedited by the Crusaders who tended to treat the highly cultured Byzantines as low-level vassals; sacked Byzantium (by then, Constantinople) and exacerbated the already strained relations. You were, of course, quite familiar with the behaviour of the Crusaders in the land of our forefathers; it may give you grim satisfaction to know that they did not treat Christian lands with any more compassion.

Those centuries, from the sixth to the twelfth, are considered the dark ages of Roman Catholicism and of west European culture. But after our time, the Roman church began to emerge, slowly, from the darkness, and most of Europe received the first ray of light with that emergence. Strangely enough, the impetus may have been Islamic theology and philosophy. Your contemporary ibn Rushd (they call him Averroes now) developed quite modern approaches for synthesizing the Islamic orthodoxy with the classical philosophies of Aristotle and Plato. He successfully combined dogma with "natural" thinking, rejecting the anti-philosophical statements of al-Ghazzali and returning to the rational methods of al-Farabi. (By accepting many of the Aristotelian teachings, Averroes did for Islam what you did for Judaism; and indeed, your teachings were also quite instrumental in changing the history of the Christian church.)

Ibn Rushd's approach was taken up by the "scholastics", especially one Thomas Aquinas of the 13th century. (He was also influenced by your work, my Master! And yet he was, and remained, dedicated to the cause of persecuting the Jews!) He not only combined Christian Scripture with the "natural" mind, but by placing Christianity on sound Aristotelian principles, he gave it a certain moral authority in addition to the theological authority based on the Messiahship of Jesus Christ.

More important, perhaps, a new movement of thinking and intellectual activity emerged, culminating in the Renaissance of the western world, just as Islam begun to fade. However, Renaissance not only produced paragons of art and, with it, unimaginable richness and luxury for the Church (not to mention, corruption), but also engendered a reaction, a movement against the trappings of the clergy, the papacy, against the concept of central authority and ecclesiastical taxing; a movement for the return to the simple values of the early church, for belief in the Christian Bible and little else. This movement was the Reformation, which culminated in a major schism in the 16th century.

The Reformation really consisted of a number of parallel efforts by various national and, indeed, city groups. When the schism was complete, there was still Roman Catholicism, based in Vatican of Rome, and then, half a dozen other churches, most without central authority, typically ruled by their respective bishops, with the faithful having important influence over church decisions.

Today, Roman Catholicism has about half of Christendom under its control, while the number of other sects, most called Protestant churches, is easily in the hundreds. Still, some of those denominations are very large: the Lutherans, Anglicans, Baptists, Presbyterians, Methodists are major churches, especially in America and Europe. Then again, many of those major denominations are subdivided, again and again; but on the other hand, what religion is not?

Still, for the last few centuries, these separate sects have, on the whole, hated but seldom killed each other. Well, yes: Christians do kill other Christians for religious reasons, here and there (for, of course, they do kill each other for other, national and political reason, that is understood). In Ireland, Protestants and Catholics have been fighting for nearly a century now. (Have I mentioned that Muslims kill other Muslims by the thousands daily?) The various denominations are all convinced of the truth of their own creed and dogma; so let the non-believer die—this is still standard Muslim tenet, with some Christian adherents.

Rabbi, I think you don't like what you are reading about Christianity and Islam. Well, Judaism is better: since the days of Hillel and Shammai, we have not killed each other for dogmatic minutiae; or, indeed, for any reason at all. We are not a murderous nation. But we do disagree with each other. And how!

The other major faiths—Buddhism, Hinduism and some others that I have already mentioned, religions of the Far East, tend to be less violent, less cruel; but then, I admit to knowing much less about them than about Judaism and its two unwanted daughters. These offsprings have certainly developed astonishing levels of intolerance for the faiths of others. I want to write to you, in my next letter, with the help of the Merciful, about the subject of intolerance.

Your devoted disciple

Yosef ben Yehudah ibn-Shim`on

INTOLERANCE NOW AND IN MAIMONIDES' TIME

27 Elul 5749 / September 27, 1989

To B'Rabbi Moshe ben Rabbi Maimon ha-Sfaradi,
Fostat, Egypt

My beloved Master:

I promised to write to you about intolerance. Let me start by quoting a few rules:

"The man who commits adultery with his neighbour's wife must die, he and his accomplice" (Lev.20:10)

". . .a man was caught gathering wood on the Sabbath day . . . The Lord said to Moses: 'This man must be put to death. The whole community must stone him outside the camp' . . ." (Num.15:32)

"If a man has a stubborn and rebellious son . . . then all his fellow citizens should stone him to death" (Deut.21:48)

"If the accusation (of a recently married man, that he slept with his wife and found no evidence of virginity) is substantiated, they shall take her to the door of her father's house and her fellow citizens shall stone her to death . . ." (Deut.22:20)

"Whoever speaks slander is deserving of being stoned to death" (Ar.15b)

"He who reads a single verse which is not from the twenty-four (books of the T'nach) . . . will have no portion of the World-to-Come" (Num.R.XIV.4)

"The following are stoned: . . . a blasphemer; an idolater . . ." (Sanh.VII.4)

"Whoever crosses a stream behind a woman will have no portion of the World-to-Come" (Ber.61a)

"For him who uses obscene language Gehinnon is deepened" (Shab.33a)

"For three transgressions women die in childbirth: because they have been negligent in regards to their periods of separation, in respect to the consecration of the dough and in the lighting of the Shabbat lamp" (Shab.II.6)

"Whoever does anything as a result of any of these happenings (divination) is punished with stripes" (Idolatry,11)

". . . a woman who adorns herself in the modes peculiar to men is punished with stripes" (Guide III,37)

"Whoever plucks out white hairs in his beard or in his head from among the dark is punished with stripes, even if he has removed only one hair . . . So, too, one who dyes his hair colour . . ." (Ibid.)

I could go on and on . . . but I believe that you do understand what I am trying to say. I am quoting from Torah, from Mishnah, Gemara and even from your own writings. I am pointing out examples of intolerance. He who is not perfect in every way, he who diverges from the current standards in his actions, no matter how trivially, or even in his words, is to receive terrible punishment, in this world or, a more recent development, in the next one.

Rabbi, I could quote for you many-many similar pronouncements from the doctrines and current opinions of the Christians, Muslims. Anybody who does not conform to *their* standards, does not believe exactly in *their* tenets has no hope of salvation, has no portion of the World-to-Come. And in the case of Islam, at least in some countries, terrible punishment is still meted out to such wrongdoers in this world as well; Christianity seems to have overcome at least those barbarities.

Why are they so intolerant? Why were *we* so intolerant? Let us consider other religions. Those which believe in One God (even if in some religions He manifests Himself as, or consists of, several different persons) believe in the same God. I am not belittling the importance of religion: it regulates a way of life, or used to; it directs individuals to God in a way that most of them could not find by themselves; and it connects the present to the past in a most worthy and realistic way. But underneath it all, surely there is only one important fact that we do know, in all of these monotheistic religions: that there is One God, who created the known world and is Lord over everything. There are, of course, many details to argue about, within any particular creed and without; but what we all should realize is that we can't possibly understand God; revelations were for another age, fashioned to mind-sets different from ours; we can argue about interpretation all we want, but at best, we can only approach the truth. Each monotheistic religion has grasped some aspects of the truth, some overlapping, some complementary; and there are, necessarily, lots of conflicts in their tenets because their understanding is faulty, or incomplete; most often, frustratingly, because they reflect a desperate attempt to express, in human terms, concepts incomprehensible to the human mind at this time.

Yet Christians want to exclude anybody else from the World-to-Come; they even assume, arrogantly, that the "wrong" Christian sects will also be excluded, but certainly Jews shall have no room there. Muslims confidently assume that only they will be welcome in Paradise; again, usually, only their narrow branch of Islam. And then, we see some of our own sages making similar claims. What conceit! What folly!

But intolerance goes further than arguing about the afterlife. It affects, one way or another, everyone in this world. Religious wars have been waged for at least the last two thousand years, and while the fervour may have abated some, Catholics and Protestants are still killing each other in Ireland, as I have mentioned; so do Hindus and Muslims in India and Pakistan; so do Hindus and Sikhs there; so do Sunnis and Shi`ites and Christians and Druze in Lebanon; so do Muslims and Jews in Israel. Many of these wars are ethnic rather than religious in character; the two aspects were never truly separate.

Take Iran. A fundamentalist Shia religious leadership took power there some ten years ago. Even though the powerful leader of that revolution is now dead, Iran is still a country whose plans and actions are motivated by hate, extreme intolerance, extending to the execution of all "heretics", Muslims whose religious opinion conflicts with those of the leading orthodoxy. Convincing their population that it is all right to kill in the name of God gives the Iranian leadership unexpected strength; they may succeed in some of their efforts. They may also set an example of the harm of intolerance; but if humanity needed such a lesson, it could have found it any time in its history, there have been such lessons too numerous to list even in a very long letter.

My Master, I have come to detest intolerance. I shall write to you about some additional aspects of it in my next letter, God willing.

Your devoted disciple

Yosef ben Yehudah ibn-Shim`on

FUNDAMENTALISM

6 Tishri 5750 / October 5, 1989

To B'Rabbi Moshe ben Rabbi Maimon ha-Sfaradi,
Fostat, Egypt

My beloved Master:

In my last letter to you, I vented my rage at intolerance. Perhaps enough has been said about that subject. (Yet can one ever rail enough against evil?) But I would like to concentrate my thoughts now on one narrow brand of intolerance, one where cruelty to one's fellow being is not the primary objective, only an unfortunate by-product in some instances.

I am referring to fundamentalism, the brand of arrogance where we assume that Scripture, our version of it, is the only true version and that it is *completely true*, in every respect.

I shall not rail against fundamentalists, for there are arguments in their favour as well as against them. More against, I think; but you be the judge of that.

Rabbi, I think I know you well, and I am sure I understand, how you view the authority of the Torah: as absolute, but subject to re-interpretation in view of the latest concepts or, at least, language of Man. Unfortunately, fundamentalists don't think of Scripture that way. To them, every word is God's word (no argument so far), and every word is to be interpreted as if it were written today.

One brand of fundamentalism is the one I wrote to you about in my last letter: fundamentalist Shi`a Islam, in Iran. Religious purity is an absolute necessity there; any nation or individual who is perceived as standing in the way of achieving such universal religious purity must be eliminated. Interpretations of Islam different from theirs are not accepted; and as for other faiths, those are to be eradicated, destroyed. Islam has always been ambivalent about Judaism and Christianity; in some writings and many situations, Jews and Christians were respected as "people of the book", permitted (along with the Zoroastrians) to practice their religion, at the cost of heavy taxes. Yet at other times, they had to be converted, their lands conquered in "jihads" for the victory of Allah; you have been familiar with both attitudes from personal experience.

I have painted a negative picture of the new Shi`a rule of Iran, and with good reason: it is a cruel, unjust, inhuman, intolerant regime. Having said that, nevertheless, I must be fair and point out that some good may have come to Iran from the inflexible attitude of their leading Ayatullahs.

You see, the western world is extremely free these days, perhaps too much so. Practically everything is permitted; it is considered bad for the individual if he is constricted in his actions in any way. A few serious crimes are frowned upon, some murderers are, on occasion, even jailed briefly. I exaggerate slightly, but only slightly: for example, capital punishment is outlawed in most western countries.

With the extreme freedom, modes of conduct that are truly outrageous have proliferated. Sexual abominations, drug abuse, not to mention the relatively minor aberrations, behaviour that makes life for the vast majority at least unpleasant, sometimes unendurable, are now rampart. Well, in Iran (and in other fundamentalist societies, as I shall show you), those thing are absolutely forbidden and practically non-existent. In forcing his people back into the middle ages, the now dead revolutionary leading Ayatullah has taken away from them all the good things of the modern age along with all the bad things. Should one condemn him or praise him? I hope you lean towards condemnation; yet my next examples of fundamentalism may very well alter those critical views of yours, if such indeed they are.

My second example, then, is in the United States of America. A branch of Protestantism, really a collection of sub-branches, does claim that every word of the Bible, the Old Testament which is our T'nach as well as the New One which deals with the life, death and resurrection of Yehoshua haNotzri, Jesus Christ and his early followers—every word of these books is true, in a literal sense. If God was said to have created the world in six days, then it was six days, a day being one of 24 hours, as we know it; it could not be, for example, a day consisting of millions of our years, neither a day having lasted only minutes or seconds or fractions of seconds.

This version of fundamentalism is a more worldly movement: its adherents are normal people in their occupations, lifestyle, dress code and most other aspects of life. But they do object to many of the more unpleasant manifestations of the modern way of living, including licentiousness, unreasonable extents of personal freedom.

These people argue about aspects of modern science, where it is in conflict with Scripture; even where the evidence is overwhelmingly in favour of science, they would not entertain the idea of a compromise, re-interpretation of the words of the Bible.

As an aside, their beliefs include the re-establishment of the State of Israel as a pre-requisite for the return of the Messiah. Because of that tenet, they are very strong supporters of Israel, our best friends in the United States.

Do you praise them, or condemn them?

My last example is closer to home. I am now talking about the Haredim, the Ultra-orthodox in North America and other parts of the world, but especially in Israel. Their fundamentalism is, of course, different in that it is not centered on Scripture alone, for that would make them Karaites. Rather, they revere all of T'nach along with the Mishnah and, indeed, the entire Talmud. Do they permit deviation? Outside their own circles, yes, up to a point. When their sensibilities are affected by the transgressions, they object. But do they ever object! They shall not permit public transportation vehicles to operate in Jerusalem on the Shabbat; they stone any kind of mechanical vehicles on their streets on that day. Nor do they permit public entertainment of any kind on the Shabbat, not even those aimed at educating the viewers. They forbid the showing of pictures which depict women immodestly dressed (or sometimes not dressed at all).

While, in other countries and, indeed, in other parts of Israel, women today dress in very scanty clothing which often reveal more than they cover, the women of the Haredim are dressed reticently, with no part of the body other than the face showing, nor hair, even when this is extremely uncomfortable because of the heat—but you know all about that.

My Master, the fundamentalist Jew of today is ourselves, you and I! Despite the relatively innovative ideas that you entertained, you were, in your mode of living, in your standards as traditional, as demanding of religious purity as today's Haredi. And so was I. You notice that I say "was", not "am". For having seen both ways of life today, I am not ready to accept one side and reject the other. In my view—for Rabbi, one inevitably develops views that may, painfully, conflict with those of one's revered Master—the Haredim are doing a wonderful, almost miraculous job of maintaining an old-fashioned, decent way of life despite the torrents of immorality and fully accepted sinfulness of today's world. Yes. But what would the Lord, blessed be His name, have us do, let the modern world pass us by entirely, in science, art, way of life? Or be part of that modern life?

I suggest, Master, that the times when the Jew needed to be a tightly knit group apart from everybody else may be past. With all of its sins and obscenities, this world is a different one than ours, sufficiently different to conclude that those "good old days" will never return. We cannot be left behind. Indeed, as I wrote to you earlier, it may be that the whole object of the diaspora has been the education of the Jews in the ways of the world, so that we can absorb the best knowledge of the Gentiles, even if along with some of the worst; and so, we can return to the Land of Israel strong, well-educated, able to stand up to the most powerful of nations and defend ourselves, deter aggression by our strength and determination. In other words, Israel must be a modern nation, at the forefront of education, culture, science, technology and, especially, defense.

Would it be possible to achieve all of these while still maintaining the traditional values? In some ways, I hope yes; we must remain true to God, blessed is He, and to His essential demands. But we must also recognize that times have changed, that many of the ancient commandments no longer apply. And in that opinion, shocking as it may sound, I have the support of the greatest of our sages since biblical times, one Moshe ibn Maimon. Yes, indeed. Just one example: Do you recall your comments about the commandments regarding Temple sacrifices?

Master, in my next letters I would like to discuss the Torah and its interpretation today. Perhaps you shall agree with what I'll have to say about it.

Your devoted disciple

Yosef ben Yehudah ibn-Shim`on

THE TORAH:

ESSENTIAL TRUTH OF THE TORAH

25 Tishri 5750 / October 24, 1989

To B'Rabbi Moshe ben Rabbi Maimon ha-Sfaradi,
Fostat, Egypt

My beloved Master:

So many things have changed over the last eight centuries, it is comforting to know that one thing has not changed at all: the Torah. Looking at the old scrolls, holding the modern printed book in my hand still sends shivers through my back: to think of all the people, our fathers who looked at those same words, fully knowing that those are the words of God Himself, His name be exalted.

Other books outlive their usefulness, become obsolete in view of the changing world; the Torah remains fresh, talks to people of all ages. It needs to be re-translated every few years into the many languages of man, but that is just a technicality. It speaks to all of us even now because it deals with real things: with God's relation to Man and with Man's relation to Man. Religion, history—big words. But a child understands nothing of religion, nothing of history, yet he will understand much of the Torah. Is it, then, a childish book? Most assuredly not: it deals with matters that many adults are not ready to handle until old age, if then. It is a book like no other.

But is it truly authentic? Is it the work of God or Man? Are God's words in it, direct quotes, truly His? Has it been revised, perhaps many times, during our tumultuous history, or does it still stand as it was some three thousand years ago?

Master, I think that just as no man today would dare to tamper with God's words, no man ever dared to do so. They, our enemies, may have tortured us throughout the ages, they may have killed us, but they could not make us change the words of the Lord.

Having said that, obviously much, perhaps most of the Torah was written by Man; but under the clear influence, nay, direction of the Holy Spirit. It has been pointed out that many of the early myths are similar to those of other people in the Middle East and further afar, from the story of the Creation itself to that of the Flood and beyond. That may very well be so; but why should those stories and myths of other people not have developed through the guidance of the Holy Spirit? Just because someone else knew some elements of the ancient history does certainly not invalidate those elements.

There is, of course, the conflict between the stories of the Creation. It would be nice to believe that Chapters 2 (except for the reference to the Shabbat), 3 and 4 don't belong there. But they are there, and to me, they are there for an obvious reason: God wanted them to be there. This leads me to a conclusion that was obvious in our time, yet would be considered strange by most learned people of this age: that the Torah is fully authentic and that it includes the words of the Lord, accurately reported.

But let me emphasize, again: the Torah needs to be re-translated every few years. Perhaps a better word would be re-interpreted. I prefer the former, for interpretation gives too much freedom to the interpreter to substitute, subconsciously, his own thoughts for those of the Lord. Translate, then. I shall attempt to deal with a few concepts and their possible translation for this age, later. Let me just pick up one example at this time, one that I hinted at in my last letter: the concept of the day of the Lord. Obviously, His day need not correspond to our day; Shaddai could make a day as long or as short as it pleased Him, for He is the Almighty.

How to translate "day" then? If expressible at all in human terms, possible current translations would be "aeon", "era", "epoch" or, more simply, 5.8 billion years or whatever is the correct number (although the number would be different for every "day"). Is He not entitled to consider such measures of time "days"? And how else would He tell us the story, tell the story to primitive early man who had little understanding of very large numbers? He could have said "year" instead of "day", but that would have been more misleading, sounding more definite; just as "50 years" would be even more so. Men of biblical times had to be satisfied with "day", while we are free to quantify it if we can (I shall attempt to do so, later); or call it simply "epoch", if we can't.

Obviously, the world was not created in six human days; also obviously, it is not 5750 human years old; and equally obviously, every word God wrote, blessed is He, is true. Why would anybody find a conflict between these statements?

I am sure that you, Rabbi, find them perfectly consistent and complementary.

Your devoted disciple

Yosef ben Yehudah ibn-Shim`on

THE TORAH SPEAKS
ACCORDING TO THE LANGUAGE OF MAN:
MODERN INTERPRETATIONS

4 Heshvan 5750 / November 2, 1989

To B'Rabbi Moshe ben Rabbi Maimon ha-Sfaradi,
Fostat, Egypt

My beloved Master:

You said: the Torah speaks according to the language of Man. Of course, you were right. It is amazing how the Torah tells the whole complex story to the most primitive of people, not only to those of thousands of years ago, but to the simple people even of this age; yet tells a different story to learned people; really, the same story, but on a totally different level. (Now, if those learned people would only listen to the story.)

The Kabbalists tried to find the hidden meaning behind the obvious words. And that hidden meaning is there, has been there all along. But the Kabbalists were wrong. You look for the secret not by searching for anagrams, not through gematria, notrikon or other wondrous devices, but through the very words used by the Lord.

He wanted to write down the story of the creation: that of the Universe, the earth, life on earth, intelligence. How to do that?

How to explain the most complex series of events to Man then so simple, so primitive that even writing was new to Him? Man who has barely gained the gift of consciousness?

Even more complex, how to explain those events in such a manner that while those primitive people will be able to conceive of them, yet later, more intelligent, more learned people will also be able to interpret them in the light of their more advanced sciences; so even people in the 20th or 30th centuries will be gainfully instructed, will learn from careful reading and consideration of those holy words?

He did it. He wrote or dictated the words of the greatest story; primitive people had understood them, and so have men and women of ever increasing sophistication, always at different levels, always getting more out of it, new insights that were not available even to their parents.

Here is what we understand: He created inorganic things first, the physical world. Then, very simple living beings; later, larger, more complex ones; finally, Homo Sapiens or, as we used to say, Man and Woman. In doing so, he utilized the method of mutation and natural selection, gradually evolving species and occasionally effecting a major cataclysm, causing extinction of species and triggering the creation and rapid re-population of earth by more advanced species. In all these, He has developed species of increasing complexity. Man and Woman came at the end. It is all there, in the Torah.

Even before those events, He separated the water from the land on earth: we know that He did. And at the beginning, even before creating the Sun and the Moon, He created light. For a long time, people thought that this must be a mistake: there could not have been light without the Sun. Now we know that among the very first thing that appeared during the first microsecond after the Creation of the world were certain elementary particles called photons, the basic units of light.

Now, one can argue about the order of events: one can say that vegetation could not possibly have been created before the making of the Sun; nor could the waters on earth be separated and brought together in oceans before the Sun was there. One could argue that at least the order of those events got mixed up somewhere, and that may be so. But it may also be, for example, that the earth was the planet of another star, with waters already consolidated, when He found it necessary, for some reason, to move it to the current Sun, attach the earth to it as a satellite—farfetched, perhaps, but who knows? What seems absurd today may well be accepted orthodoxy tomorrow.

In any case, when He first created the world, in the beginning, there was chaos, "Tohu vaBohu", which I take to mean an abundance of some kind of matter in a state of maximum disorganization, or *entropy*; I shall have more to tell you about that concept later on. He created this material out of nothing—it took scientists a long time to finally accept the possibility of "creatio ex nihilo", but now they see that it had to be that way. Then, He found a way to reverse entropy, to bring that chaos together, into a space so small that could not be seen by human eyes (indeed, He most likely created space itself at that time of creating the first matter; I think that even time was created then, so there was no "before"); and there He created such a tremendous energy differential (and matter differential; but I don't want to be too technical here) that the resulting explosion, something scientists now call the "big bang", created all particles needed for the universe able to support, eventually, life. First, there were photons . . .

Much later, He created Man: of course, Man was the end-product (up to then) of a chain of creations of ever increasing complexity. So it was not a single individual that was created, but thousands if not millions. But what He really created along with Man was intelligence, a concept a whole level above life. Did all of these "men", having evolved from an ape-like being, become intelligent all at once? On the same day? In the same year? The same century? Most likely not. There had to be a first one to become conscious. And his descendants, having the advantage of intelligence, surely managed to assure for themselves a dominant position, very soon after. Very likely there was an "Adam".

What about Eve? I don't claim to have all answers; the story of her creation bears some intelligent re-translation. Let us remember, though, that like Adam, her creation must mean her gaining consciousness. Rib? Perhaps some cephalic cells . . .

I am not the man to translate the Torah; scientists should do that. But it could be done; for it is true. They would find that all modern concepts, including nuclear physics, computer hardware and software, management theories and other concepts we have not even heard about so far, would find application in such re-translation.

But we must also remember that no re-translation shall be the "final" one. The best translation of this age couldn't fully justify some early parts, such as the second description of the Creation, including the Eve story with the serpent, forbidden fruit, expulsion; the Lord included that story for a reason, perhaps to serve as the eventual basis of Christianity (as I have already suggested earlier; I intend to comment on that possibility again in my next letter), perhaps some other; some day that reason will emerge and will be translatable in a way that will make good sense. It would be nice to be around then, to be able to read it; but then, with our limited understanding of the world, we could probably not make much sense of such future translations.

Your devoted disciple

Yosef ben Yehudah ibn-Shim`on

INTENT OF THE LAW vs. LETTER OF THE LAW

18 Heshvan 5750 / November 16, 1989

To B'Rabbi Moshe ben Rabbi Maimon ha-Sfaradi,
Fostat, Egypt

My beloved Master:

You and I believe, then, that the Torah speaks according to the language of Man; and that because the language of Man has changed since the days of the Torah, it needs to be re-translated. But I also believe, and perhaps you do, too, that not only the individual words need to be re-translated, but also the meaning behind those words, including whole expressions, sentences, even chapters.

I think there is no question that the Holy One, blessed is He, included many things in the Torah that He considered necessary for early Man, yet not needed in later ages. Similarly, He probably included things there aimed at men at various later ages; there must be many items in the Torah specially directed to people a thousand years and more in our future.

It is even possible that a section of the Torah conveyed some most important message for an earlier generation of humans; the section then ceased to be of current importance; yet it may contain another, perhaps quite different message for a later generation. That alone would make it impossible to remove any part of the Torah, would anyone have such a silly idea.

Let me try to show some possible examples:

The ceremony of the sacrifice was, as you know, necessary for people of the first millennium before the destruction of the Second Temple. After all, each of the surrounding people in the Middle East sacrificed to their gods; how could Jews do less? But the prophets increasingly grumbled about the symbolic good of the sacrifice, as opposed to the real value of good works; and indeed, it has gradually become obvious to thinking people that sacrifice is not only no substitute for charity, it may be a negative good. The destruction of the Temple provided, I am sorry to say, an almost convenient finish to the practice.

Master, I do know that were the Temple to be re-built today, and were you to have a say in its functions and ceremonies, you would strongly object to the re-establishment of ritual sacrifice. I think you would not encounter much opposition; there are some, but not many people today who would want the barbarous old custom revived. Perhaps some new symbolic acts, some new prayers offered in lieu of sacrifice; and of course, money, for the Temple and the priests would require maintenance and salaries. But why kill and burn innocent animals?

Such sentiments would, of course, have been considered sacrilegious in earlier times. Yet were we actually to remove all commandments that have clearly lost their relevance to people of this age, the 613 would become a much smaller number, I shall suggest that number for you later. Remove them from the Torah? Impossible! Yet we must realize that there are things there not relevant to this age; there are commandments there no longer observed.

Let me comment again on Chapters 2 to 4 of Genesis. Why is there a more-or-less different version of the Creation? That second version deals with Adam's and Eve's eating of the forbidden fruit and their subsequent punishment. Those elements did not mean much to early Jews; indeed, they have been greatly ignored until later Talmudic days. But they were vitally important for early Christians; much of the Christian theology is built on the concept of Original Sin and Man's redemption from it through Jesus Christ. (Perhaps, as I have already mentioned, the Original Sin based on Adam's and Eve's little sin is now obsolete; perhaps the Christian churches will have the sense and decency to adopt a new basis, an Original Sin commemorating their crime against the Jewish people in the 20th century Holocaust.) Regardless of what you may think of the concept, Christianity now has some one thousand million adherents. It appears clear that the Lord did not want those masses of people to remain pagans; nor did He want them to become Jews; so He wanted to give them a religion which provided for their acceptance of the rule of the Lord, making them faithful followers and subjects of the One God. Hence He designed Christianity for them; as He designed Islam for others, and still other religions for people of greatly different mentalities. The establishment and content of the Christian religion was really more complex than what I have just written; but the point is that without any doubt He established it for the pagans who were to become Christians.

And therefore, what I am telling you, Rabbi, is that the Holy One, blessed is He, inserted elements in the Torah fully knowing that at some future date, they will be needed for a specific purpose.

Going back to the 613 commandments, then, how many of them still talk to us? About 200! Why? Even excluding those relating to the Temple, the priests, sacrifices, the Nazirites—so many others are ignored by the most devout, simply because the context where they should be observed no longer exists. Yes, people make a judgement about the Lord's intentions; if they find the commandment no longer valid, they ignore it. No, that is not quite true: the Haredim would not dare to ignore a commandment; that is why they tremble, after all; no, they'd rather find a way to observe it without actually doing so.

Take the sabbatical year. Israel couldn't afford not to grow food every seventh year. So all land in the State of Israel is sold, through a symbolic paper-transaction, to Arabs, for a year or so, and then bought back. Personally, I would prefer simply to ignore the commandment, but the Ultra-orthodox don't dare to do so, rather use the technicality.

I really don't assume that they truly hope to successfully fool God, rather, they hope that the Lord will appreciate their efforts of trying to go around the Law instead of simply ignoring it.

Marrying one's dead brother's widow cannot be done in an age of strict monogamy (unless the surviving brother is unmarried, of course); nor would the widow be normally interested; nor does she, in an age of feminine equality, would need that measure of protection. Of course, part of the reason was the continuation of the name of the dead brother and ensuring that his inheritance finds the rightful recipient; but the wife would normally inherit now, anyway, child or no child.

The ceremony of decapitating a heifer has long since been invalidated by the sages. So has the practice of forcing a woman to drink "bitter waters" to establish her adultery or innocence.

Slavery! I shall have a lot more to say about that subject. For now, enough to say that no commandment applies since there is no slavery (at least in the civilized world).

What about idolatry? So many of the commandments, so much of the entire T'nach is aimed at stopping idolatrous practices. Master, they *are* stopped, they have almost completely disappeared from the face of the earth. No Jew has to worry about the danger inherent in adoring graven images. What this means is that graven images are everywhere today: not as subjects for religious adoration, but as works of art. There are beautiful sculptures, images of men and women and animals and inanimate objects. Nobody considers them forms of any deity; only the skill of the artist is admired. It is perfectly safe to have them around, along with other sculptures that don't propose to depict anything, only offer pleasing shapes; and along with paintings, two-dimensional depiction of a variety of subjects, or of nothing specific, providing only pleasing forms.

I could show many other examples, and I may give you a detailed list of valid and obsolete commandments later. But these few should suffice, for now, to illustrate the conviction I have slowly arrived at in this new world, this new age: the letter of the law is less important than the intent of the law. The intent is to bring Man up (I really should say Human Beings; today, women object to people in general being referred to as "Men"; but I am old-fashioned enough to continue to use the term; so when I say "Men", note that I mean "Men and Women"); to bring him along, continuously, on the path of development, so he shall become less animal and more spiritual, all the time. God has created all of us from dust; brought us along through forms of a great variety, from the lowest forms of life through advanced animals, and now we are human. One day, we shall be more than that; we shall become something which will be very close to the Lord, blessed be His name. That has been His intent; He has created us in His own image, and one day we shall live up to that plan. And so long as we follow those rules that facilitate the Lord's plan, we have fulfilled His requirements from us.

Or so I understand the meaning of the Law.

Your devoted disciple

Yosef ben Yehudah ibn-Shim`on

BRANCHES OF JUDAISM

24 Heshvan 5750 / November 22, 1989

To B'Rabbi Moshe ben Rabbi Maimon ha-Sfaradi,
Fostat, Egypt

My beloved Master:

I have already written to you about the various types of Jews in this age, the extent of their observances or lack of it, their belonging to groups or congregations of various degrees of strictness in following the Law. Yet today I would like to discuss the matter further with you (discussion is not quite the right word; I wish it were, I wish you could be here with me, or at least, somehow, be able to answer my letters, so I could argue with you rather than with myself). Yet I am eager to gain your agreement to my latest views.

I am sure that at first, upon reading my letters, you thought that only the Ultra-orthodox, the Haredim, follow the ways of the Lord, blessed be He; that the rest can hardly be called Jews at all; for what kind of Jew would ignore the words of the Lord, ignore His explicit commandments, refuse to study Torah, live like a Gentile, call himself a Jew without a care, without a thought for the obligations that word carries? So I believed myself when I arrived to this strange time and place. My views have changed, though; and I shall try to change yours, if I can and if I have not done so already.

Rabbi, I would like to suggest that nothing important happens in the world without the approval of the Highest. He establishes the directions, sets His people going on a certain road and monitors their progress. There are those who stray. He helps them back onto the path of righteousness, if possible, punishes them when necessary. Sometimes, He makes major changes in the overall direction, changes that are usually painful, necessarily so; the people affected cannot understand why they have to suffer.

I am talking about these things to say, in a roundabout way, that today's Jewry is exactly where the Lord wants it to be. It occupies a position, a spread over a wide range of practices and groupings, if not of belief. The range is from the Reform and Reconstruction (or even "Secularism") at one extreme, to Ultra-orthodoxy at the other. This is a very different range than in our time, or the time of, say, Hillel of blessed memory, but a necessary range.

So we look at the range, and try to establish what is best, where the true tzaddik should be. Rather than taking the inflexible view of accepting the Haredim and nobody else, we could apply the teaching of the "Chief of the Philosophers", Aristotle, and seek out the golden mean, while rejecting both extremes. Yet in this case, I would like to suggest not to do so. I think the whole range is necessary, each element is valuable; the Lord has organized each group. But for what purpose?

It is always dangerous to speculate on the purposes of the Lord. How could we understand His lofty program, His complex planning? Still, one must always try to understand Him, seek Him; some of His moves become self-evident after a while.

Why may He have directed Jewry towards the strange position it occupies today? Among many possible objectives, we can identify at least two: the general forward motion of the human race, with its technological and social progress, for which He still wants His chosen people placed in a special position (of leadership? irritant? social consciousness? unconventional thinking?) to assure that the progress will be fast enough.

And the second objective? The re-establishment and maintenance of the State of Israel. I have already written to you about that: the view that what may be the primary concern of the Lord, at least at this general time, is perhaps not Jewry but Israel.

It may be that the diaspora Jews will become unimportant, that the very word "Jew" will become secondary to the other name, "Israel". We cannot know for sure that this is what He has been planning for all this time; but a review of our history is certainly in strong support of such a view.

Of course, even if it were so, the term "Israeli" must mean a Jew, or something very close to it, if only for the ancient Covenant. I doubt that any useful plan could be brought closer to fruition if the Lord were to permit, for example, a demographic change in Israel with the Arab population becoming the majority and taking control; that would, effectively, re-establish the diaspora; I think we know the Lord sufficiently to be able to predict, confidently, that He will not create an Arabic Israel. And so, the people of the Covenant must be preserved at all cost. But what is the best way of doing so? Increased Jewish militancy in Israel, perhaps culminating in the expulsion of the non-Jewish minority? Or increased religious fundamentalism, re-establishment of the power of the devout?

In the latter case, the vast majority of the Jews would not necessarily follow; many, perhaps most, would simply turn away. Without religious discipline, on the other hand, the only thing that maintains a Jewish identity over several generation is Israel itself, our pride in a glorious state of our own. Or does it?

As things stand now, Israel, while strong enough in its defense against external enemies, may be unwilling to maintain its Jewish character. Perhaps the Ultra-orthodox are the only ones willing to take unpopular steps in that direction. So it seems to me that the most fundamentalist extreme of the Jewish spectrum is also an absolutely necessary one.

But what about the other extreme? And what about the centre, the "golden mean"?

One could easily find good justification for each segment of the spectrum; for example, in the areas of modern scientific and technological advances, for which the Ultra-orthodox have neither the time nor the inclination. Nor are they well equipped for the task of national defense. And, in the Diaspora, only the least religious can fully participate in the business life of the Gentiles, providing us with most valuable education and contacts, ultimately useful to the State of Israel, if not in this generation, then in the next.

The spectrum is as the Lord has defined it. As long as there is Jewry and Israel, as long as there are those willing and able to defend us militarily and spiritually, we shall continue to serve the Lord as His chosen people, different as we may be from what we were eight centuries ago or two millennia ago.

Your devoted disciple

Yosef ben Yehudah ibn-Shim`on

OUR STANDARDS HAVE CHANGED:

ECONOMY, INCLUDING FINANCE

6 Kislev 5750 / December 4, 1989

To B'Rabbi Moshe ben Rabbi Maimon ha-Sfaradi,
Fostat, Egypt

My beloved Master:

You may understand by now how this 20th century is different from our world of the 12th. Yet I would like to give you some of my views on several key changes, to add support to my arguments about the inapplicability of the old laws to this new world; how they may have to be re-interpreted, so they will become the rock foundation of a dynamic, constantly changing set of laws, written or otherwise, to serve the permanent, unchanging long-term wishes of the Holy One, blessed is He.

Several aspects of this world should be considered. I would like to start with the economy of this age.

Now I am not an economical sage; I was not one in our time, so how could I be expected to become an expert on matters of economy and finance in the 20th century? But some of these matters are quite simple and clear to everybody here. For example, the role of the banks.

Banks fulfill two main functions for their customers (apart from the old role of money-changing, still extant, but of minor importance):

they take money in and they give money out. When they take it in, it is usually for safekeeping, sometimes loan repayment; when they give it out, they either return the customer's own money on demand, or provide a loan.

Interest is paid on both types of transactions.

Please try to forget about the old concept of usury. These interest rates are not high enough to be cruelly destructive, but they are not insignificant, either. Interest is what drives the business world, allows development, progress, human well-being.

Let me give you some typical figures. People earn good salaries, so they save some of their earnings. Almost everybody saves at least a little, some of them save a large portion. Let us take a typical citizen of a Western country and of this age. He would manage to put aside, say, eight out of every hundred units earned, or as they say here, eight percent. He puts this money in the bank, and earns on it, annually, 6 percent (they use the sign % for this concept). This figure changes often: interest rates vary with the availability, or scarcity of the money supply.

The bank, in turn, lends this money to individuals or companies. A customer, for example, wants to buy a house. The family has saved enough for about a quarter of the purchase price. The rest will come from the bank, which will provide the money and charge an annual interest of, say, 10% on the loan. It is repaid over a very long period, twenty or thirty years. Yes, the interest adds a lot to the cost; it builds up over the years, it compounds, so the actual amount of money paid back to the bank may be twice or even thrice the original amount, unless the customer can repay it sooner (he usually can).

But you have to consider another aspect of today's economy: inflation. It is not really new, ever since symbolic money replaced the barter system for convenience, currency has always been losing part of its value, not steadily but in waves. This trend is now fully recognized and taken into account. If, on the average, we have an inflation rate of, say 5% per year, then a person paying ten thousand units of money over a 25-year period really only pays five thousand seven hundred in terms of the original money. In other words, a large part of the interest charged only compensates the bank for the money it loses to inflation.

Now, the bank does charge higher interest rates on the loans it gives than the interest it pays to customers on their savings. That is as it should be. That difference pays for the bad loans: some loans, say one or two out of every hundred does turn out to be uncollectible, the bank may have to forget about it. Indeed, the interest a bank charges on its loans does depend on how high the risk may be of such loan "going bad". Large, major business companies tend to pay lower interest than individuals, especially those with no assets of any kind. But even a very large company may collapse. And even a relatively poor individual does not pay a very high interest; his rate may be, say, two percent higher than that of the major company.

Another reason for the spread between interest rates charged and paid is, simply, that the bank needs to pay for its administrative expenses. A bank tends to be a huge organization, with many branches and with a head office employing thousands of people, all of whom need to earn salaries, all of whom need to be housed for the duration of their working hours in heated or cooled offices; taxes must be paid, office supplies must be bought; and so on.

Yet a third reason for the spread is that the bank wants to make a profit. The bank is not a charitable organization (although, typically, it contributes heavily to worthy charitable causes). It is owned by hundreds, thousands of individuals, ordinary people who buy a few, or many shares of the bank's stock. The entire bank (just as most major business organizations of any kind) is represented by a certain number of shares, sometimes millions; if a person owned all shares, he would own the entire bank. But that practically never happens; in cases of large organizations, not even half, often not even 20% of the shares are owned by one person.

Why would ordinary people buy shares of a bank? They invest their money there to earn something similar to interest, it is called "dividend", participation in the company's profits; and also, they hope that if the company is doing well, the value of the shares will increase significantly by the time they want to sell them. They could simply deposit the saved money they have into a bank account, and earn interest; dividends are not always higher than the interest rate; but the money in the bank account could not "grow". Investors hope that such growth will at least match the inflation rate, perhaps be much higher.

And so, as you can see, Master, the bank's profitability is essential for its investors. The management of the bank, who are senior employees, but not owners (unless they buy shares of their own employer) are under pressure by the investors to improve the profitability of the bank. They could do so by increasing the spread between deposit and loan interest rates, say charge 14%, yet pay only 4%. That would not be considered fair business practice; a bank trying to do that would not be very successful.

Large companies (and also governments) always owe money to banks; and not only to banks, but to individuals as well, who invest still another way: buy promissory notes, or "bonds", of those companies, at interest rates significantly higher than those paid by banks. Why do large companies borrow money? They use it to expand, build new facilities, hire more people; they believe that they can earn a higher profit on that money than the interest they must pay to banks or individuals.

And so, an ordinary person who has a little saved money can do many things with it. He can deposit it in a savings account, earn interest. He can buy corporate bonds (or sometimes the bonds of the country's government) and earn higher interest. He can lend it to another individual, say somebody buying a house or investing into some business venture, and earn a little more interest still (but his risk would also be a little higher). Or he might buy shares in one, or several companies—manufacturers, construction companies, food distributors, telephone companies, banks, thousands of others—and become part owner of those. If one were to accumulate a significant part of the shares of a company (for not all such shared companies are huge), one could then have a major say in its management decisions. One can choose between investing in stable large companies, earning perhaps a smaller dividend and expecting a little less growth, or smaller, newer, rapidly growing companies providing either high return or fast increase of share value or both, but taking a greater risk of something going wrong with the company. Or, of course, one can simply buy bonds of good companies; or just deposit his money into the bank. That is where we started.

This process results of money, "capital", constantly shifting to accommodate the need. The result is permanent growth of the economy (with occasional interruptions). Everybody is always getting richer; poverty is greatly eliminated. Hunger has been almost completely eradicated in most of the world (with the exception of a few countries not only backward, but choosing to remain backward by their shortsighted leader). Gone as well are most of the epidemics, infectious diseases that used to spread due to lack of hygiene, again due to poverty.

The economic system I've just described is called "capitalism". It is about two hundred years old now, although in some parts of the world it has not been adopted until ten or twenty years ago, with tremendous success. It has been opposed by the Communists who have established alternative economic systems of their own in all of their countries. Everywhere, they have failed miserably. At this time, most of those countries have begun to establish capitalism in their lands; they seem to be doing better than before.

Most of the elements of today's economy have been around for a long time, we have seen many in our times. But those elements have now come together into a coherent system, figures rationalized, profits fine-tuned, so that the companies all prosper, but not at the cost of impoverishing their customers; just the opposite: by making all their customers richer, they enlarge the buying or investing power of the customer base and, thereby, help themselves. (Master, I am over-simplifying this. There are many special situations where the system works less perfectly then as I have described, for various reasons; but I think that it is always improving.)

Well, such capitalistic system could perhaps have developed sooner, perhaps even in our time; except for the on-again, off-again persecution of the Jews. It turns out that throughout the ages, up to nearly the present, most of the bankers were Jews in all parts of the world. They prospered for a while, helped the local economy build up; financed growth, peace or war; then, when the rulers became too indebted to these Jews, our people were typically expelled, often murdered, their assets taken, while the loans, of course, were simply annulled. Then, the economy slowly began to deteriorate; eventually (but not in the lifetime of the same ruler), Jews were needed again. This pattern, I think, is familiar to you, for Muslims and Christians have always taken identical short-sighted views, or have until recently, when stable banking has gone hand-in-hand with relatively fair treatment of Jews, in several western countries for a hundred years or more now. Let us hope that this stability continues.

So I would like to conclude this letter with talking about interest again. You have been familiar with lending at usurious rates that is the reason for the biblical prohibition against interest. People in successful economies have always ignored the prohibition, sometimes through pretending that the interest earned was something else, a fee for services or the like. Really, the problem has always been that the law regarding interest has been a bad one; that is why Jews have been forced to find ways getting around it; look at the Baba Metzia tractate of the Talmud, worrying about what is and is not permitted in such efforts. Had we the courage to do it, we could have proposed—you could have—to re-interpret the law, permitting small interest charges and payments, perhaps establishing the maximum spread between the two, perhaps recognizing the concept of inflation in the calculation of interest rates; we could have done that, but we took the easy way out. We said the law was unchangeable, which is true; but by not making it meaningful for the newer ages, we have made the law less relevant, less respected.

Your devoted disciple

Yosef ben Yehudah ibn-Shim`on

AMBITION

20 Kislev 5750 / December 18, 1989

To B'Rabbi Moshe ben Rabbi Maimon ha-Sfaradi,
Fostat, Egypt

My beloved Master:

Today's western world is characterized by progress, advance; as well as constant hustle and bustle, everybody working hard, without suffering as a result. Some like to brag that they work hard and "play hard", take their entertainment and relaxation seriously, don't sit around doing nothing, but constantly do enjoyable things. Perhaps today's world could be described as one of constant activity.

And it could be argued that it is this activity that moves the world ahead, that results in the permanent state of visible advancement. Advancement for the society; advancement for the individual.

So then we are faced with the necessity of deciding: is advancement a good thing, pleasing to the Lord, blessed is His name? Or would He prefer if we just languished, did the minimum amount of work, waiting for things to happen?

To me, the answer is clear: Judaism is based on action, good deeds, positive steps moving the society constantly ahead. Fatalism is for the Muslims, otherworldliness is for the Christians (and even for them, activity and ambition are increasingly becoming the standard way of participating in society these days). We have always understood that the Lord wanted us to do His work. When Man succeeds in creating a set of circumstances where his work is appreciated, where success pays off, where material rewards are available to all who want them and are willing to work for them, then Man has succeeded in creating an ambience pleasing to the Lord. Some ways, that world is here now.

But have we always encouraged Man to work hard, to build a better world? Sometimes we have; other times, no. The great Rabbis in Hillel's age all worked hard at trades and were proud of it. Encouraging productive physical work is an idea that permeates the T'nach. Early Christianity missed it completely, but decided that it was an essential element in later centuries. (This is especially true of Protestantism.) Of course, in early Christian times the end of the world was thought imminent, so there seemed to be little incentive for working hard, building a better world here on earth.

That old Christian belief, perhaps reinforced by the Ash`arite determinism of Islamic lands, resulted in an anti-work atmosphere that permeated most thinking Christian and Muslim societies in our days. It even influenced some of our greatest thinkers. Bahya ibn Paquda, perhaps voicing the Sufi movement's teaching, counselled against taking work, trades seriously. He suggested that work should be exerted just sufficiently to provide for the minimum necessities.

Another, even greater such sage, no doubt influenced by Bahya, was nobody less than our own Maimonides! You have admonished those who would pay too much attention to the earning of money, building up a fortune; suggested that one should work only enough to provide for one's family needs. Rabbi, I hesitate to say this, but I think that you were wrong. With no ambition, Man does not move the world ahead. Should we just sit back and wait for the Lord to create the perfect world for us? Today's world, while far from perfect, has been created by Man's ambition and willingness to work for it.

Of course, you may reject today's world as a desirable objective; but the alternative is what we saw in the middle ages: brutish life, oppression, ignorance, illness, early death for the majority. Ambition begets ambition; the poor, seeing the middle classes freeing themselves from poverty and suffering, through willingness to work hard, will always emulate those middle classes; and so, it is inevitable that eventually all poverty should be eliminated along with ignorance, lack of hygiene, superstition and the other ills of society (when this is not artificially prevented by a short-sighted, selfish, cruel ruler or ruling class).

But why does a man work hard? For material goods? Well, yes, of course, to provide not only for his family's current needs, but to build up solid reserves, to assure, as far as possible, the future well-being of those he loves. But there is more. Man craves recognition, the respect of his peers. He wants to be successful, so those who know him, or even strangers, will increasingly respect and admire him, recognize what he has created with his own hands or head. Sure, if he is wise, he'll know that he could not have done any of that without the help of the Lord; but the Lord will only help those who help themselves.

Man craves respect and recognition, and I suggest to you, Master, that there is nothing wrong with that.

You have repeatedly chided those who would seek fame, as fools of the worse kind. Certainly, that has been the accepted view, at least the stated view, of all the sages of Judaism as well as Christianity and of most other religions. My Master, Rambam, I would like to suggest to you that the view is hypocritical! You and all other sages craved fame and recognition, fought hard against those who would deny your due in respect. You were the most famous theologian of your age, and with good reason; but you certainly did not reject recognition, did not hide yourself behind a false identity, did not go around pretending to be, say, a simple carpenter; no, you were pleased that people turned to you for advice on many different topics, from Torah to Law to medicine.

I suggest to you, Master, that a scholar whose work is ignored or rejected—not by a few critics, for that is the fate of all scholars, but by all—is soon discouraged. The love of God may keep him working, but the love of his family will more than likely force him to switch professions, seek success as a builder of houses or grower of figs.

Yes, there have been respectable exceptions: otherworldly thinkers, mainly among the Roman Catholic clergy, some priests and monks with no material needs at all, who laboured, often unrecognized, for the greater glory of God. But even that Church has always encouraged what it considered correct thinking by formal recognition, rewards, promotion, fame. Very few did original work against such recognition.

Do you counter that a seeker of fame is a vain, proud person? Vain, probably; proud, yes, when he already has something to be proud about. Pride is an excellent possession of Men: it can easily be accommodated, it is available in great supply, does not cost money, seldom causes suffering. Is a proud man a fool? I think that those well-accepted opinions are nothing but the defense put forward by the unsuccessful, the meek. If the meek are to be rewarded in the World-to-Come in preference to the proud, as Yehoshua haNotzri is said to have claimed, then it may not be worthwhile to strive for anything in this world. I refuse to believe that. Our Lord, blessed be His name, wants progress in this world, progress which advances His plans and designs; and if it is pride of achievement that motivates Man to do God's bidding, then all honour to such pride. Let the scholar, the builder, the grower and the teacher seek recognition as well as financial reward, let ambition grow, so the Lord's plan can move ahead at a healthy pace.

Let us be wary of hypocrisy.

And finally, let me make a comment about humility. You were proud (yes, I am afraid it was pride) of being humble. You brought up an example of humility: that of a man being pissed upon by an arrogant person on a sea voyage, by one who would look down on him, consider him as nothing; being happy about accepting such a fate without complaining. Nonsense, my Master! Total nonsense! That is not humility, that is stupidity. Would you stand for such treatment? Never! But let me tell you what true humility is: when a scientist, a philosopher makes a proposition, he should never state it as an absolute fact; rather, he should call it just what it is, a hypothesis, unless proven with absolute evidence beyond any doubt. Here is what Aristotle said: "The actual facts are not yet sufficiently made out. Should further research ever discover them, we must yield to their guidance rather than that of theory; for theories must be abandoned unless they tally with the indisputable results of observation." Was he really that humble? I suspect not. I know that Galen was not that humble (and look at the damage caused by his false certainty, by his arrogance). Practically none of the philosophers, metaphysicians or other scientists of the next millennium were that humble. I want to point a finger to one of the greatest philosophers who was not that humble: one Moshe ben Maimon. No, he was not humble at all. Was he actually arrogant? Well, let me just repeat: he was not humble.

Your devoted disciple

Yosef ben Yehudah ibn-Shim`on

HEALTH, HYGIENE, DIET

7 Tevet 5750 / January 4, 1990

To B'Rabbi Moshe ben Rabbi Maimon ha-Sfaradi,
Fostat, Egypt

My beloved Master:

If I called you the most respected physician in the Court of Saladin, I would greatly understate the importance of your medical work and the universal recognition accorded to you. Nobody in the 12th century knew more than you about health, hygiene and the role of diets (certainly not I, your servant who have benefited from the teaching of the great Maimonides, learned all I knew about medicine from you, cherished your words of wisdom). So it is not unreasonable to expect that you would like to know about the state of those disciplines today; and I am eager to tell you about them, for they relate to religion. But be prepared to swallow your pride (if you admit to having any of that commodity), for things have advanced by much.

Medicine has become a major science, requiring its practitioners to study until about age twenty-five, then apprentice in hospitals for several more years. That way, they may become qualified general practitioners at the age of twenty-eight or so; but if they wanted to specialize in any particular type of illness or part of the body, that would necessitate several more years of study. Without disrespect, please contrast that to your own medical training, not very long, not very thorough, at least in comparison. Of course, not only have the number of years spent in school increased, but so has the amount of knowledge to be absorbed there, the volume of medical science. There is so much to medicine today! What we knew seems almost insignificant. I am afraid that even ibn Sina's writings have been obsoleted by now (yet they greatly respect him still, although, for some reason, they call him Avicenna in these days).

In our age, health was considered maintainable if one observed all rules—religious and otherwise—for good medicine was based on the Lord's commandments as well as on good common sense; at least the sort of medicine you practiced. (For there was also bad medicine, right up to the 18th century, with its advice based on primitive magic, Shamanism, superstition and other kinds of nonsense.) Somehow, it was not recognized that a man could become sick even if he were to observe all rules; that he could get an infection, or hereditary disease would make its presence known; he could develop heart disease, or cancer. And having been so struck, you and the other philosophers could not do much more than have the man lie down and hope for recovery. Some of the cures were worse than the illnesses. Just one example: people were bled, a procedure that seldom provided anything of value, but contributed very often to the weakening of an already weak patient.

Cancer is usually treated by surgery today, often followed by chemical therapy and irradiation, a procedure I shall not even attempt to explain here. After cancer, the second major cause of death is heart disease, along with circulatory problems. The cause is partly hereditary, partly dietary; the latter is well-understood and controlled today. Chemical treatment is improving and surgical treatment is also quite common and effective. Indeed, surgery is so advanced, any part of the human body can be reached and repaired, or removed and, if necessary, replaced. Replaced by what, you ask? By a similar organ of somebody else's, say one of two kidneys voluntarily offered by a relative, or by an organ of a stranger, a healthy person, who has suddenly died as the result of an accident (I've told you about cars running around the cities and roads at tremendous speeds; unfortunately, many accidents happen; victims can usually be treated and healed, but sometimes, such help comes too late).

Another way of replacing a damaged organ is by using a totally artificial device, say a mechanical heart! Again, the surgery of Abul Kasim, advanced though it may have been for our age, has long since been eclipsed.

You see, we did not understand infection, micro-organisms, tiny living beings so small that even a million of them, side-by-side, would still be invisible to the human eye. And so we could not appreciate the need for extreme cleanliness in surgery, including boiling each instrument in water extensively, using sterile (heat-disinfected) gloves, sterile bandages and hundreds of other protective measures, to assure the recovery of the patient. Nor did we have the chemicals needed for local or general anesthesia.

Those micro-organisms, called bacteria, cause many conditions that were once deadly, such as pneumonia, today easily cured by chemicals. Still smaller micro-organisms, called viruses, cause many other diseases, from the common cold to (probably) cancer; these can be prevented to some extent, treated without surgery sometimes; and many of them cause only inconveniences. But others are still fatal. Thousands of scientists are desperately researching those viruses, those diseases; I am sure that their effort will produce results, understanding, perhaps even full cures by the end of this century, if God so wishes.

One type of virus-caused disease is a deadly, new, sexually transmitted ailment, striking mainly homosexuals—yes, Sodom and Gomorrah, again. It is not yet clear whether this will cause a major threat to the heterosexual population; almost certainly not to the law-abiding, sexually faithful ones.

It is interesting to note that Jews and others who are circumcised are far less likely to be infected by this disease (and by various other diseases) than other people are. Incidentally, the wives of Jewish men are also much better protected against cervical cancer than the wives of uncircumcised men. It is worth considering that a regulation like that could never have been invented by a man, by a physician; how could he have predicted such results? But it came directly from God, blessed is He. So it seems that much of the medical knowledge of our days is now obsolete; but the knowledge of the Lord is as relevant today as ever.

I think you were incorrect in stressing the harm of sexual excess, depending, of course, on one's definition of such excess. Your insistence on abstinence excepting the strongest need has certainly proved overly cautious; your list of teeth falling out, foul odours, other diseases—well, these things just don't happen. However, I know that you wrote those things with certain sexually active members of the Court in mind; and such a person is more likely to contract venereal diseases, in which case, yes, he will become susceptible to various other illnesses, so everything you said will probably happen. But there is no danger of that for sexually active, faithful married couples.

Also, I am afraid you were not correct in your suggested cures for emotional diseases. The soul, or rather mind, can certainly be diseased just as the body can; some think that in fact, diseases of the mind are almost always of physical origin. Those illnesses are treated through a combination of physical, or chemical, and mental therapies, as the particular case demands; but not, I am sorry to say, through instruction of the Law, worthy as such remedy may be for those with healthy minds.

You were quite right in suggesting hygienic measures, including frequent bathing; but your insistence of doing so once a week would not be considered very sanitary today. People bathe or shower (a constant stream of dispersed water coming from above, with adjustable temperature) *every day*, sometimes twice a day! A person doing so only once a week would be considered very bad-smelling.

Of course, this modern custom, and the fact that every house includes at least one bathroom, obsoletes some of the old laws, for example the very important one relating to women taking a bath once a month after menstruation. I remember your comment regarding the Karaites' custom of simply taking baths, but this is what all but the Ultra-ortho-dox do today.

It is so clear that the Lord's laws were of practical nature, and as such, susceptible to updating from time to time, as the need, the circumstances warrant. (Not really the words: the interpretation. Not the Bible: the Halakha.)

Incidentally, those bathrooms, or other nearby enclosures, include very hygienic, odourless toilets to take care of the excretionary functions. Soon, it will be standard for every bedroom to have an attached bath-room, perhaps one for every person in the house. As I have already mentioned, those bathrooms also include a washbasin, with running warm and cold water; and often other hygienic devices.

Teeth were not washed that often in our days; now, they are brushed twice a day, with a cleaning powder or paste, so they won't readily decay. When they do, they can be replaced by prostheses, so the difference is not visible.

Regarding diets, many of the foods proscribed by you as unhealthy or poisonous is eaten in large quantities by everybody today, with no bad effect. Mushrooms, cheese, all kinds of fish, lentils, onions—the list could go on and on. Cabbage is especially healthy, often preventing cancer of the colon.

Why did you proscribe tree fruits? Apples, pears, apricots, peaches, —they are all very healthy.

Which takes me to food proscribed not by you, but by the Holy One, blessed is He. His reasons for certain proscriptions are obvious; for example, pigs really were unsanitary in our days, but not today. Many shellfish, when not quite fresh, were poisonous indeed.

We can make good working hypotheses regarding those laws: first, that all of them had dietary reasons, in which case they are variable with changing conditions; second, that they all had practical reasons, but we don't necessarily understand those reasons in each case; and last, that it is not for Man to speculate about the reason, but for Man to accept the Law and follow it, because it makes one holy (and perhaps because it makes one separate from the others). I know that you lean towards the second of those hypotheses, that there is a sound reason for every law, but we cannot understand many of them. You may be right; I shall make a few more comments on this subject later; enough to say, for now, that the Lord told us so many important things, most of which we could not have thought of by ourselves to this day and even into the future (if He did not command circumcision, I am sure that nobody would have thought of it).

You were right, of course, in warning against overeating, overdrinking. But perhaps you were too strict when you prohibited the enjoyment of food? I would say that there are five views on how much one should indulge: first, the views of the epicureans, who would deny nothing to Man; second, the views of this 20th century world, which caution against only certain food, for example those very rich in fat, such as butter; third, a sensible middle ground that has not yet been reached; fourth, the views of our sage Maimonides, you, who seem to consider anything that is enjoyable perhaps somewhat sinful (except for the sick); and last, the views of the truly ascetic, the early Christians, the Sufi Muslims and also certain Jewish thinkers, such as Bahya, who counsel towards austerity and self-denial. There are few Jewish theologians today who would accept a legitimate scriptural basis for asceticism. We are thankful to the Lord for the good things He has provided, and don't insult Him by refusing His provisions.

Your devoted disciple

Yosef ben Yehudah ibn-Shim`on

FEMINISM; PLACE OF WOMEN; SEX

21 Tevet 5750 / January 18, 1990

To B'Rabbi Moshe ben Rabbi Maimon ha-Sfaradi,
Fostat, Egypt

My beloved Master:

In this letter, I would like to write to you about women, their role and place in this most interesting age where I now find myself.

In a very few words, women work alongside men in all professions, all jobs; think alongside men in all sciences.

There have been four motivating forces behind this development.

First, *women needed to work*, to support their families. Of course, they always have, in all cultures, except in the higher social and economic classes. Menial work, both around the house and outside, was expected from all women not too old or ill, in all ages. But in more recent days girls, even in well-to-do families, were expected to work until they got married.

The second force was the *development and social acceptance of birth control methods*. Today, conception can be inhibited by a variety of technical devices, some physical, others chemical; all are permissible by civic laws as well as by religious authorities, with the exception of Roman Catholicism (the Haredim oppose certain methods, but not others); yet even their adherents use the devices, if at the risk of committing sin.

There is also widespread use of abortion, the artificial termination of pregnancy in the first few weeks or even months. The foetus is removed by a physician, safely, with no danger to the health of the woman. However, here the opposition of religious authorities —including Orthodox Jews—and also many governments is much stronger; it is as often forbidden as permitted. The ban is based on the assumption that the foetus is a living human being, so abortion is murder. The argument for and against that proposition has been raucous and even violent for a long time now; it may never be resolved.

In any case, birth control permits a couple to limit the size of their family, and indeed most families in advanced countries have one or two, at most three children. You must also remember that those children don't normally die young; barring an accident, war or rare disease, all children are expected to grow up and most likely die in relatively old age.

With only one or two child, a woman's home workload is not as heavy as with six or eight. But that workload has been lightened further by the development which is the third major force influencing the role of women: *Housekeeping chores have been all but eliminated by mechanization,* by automation. Let me give you a short list of some of the machines found in every household:

Vacuum cleaner: a machine to suck up all dusts from the floor, carpets and furniture.

Floor polisher: it makes wood and stone floor shining clear, with very little effort.

Washing machine: it washes all clothes, with no human effort at all.

Dryer, a machine that dries the freshly washed clothes.

Electric iron, that becomes hot by simply pushing a button; this is seldom needed now, for most of today's clothes are permanently pressed.

Dishwasher—for all dishes and cutlery.

Stove and oven for cooking and baking: all electric, so there is no need for making a fire. An oven can even clean itself.

Refrigerator: it keeps food cold, even frozen, if wanted, so it lasts for a very long time; hence, there is no need to shop daily.

Canned food, any kind of food in sealed metal cans, usually pre-cooked: while perhaps not quite as tasty as fresh food, freshly cooked, yet quite edible and healthy, it practically lasts forever.

And there are other machines available for mixing, mashing, beating, grinding and other chores in the kitchen. And everything can be bought ready-made; for example, nobody bakes bread anymore, huge factories manufacture tens of thousands daily. And still more: the proliferation of restaurants: easy as cooking has become, much of the time the family goes to a restaurant to eat, there are thousands in a major city.

So you can see that woman's work at home has become easier. In some cultures, that work is now shared by her husband. Yet you must also remember that all of those machines cost money; so she must go back to work to earn additional income for the family, to help pay for these machines and all the others that I have already mentioned, machines for entertainment (televisions) and for transportation (cars) and so on.

On the other hand, very few households have servants today: only the very rich can afford that luxury in the developed countries. In more disadvantaged, more primitive lands, the middle classes do have servants, for poor women in those countries have few choices of work, they must accept employment is households for pittance. In western countries, typically only recent immigrants from poor lands work in households, they usually go to a household once or twice a week, to help with the cleaning chores (for even machines need to be guided, taken upstairs and down, moved about, controlled). As soon as they learn the language of the land, they tend to find better jobs, in factories or offices.

And then, the fourth major force: *education of the girls*. This is a relatively recent development, having occurred mainly in the last two centuries. It has provided ample proof that girls have brains every bit as good as boys do. And it has resulted in two unplanned consequences: pride and indignation.

Women are now proud that they can think and do as well as men can. And they are indignant that they have been oppressed by men for all those centuries and millennia.

For oppressed they were. Not only that, they were looked down upon, first denied an education and then called stupid for not knowing things that men knew. Let me put the blame squarely where it belongs: on all old cultures, especially their spiritual leaders. On the Torah. The Talmud. The Midrash. The writings of the sages. Maimonides. Yes, Maimonides! Your writings are full of derision for women; they are presented as creatures of secondary importance, justified only by their beauty (for your women did not work, not even at home) and by their ability to give birth to babies. Even their sexual needs were considered unimportant by you. (This attitude was corrected by later Jewish authorities, such as Joseph Caro, writer of the important Shulchan Aruch that defined every aspect of Jewish life, including the duty of a husband to satisfy the needs of his wife.)

Strong words, strong criticism of a sage as great as Maimonides. Yet, I think, just. Was your attitude a reaction to your main antagonist, Samuel ben Ali, the Gaon in Babylon? I know that he really annoyed you by letting his daughter make important pronouncements, even decisions. Perhaps you felt that you had to get back at him through her?

I am sorry, Master. I shall have to apologize to you for these words, and I shall do so, when I cool down a little. Right now, though, I am very agitated; it seems that women have convinced me, quite successfully, about the justice of their cause.

For consider some of the things that women are doing these days. They teach children in schools. They are very successful physicians; excellent lawyers, bankers. They design computer systems including the extremely complex logic functions that I must have mentioned to you in an earlier letter.

They manage stores, schools, hospitals, business organizations. They run factories, farms. They write books, compose and perform music. And they are philosophers; thinkers, metaphysicians.

They are even soldiers, although in most countries they are not allowed to participate in combat duties. They seldom do heavy physical work; but then, there is very little physical work left to do today.

They do lots of menial work, of course—sewing, low level work in offices, cleaning (as I have shown), looking after small children—but then, so do man. My point is, women can be as intelligent and as stupid as men can be. Oh, I would love to see you debating some matter with, say, a university professor today, one who just happens to be a woman.

And to go on: they are members of governments, even heads of nations, elected leaders; for in many cases, it turns out that of all contenders, they are the most highly qualified to undertake the leadership of a country. Let me tell you something: a few years ago, the head of the Israeli government, one of the strongest, brightest ever, was a woman.

Even in sports, women compete in practically all contests that were previously open to men only. They compete against other women, for their physical strength is not equal to that of men; but women constantly upset records of speed, distance, height that men have achieved perhaps as recently as ten years earlier.

One other thing: women are ready to compete with men in positions of religious leadership. Some denominations actually permit women to act as spiritual leaders; there are numerous ministers in some Christian sects, if not priests. The latter designation applies mostly to Roman Catholics: they still forbid women in priestly roles; that stance may not hold for very much longer.

In Islam, admittedly, I don't see any advance for women; worse, they are now forced to wear the hated chadors again in Iran, covering face as well as body. There is no role for them in any important activity, let alone in the mosque; let alone in the government. (And even so, one non-Arab Islamic country, Pakistan, has a woman leader now, even though the more traditionalist elements are trying to unseat her, and seem to be succeeding.)

In our own faith, woman rabbis have begun to appear in Reform congregations and increasingly, in Conservative synagogues. I don't see much chance of woman rabbis among the Orthodox for a long time to come.

Judaism, the most progressive of Man's religions, turns out to be regressive in some respects; we don't have the mechanism for making radical changes. Perhaps if we had a Sanhedrin . . .

Well, Rabbi, I don't know how you'll react to these developments: will you applaud women's advances, or are you still appalled? The progress is real, it cannot be stopped, whether anyone likes it or not; but I would be happy having succeeded in convincing you that you were wrong, that all other great authorities were wrong. That you will, quietly, in your own mind, apologize to women, just as I shall have to apologize to you for being rude. I shall do so; will you think about doing your part?

Your devoted disciple

Yosef ben Yehudah ibn-Shim`on

SLAVERY

27 Tevet 5750 / January 24, 1990

To B'Rabbi Moshe ben Rabbi Maimon ha-Sfaradi,
Fostat, Egypt

My beloved Master:

I know that an apology is due, and shall be offered; but not yet. I still have more things to say that you may not like at first, but will come to agree with me in the end, of that I am certain.

I have been saving my scorn for the subject of slavery.

In most parts of the civilized world, slavery has been illegal for a long time now, a thousand years or more (so perhaps our world was not quite as civilized as we thought, after all). It is true that in Europe, as recently as the 16th, 17th, even 18th century, Christians and Muslims found it profitable to capture Jews and sell them into slavery, especially in the hope of a fat ransom; the Knights of St. John, a Christian organization in Malta, continued the practice until the end of the 18th century, when a French conqueror by the name of Napoleon put an end to it. Yet in the most modern, most free, most democratic centre of the modern world, the United States of America, slavery was accepted up to the middle of the 19th century. For several centuries before that, it was a normal practice for certain European and especially Arab groups of criminals to undertake raiding expeditions to Africa, where Negroes were captured, shipped to America and there sold to the highest bidder. (I am sorry to say that according to certain historians, even Jews were to be found among those criminals.)

Many Americans of decent feeling objected; but others insisted on maintaining the custom for the obvious financial benefit. Eventually, a civil war was fought over the issue; the abolitionists won and thus slavery finally became illegal in the land. Soon after that, it was banned even in the remaining uncivilized areas of the world (although one hears occasional rumours about the practice persisting even to this day in some primitive Muslim societies.)

After the abolition, Negroes (who now prefer to be called blacks) became members of a conspicuously lower economic and social class and remained there for a long time. But eventually, and not too long ago, major steps have been taken to eliminate that unfortunate differentiation. It was necessary to legislate full equality to remove segregation of blacks from various walks of life. That has now been fully achieved; and it is hoped that gradually, that group will achieve full economic equality.

The point I am making here is that segregation is distasteful to most members of today's society, while slavery is truly abhorrent. Admittedly, this has not always been the case; yet I would hope that no decent, fair-minded person would ever have approved of the practice.

Which takes us to your views on the subject. Yours and those of the other sages, from the T'nach to the Mishnah and Gemara. No, I am not accusing you of having been a proponent of slavery. Not that.

But I am, nevertheless, accusing you of being short-sighted. While slavery may have persisted, here and there, into the 19th century, were we not supposed to be ahead of everybody? Especially in matters of social significance? If Americans freed their slaves in the 19th century, how could we tolerate slavery in the 12th? (Let alone later?)

You answer that we did not. To some extent, that is true. You did not own a slave, neither did other Jews; and when you heard of any Jew being sold into slavery, you organized efforts to collect money and buy their freedom. Very noble work, I am not taking that away from you. But what about the institution?

It was not a primarily Jewish institution in our time; and we had no control over it. But did we fight it? What have you done in order to eliminate slavery from the face of the earth?

What has the Talmud done? Well, quite a lot. It has protected slaves. It has created two classes of slaves, Jewish and Gentile. It has provided extensive protection for the Gentile slave and even more for the Jewish one. For one thing, they were to be freed every seventh year. That is, no doubt, enlightened. Yet slavery in the 2nd, or 4th century? How barbaric!

And so did the great Maimonides provide extensive measures of protection. A slave—a Jewish one—had a say about following his master to a foreign country. He could demand to be taken to Eretz Yisrael. Or he could escape to that land, and then had to be freed. Perhaps you could argue that these measures almost negated the practice. Almost, but not quite. And what about the Gentile slaves?

Perhaps I should not extend the blame back to the Torah itself, for it is talking about totally different times, different social relations, different laws, different world. A primitive, barbarous world. But surely not the 2nd century, let alone the 12th!

Judaism has long been a religion of equality. We have said that the Lord's laws apply to Jew and Gentile equally. What right do we have to tolerate one person "owning" another? At least the Greeks, even the wisest ones, professed to believe that a slave—by definition from a "barbaric" country—was at a much lower intellectual level than a Greek, that such a barbar was hardly better than an animal, and so it was just and right that a Greek should be master over such other. I wonder if they really believed that lie; yet it gave them a justification. We have never had such horrible but useful hypocrisy. We did not pretend to be more noble, more just than everybody else; we simply accepted the concept of slavery. How could we justify it in our minds? By trying not to think about the subject?

Rabbi, that topic really upsets me. I would have expected you, who had considerable influence in the most important, royal circles, to fight, constantly, for the elimination of slavery, until finally you suc-ceeded. You did not do so. Neither did I, and that is even harder for me to understand; but, for an excuse, I never had your position, your influence. Why I did what I did is less important now, since I am a resident, so to speak, of the 20th century. But you are, Master, if you read this letter, still in the 12th. Why did you do as you did? Why did you not do as you should have?

Your devoted disciple

Yosef ben Yehudah ibn-Shim`on

OUR LAWS HAVE CHANGED:

THE MISHNAH IN THIS AGE

6 Shevat 5750 / February 1, 1990

To B'Rabbi Moshe ben Rabbi Maimon ha-Sfaradi,
Fostat, Egypt

My beloved Master:

My overdue apologies: please forgive me for taking liberties, for using a harsh tone in my last few letters. I know I have been impertinent; how could I assume a position of moral superiority towards the Sage of Judaism, simply because I now live in a more enlightened age?

For it is the age that forces one to think ideas through, ideas that may have been around in an earlier age, but were not considered important.

If you *had* considered this exhaustively, then my words about the matter would be superfluous or even foolish, as Alfarabi puts it in the introduction to his book on music: "To speak about something that has already been spoken about, and exhaustively at that, is superfluous and foolish, and both are bad." But precisely because you have not exhausted the subject, I felt induced to write, to step before our Master, the Head of the Law, with what had been imparted to me from your wealth, and the correct understanding, to which I have been guided by your light. I am not laying claim to any merit, or to shine in scholarship—my aim is far more in keeping with what the poet sings about the ocean: the cloud pours out over the sea, which has no profit from this, for it is, after all, its own water.

Having said so, my dear Master, you still have to accept the fact that this age is more enlightened; many of the newly learned concepts obsolete old views; many of the newly adopted practices obsolete old rules. It may even be that, some ways, in the 20th century we are a little closer to the Holy One, blessed is He; perhaps a 20th century person knows Him a little better than one of equal education in the 12th century would have. And perhaps by now I may not need to convince you that a 12th century man understands things about the Lord that a 3rd century man may not have.

My Master, you had the highest respect for the wonderful teacher Yehudah ha-Nasi, "that man of perfection in wisdom and piety" (your words); yet you thought that there were many things that you understood better than he did. Similarly, you thought most highly of the tannaic rabbis and their successors, the amoraim, the savoraim (the little that we know about them) and the geonim, with some exceptions perhaps. But is it not true that you have understood all aspects of the Torah, the K'tuvim and especially the Halakhah better than they did? Did you not, in effect, re-write the Mishnah?

I am not proposing to re-write the Mishnah all over again; nor your Mishneh Torah, nor Caro's Shulchan Aruch or other great codes for the use of 20th century man. I wish I could. I wish anybody could. Such revision becomes necessary when it is sensed that the old rules are no longer observed by most people, for they are no longer relevant. We are in such a period now. The Mishnah reflects the Oral Law; it is interpreted for each age by the Halakhah; for custom annuls the Halakhah.

Rabbi, it is nice to say that our laws are the laws of the Torah; that the Torah is immutable, hence the laws don't change. It is a pretense, a pleasant line, one to which people pay lip service. You have spent your life insisting that the law remain valid without change; meanwhile you have re-defined the law! (and have done so very properly). So long as we are permitted to re-define, re-interpret, re-translate, re-explain, re-justify, I can go along with the practice; that is what *pilpul* is all about. But let us not be hypocritical. Let us admit that much of the Mishnah has lost its meaning, its validity, its relevance for the current age.

Just a couple of examples: the Mishnah clearly states that an unmarried man is not qualified to be an elementary school teacher. Even the amoraim were not happy with statements like that—what, they asked, are we pederasts? But the Tannaim go further, and forbid women —married or otherwise—from being elementary school teachers. Later, one amora excuses the proscription on the basis that the woman teacher would encounter the father of the child who brings him to school. I really don't know, Master, if this ever made sense; but it certainly is ridiculous today, and is simply ignored by Jews everywhere.

(Do you recall what the Mishnah said about the mouse, that it was half flesh, half earth? Our ancestors believed that the mouse is somehow generated from the ground, without the usual biological reproduction. I don't blame the tannaim for lacking competent zoological knowledge; but you cannot legislate such a mouse.)

But then, a large part of the Mishnah deals with the rules governing sacrifices. Oh, Tannaic Rabbis! From Shimeon ben Gamaliel through Eliezer and Akiva and Meir and all the others, and especially Rabbi, Yehudah ha-Nasi! How wise you all were; yet how foolish. For you did not understand that the time for sacrifices was over; that it was part of the T'nach only to appease the needs of the former idolaters; that the prophets declared the ceremony useless centuries earlier.

My Master, the Mishnah is a beautiful and most valuable document; it does *reflect* the oral law, but it *is not* the oral law and has never been. It does not apply today, certainly not in a general way. You knew that even in your time; we all know that today; the sooner we admit it openly, the better.

Your devoted disciple

Yosef ben Yehudah ibn-Shim`on

INCONSISTENCIES WITHIN MAIMONIDES' TEACHINGS

20 Shevat 5750 / February 15, 1990

To B'Rabbi Moshe ben Rabbi Maimon ha-Sfaradi,
Fostat, Egypt

My beloved Master:

Perhaps I should apologize again, in advance, for what I am about to write to you in this letter. Last time, I may have been too critical of the highly respected Rabbi, Yehudah ha-Nasi and other tannaic and amoraic rabbis. This time, I am afraid, it is your turn again. But, Master, please understand how a dwarf sitting on the shoulder of a giant can see farther than the giant can. Having your teaching as the basis of my thoughts, it is easy for me to gather a little more facts than you have had at your disposal, especially eight centuries in our future, and then being able to correct you, point out to you where you were wrong.

You may counter, of course, that a sage is beyond criticism; that he is, almost by definition, a saint, and attacking him is tantamount to attacking the Shekhinah. If so, I must respectfully disagree. Your arguments, relating our many respected teachers to Moses our Teacher, are farfetched, if not immodest. Granted that Moses could not be criticized, yet the millions of teachers following him certainly could be, often for very good reasons.

Having commented already on your opinions regarding women, slaves, loans, health, hygiene and diet, let me raise some other issues in this letter.

You claim that the Torah is valid and immutable forever; good. But then, despite your own comments that the Torah speaks in the language of Man, you refuse the right for any of the commandments to be re-interpreted. And that, in the view of the many-many re-interpretations of your own!

You do permit temporary changes, but only by the Sanhedrin. Was that a jest? *There is no Sanhedrin!*

Your views on the Messiah do correspond to that of the earlier sages, in that He will be an earthly king, will form a dynasty, bring political independence. Yet you would not consider re-interpreting that dogma in the view of current (12th century) man's language, understanding and concepts. You clearly refuse to have an open mind on that subject; indeed, you go as far as proposing that the Messiah will re-establish all the old rules, re-build the Temple and re-institute the custom of sacrifices there! Surely you knew better!

You have tried, valiantly, to cope with the age-old dilemma of choosing, for man, between free will versus divine providence and predestination. Yet you have not managed to surpass Akiba's statement "all is foreseen, yet freedom of choice is given". Why not rationalize that statement, expand it into something like this: "all of the most important things are foreseen, yet in most things freedom of choice is given"? If the Holy One, blessed is He, controls the Universe, He certainly will not let things go wrong, will not permit the emergence of perhaps irreparable damage; yet within broad directions and with maintaining tight control over a few key events, He could allow free will to Man. I am certain that He does allow it.

May I mention some other points where, I think, you should have been more fair, more just, more consistent?

Judaism has always been the religion of equality. Yet you propose a great measure of meritocracy; you despise the unlearned, those who are not scholars, have not spent their days studying Torah and

Talmud: the *Am ha-Aretz*. You would even exclude them from testifying in court, in effect making them second-class citizens, who must share your contempt with women. This is not a Jewish approach, but a Greek one; yes, your ancient philosophers treated not only the unlearned but tradesmen and businessmen with scorn similar to yours. Surely we are above such patronizing attitude towards anyone outside our class!

You approve of wars without making any distinction between just and unjust causes. You seem particularly in favour of religious wars —shades of Islam—but also approve a King's attacking his neighbour simply to enhance his greatness and prestige!

And still another point: you insist that a Jew must live in, as you put it, Palestine. You allow him business trips outside, but otherwise he must reside there, even if among only a minority of Jews, in preference to better foreign locations, even if they were to find a Jewish majority there. How, then, do you justify your own very brief stay in Palestine, followed by a quite rapid departure, I should say descent, for Egypt?

On this last point, as in all others, I am not blaming you, for you did what hundreds of thousands of Jews do even now: pay lip service to the cause of Zionism, but live in the Diaspora, for the living standards are higher there, and it is more peaceful (at the moment). Even I, your disciple, have chosen not to live in Israel so far; although I would expect to go up to Israel in the not-too-far future. So there is a measure of hypocrisy among most Jews today. It is quite likely that were you to live in this century, you would have chosen Israel long ago; it was much more difficult in the 12th century. But then again, one would expect more from you, Rabbi, than from ordinary people, such as your humble disciple.

One last complaint: you were, perhaps, too quick to accept the teachings of non-Jewish philosophers, even where those teachings were in conflict with those of the Torah. The one glaring example is your granting the possession of "higher intelligence" to the celestial "spheres", without even allowing argument about that subject, having considered it proven beyond doubt. Proven by whom? How? It was a ridiculous concept, long ago shown up as nothing but figments of human imagination. Is it not safer, on the whole, to go with the Torah?

Rambam, Rabbi Moshe ben Maimon! How wise you were; yet how foolish. For the simple truth was there before your eyes, yet you refused to see it, preferring to adopt obscure nonsense.

Your (nevertheless) devoted disciple

Yosef ben Yehudah ibn-Shim`on

WHAT IS SUPERSEDED?

3 Adar 5750 / February 28, 1990

To B'Rabbi Moshe ben Rabbi Maimon ha-Sfaradi,
Fostat, Egypt

My beloved Master:

If you are reading this letter, then I am relieved. I am very glad that you are still willing to accept letters from me. It takes a great man, a humble man, a true *tzaddik*, to accept criticism, especially from one lesser than he is.

I would like to involve you in the re-examination of the Law: how much of it is still valid, what relates to this age and what does not. This is a very difficult question, especially because of implications of Christianity.

As you may be aware, the creator of Christianity, Saul of Tarsus (later Paul) stated, in blatant contradiction to Jesus himself, that the Law of Judaism, the Law of God, has been superseded by the birth, life, atoning death and resurrection of Jesus Christ. He went further by saying that the Law is really a curse; if there were no law, there would be no sin (a surprisingly foolish and trite statement from somebody as brilliant as Paul). Indeed, the Christians soon found that, as the end of the world did not materialize immediately according to their expectation, and as their number grew, they needed a set of laws like every other group or nation.

Still, considering that statement about the Law having been superseded, one really hesitates to use the term "supersession". Yet many individual provisions of the Law are clearly no longer valid, not applicable to this age. There are others that could be applied if one were to insist on an anachronistic lifestyle, or one that makes a mockery of the Law by pretending to follow its words, while blatantly ignoring its intent.

I have already mentioned a few of the commandments that are now, apparently, obsoleted. Some of them were obsoleted by the tannaim and amoraim, such as the commandments having to do with jealous husbands and bitter waters, also about beheaded heifers. Some others were obsoleted by yourself, although inconsistently; you have ridiculed and invalidated the entire sacrificial system by realizing and stating very clearly, yet not consistently, not in all of your writings, that it was an important law for primitive man, but an embarrassment for the last 1700 years (by now closer to 2500).

Let me classify your 613 commandments, the *mitzvot*, in eight categories. I shall include examples with each.

Essential commandments, observed not only by Jews, but by every decent person:

your prohibitions #
243, 244, 245, 246, 247, 248, 249, 250, 251, 252, 253, 285, 289

(e.g. you must not steal; rob; murder)

Commandments valid today as before, and observed by every good Jew:

your decrees #
1, 2, 3, 4, 5, 6, 7, 8, 9, 94, 194, 195, 198, 200, 201, 202, 203, 204, 205, 206, 207, 208, 209, 210, 211, 212, 215; and

your prohibitions #
1, 2, 3, 4, 5, 6, 7, 8, 9, 10, 31, 32, 33, 34, 35, 36,
37, 38, 57, 58, 60, 61, 62, 63, 64, 65, 157, 219, 232, 234,
238, 239, 256, 267, 268, 269, 270, 271, 272, 297, 298, 299, 301, 302,
303, 304, 305, 318, 319, 330, 331, 332, 333, 334, 335, 336, 337, 338,
339, 340, 341, 342, 343, 344, 345, 346, 347, 348, 349, 350, 351, 352,
353, 355

(e.g. belief in God, love and fear of Him; charity and decency)

Other main commandments, interpreted variously by Jews today, fully observed only by the Orthodox:

your decrees #
10, 11, 12, 13, 14, 15, 19, 54, 73, 146, 147, 148, 149, 150, 151,
152, 154, 155, 156, 157, 158, 159, 160, 161, 162, 163, 164, 165, 166,
167, 168, 169, 170, 190, 191, 192, 193, 213, 214; and

your prohibitions #
42, 43, 44, 172, 173, 174, 175, 176, 177, 178, 179, 183, 184, 185,
186, 187, 188, 189, 190, 191, 192, 193, 195, 196, 197, 198, 199, 200,
201, 320, 321, 322, 323, 324, 325, 326, 327, 328, 329

(e.g. religious rituals; dietary laws; observance of the Shabbat)

Completely obsoleted by modern hygienic standards; yet observed by the Ultra-orthodox:

your decrees #
96, 97, 98, 99, 100, 101, 102, 103, 104, 105, 106, 107, 108, 109

(e.g. commandments relating to menstruous women and other aspects of ritual purity)

Impractical today; in most cases replaced by modern charitable and other measures:

your decrees #
18, 120, 121, 122, 123, 124, 134, 135, 136, 138, 139, 140, 141, 142, 171, 184, 197, 199; and

your prohibitions #
210, 211, 212, 213, 214, 220, 221, 222, 223, 224, 225, 226, 227, 230, 231, 235, 236, 237, 240, 241, 242, 311

(e.g. agricultural regulations, especially the "shemitah" and "yovel" years; financial transactions)

A few commandments that I personally consider unfair.

your prohibitions #
312, 313, 314, 315, 316, 317

(e.g. the 'sanctification' of the judge and teacher)

Totally archaic commandments:

your decrees #
16, 55, 56, 57, 58, 110, 111, 112, 137, 181, 185, 187, 188, 216, 217, 218, 219, 220, 221, 222, 223; and

your prohibitions #
11, 12, 13, 14, 15, 16, 17, 18, 19, 20, 21, 22, 23, 24, 25, 26, 27, 28, 29, 30, 39, 40, 41, 45, 46 (Master!), 47, 48, 49, 50, 51, 52, 53, 54, 55, 56, 59, 66, 118, 119, 120, 121, 122, 123, 124, 125, 126, 127, 128, 129, 130, 171, 180, 181, 182, 194, 215, 216, 217, 218, 265, 266, 306, 307, 308, 309, 310, 354, 356, 357, 358, 359, 360, 361

(e.g. commandments relating to idolatry; slavery; treatment of women; intolerance)

And finally,
Commandments that are technically impossible today; or cannot possibly apply:

your decrees #
17, 20, 21, 22, 23, 24, 25, 26, 27, 28, 29, 30, 31, 32, 33, 34, 35, 36, 37, 38, 39, 40, 41, 42, 43, 44, 45, 46, 47, 48, 49, 50, 51, 52, 53, 59, 60, 61, 62, 63, 64, 65, 66, 67, 68, 69, 70, 71, 72, 74, 75, 76, 77, 78, 79, 80, 81, 82, 83, 84, 85, 86, 87, 88, 89, 90, 91, 92, 93, 95, 113, 114, 115, 116, 117, 118, 119, 125, 126, 127, 128, 129, 130, 131, 132, 133, 143, 144, 145, 153, 172, 173, 174, 175, 176, 177, 178, 179, 180, 182, 183, 186, 189, 196, 224, 225, 226, 227, 228, 229, 230, 231, 232, 233, 234, 235, 236, 237, 238, 239, 240, 241, 242, 243, 244, 245, 246, 247, 248; and

your prohibitions #
67, 68, 69, 70, 71, 72, 73, 74, 75, 76, 77, 78, 79, 80, 81, 82, 83, 84, 85, 86, 87, 88, 89, 90, 91, 92, 93, 94, 95, 96, 97, 98, 99, 100, 101, 102, 103, 104, 105, 106, 107, 108, 109, 110, 111, 112, 113, 114, 115, 116, 117, 131, 132, 133, 134, 135, 136, 137, 138, 139, 140, 141, 142, 143, 144, 145, 146, 147, 148, 149, 150, 151, 152, 153, 154, 155, 156, 158, 159, 160, 161, 162, 163, 164, 165, 166, 167, 168, 169, 170, 202, 203, 204, 205, 206, 207, 208, 209, 228, 229, 233, 254, 255, 257, 258, 259, 260, 261, 262, 263, 264, 273, 274, 275, 276, 277, 278, 279, 280, 281, 282, 283, 284, 286, 287, 288, 290, 291, 292, 293, 294, 295, 296, 300, 362, 363, 364, 365

(e.g. sacrifices; priests; kings; jurisprudence).

Anybody could pick arguments with this list; suggest moving this or that commandment from one classification to the other. There may be a few commandments that I consider impossible, yet somebody finds a way of fulfilling. Nevertheless, I think it may be hard to argue with what I am saying here: some commandments are more valid today than others.

Or, to put it in a more traditional way: Custom annuls Halakhah. A non-functioning rule is a non-binding rule. This statement, as you know, is part of the Halakhah itself.

Today's Jews have matured enough, or have been thrust into a position of forced maturity by the Holy One, blessed is He, to be able to decide on the set of commandments that they think are applicable to this age and applicable to them, personally. I think that this development, while fraught with danger, is still a great positive step forward.

Your devoted disciple

Yosef ben Yehudah ibn-Shim`on

EXCOMMUNICATION

17 Adar 5750 / March 14, 1990

To B'Rabbi Moshe ben Rabbi Maimon ha-Sfaradi,
Fostat, Egypt

My beloved Master:

I would like to close this second series of letters to you with a note
of appreciation for your broad-mindedness and flexibility, understanding of a changed world and changed laws. But of course, I cannot
really be sure that you do indeed understand those things, much less
accept them; these communications over the centuries, quite unnatural-
ly, work only (if they do) in one direction: future-to-past.

Or, God knows, they may really work the other way. Perhaps you *are*
sending me messages. How? Simple: Through your writings. After all,
so many of your later works *were* addressed to me; perhaps I have
misread them, perhaps they were addressed to my 20th century presence, not the 12th century one? But then, you must have received my
letters from the future; yet I am quite sure that you never have; surely
your opinions would have changed as a result of them, or I am a very
poor persuader. Then again, could your opinions, your rules have been
harsher, less tolerant without my influence? Come to think, it must be
admitted that your views on the role and immutability of the Law did
change between the Mishneh Torah and the Moreh Nevukim, or Guide
for the Perplexed; was that because of the influence of my letters?
This is all very confusing, hard to understand.

On the other hand, while hoping to influence you with my letters, I must consider the possibility that you will refuse to take all this 20th century life-style seriously; that you will simply decree that a way of life that was good for us in the 12th century should also serve those no-goods in the future.

I have to consider the possibility that you wrote the Guide for the Perplexed as a warning to me, as a series of *responsa* defining your views about which thoughts are permissible and which ones are not. In a sense, perhaps, a *niddui,* a formal warning: a chance for me to change my ways; if I refuse, you may then issue a *herem,* an excommunication, against me. Many would have, in the past; there are some herems even today.

Don't do that, Master. Excommunication never achieves anything. If the subject of the herem is truly different, so divergent in his views that you don't want your people anything to do with him, he would move away with his followers with or without a herem. This happened to Jacob Frank and the so-called Frankists who tried to keep the failed Shabbatean pseudoMessianism alive in the 18th century.

Yet nidduis and herems were pronounced against many others, quite needlessly; you can't stop the emergence of new ideas with the threat of excommunication. (Nor can the other religions, from whom we Jews have learned the detestable practice.) We excommunicated the towering philosopher Baruch Spinoza in the 17th century along with other great minds. I may already have mentioned that the extatically joyous religious practices of the latter-day Hasidim were found objectionable by other religious leaders, resulting in the excommunication of the Hasidic movement! A movement which has nevertheless thrived, and is among the most religious trends today.

A more poignant example: the works of a certain Moshe ibn Maimun, the great sage—yes, yourself, my Master—were excommunicated by the Jewish authorities in Spain and Provence and also, even in stronger terms, by those in northern France. Their main objection was your partial acceptance of Aristotelian thought which they did not know and had no interest in knowing. They did know that Greek thought and lifestyle had a deleterious effect on the Israelites of old, and they refused to grant you the right to study and adopt any such thought.

They may have regretted their herem later, when your books were burned by the Christians (who, nonetheless, eventually came around to accepting much of your philosophy). I am not sure if the herem against you was ever formally lifted; but there were herems against the study of philosophy, the sciences, mathematics and medicine.

Eventually, rival authorities issued nidduis and herems against each other, to such an extent that the whole concept of sanctions became meaningless. Our sages! How wise they were; yet how foolish! For excommunication cannot work without an authoritative central religious body—a Sanhedrin—and I think it could not work even with such a body. The Roman Catholics do have such a central authority, and their excommunications have brought shame to that body.

But then, how do we know if anybody's proposals for changes in Jewish life, Jewish rituals, Jewish thought are acceptable? Well, in the long run it will become obvious whether or not they were acceptable. If they become adopted, if the new proposals become part of the Jewish mainstream, then they were correct. Otherwise, the Holy One, blessed is He, would not have permitted Judaism to change in that direction.

It is more difficult, of course, to decide on the correctness of a new set of proposals in a timely manner, without the benefit of centuries' worth of hindsight. One could refrain from expressing an opinion on them, leaving the matter to the Lord and to history. Alternately, one could make a decision on the validity of new teachings based on one's healthy intuition (perhaps aided by the Holy Spirit?) Does this new proposal, new definition of the law, new life-style feel Jewish? Do these writings sound like Jewish writings? Admittedly, such feelings are not very scientific; yet it is the only measure we have. We could have used it in the past; then, perhaps, Kohelet, Ecclesiastes would have been rejected from the holy writings: beautiful as it is, it's certainly not Jewish.

I hope, Rabbi, that you will accept my writings as Jewish.

And now, I have completed the second group of letters to you. Blessed be the Merciful who aided us.

Your devoted disciple

Yosef ben Yehudah ibn-Shim`on

BOOK III.

To understand God—and man

JOSEPH BEN YEHUDAH'S LETTER TO RAMBAM

22 Tammuz 5751 / July 4, 1991

To B'Rabbi Moshe ben Rabbi Maimon ha-Sfaradi,
Fostat, Egypt

My beloved Master:

I have not written any letter to you for over a year now. I have been
thinking, more hard than ever before. There is so much to consider,
to re-evaluate, to understand. Asking for the help of the Holy One,
blessed be He, I am, finally, embarking on a new series of letters to
you. Up to now, what I have been doing was telling you about the
Jews of this 20th century and trying to justify their strange ways to
you. Now I shall have to try to tell you about what I think is behind
it all. About the views I have developed with the help of the Holy
Spirit (even though you have always been skeptical about my claims
to such a privilege). About views that can now be based on the
enormous amount of knowledge accumulated over the last centuries,
especially those of the 19th and 20th ones. About life. About Man.
About God.

In a way, you may find these views not radically different from those
of your own; they may merely be expressed differently. They have to
be. For many of the concepts that I shall use, you could not possibly
have, as they were unknown to you or to me eight centuries ago. I
hope I can make them understandable to you.

I would like to make a possibly presumptuous statement that you and
I, my Rabbi, have always searched for the hidden meaning of
everything, tried to understand what is "behind it all". Do I understand

it now? Certainly I am a lot closer to it. That is where we differed even in the 12th century, my Master. You needed deep understanding; you did not envision the approaching rapid advancement of science, so you turned, first, to metaphysics and philosophy and then, when you were finally disappointed about the conflict between the basic tenets of Aristotelian philosophy and those of our faith, then to prophesy. You realized, or believed that it was impossible to understand the mysteries without additional information, and so you prayed to the Lord for understanding through the visitation of the Holy Spirit, through prophesy.

I, your humble disciple, on the other hand, thought that I can figure those mysteries out for myself, simply by using my mind. If that could be achieved only through the good offices of the Holy Spirit, so be it: I was convinced that the Holy Spirit has visited me on numerous occasions. By referring to myself on one occasion, incautiously, as one who is, or will be, a prophet, I really aroused your ire.

Yet, as it turns out, it really is possible to develop deep understanding of the mysteries of the Lord through the process of thinking. Does one need the help of the Holy Spirit to do so? I do not have the answer to that question, Rabbi; perhaps not, as long as one is willing to restrict his search to a depth based on current knowledge, what they call in this age as the "state-of-the-art". Beyond that, one needs divine help; but then, one will have trouble understanding the answer given, the picture provided. Look at the vision of Ezekiel: he saw something, no doubt something real; but he lacked the scientific training to interpret the vision, so ended up confusing himself and many generations after his time.

Still, it could be that one cannot get anywhere trying to understand the world, even when using current scientific concepts, without the help of the Holy Spirit; so I shall have to assume that such help has been available to me, and for that I thank the Almighty. And so, what I hope to achieve in these remaining letters to you is to make you (and perhaps others who may read these letters) view the Lord the same way I view Him, understanding what He has been doing and how (if not why); in the process come to understand ourselves, men and women; and especially understand what being a Jew means, what the role of the Jewish people has been and will be in the greater scheme of the Lord.

It will not be an easy task; I ask for your forbearance. For it will be necessary to consider most, if not all, views of the world. I have tried to understand separate aspects of the Universe's existence, but have found that it did not make sense that way. Everything is part of an overall design; it makes sense to look at the individual parts, but only after having understood that design. And while many of us —especially such people as my Master, Rambam—have managed to approach such understanding, I feel that wise as we all may have been, we were all foolish. Perhaps we still are; for certainly we shall never fully understand the majesty, the true nature of the Lord. But with His permission, we may now get closer to such an understanding than ever before.

I am sure that I have secured your attention, Master. But can I deliver the promised insights? Let me try.

Your devoted disciple

Joseph ben Yehudah

TO UNDERSTAND HIM:

NEED TO APPROACH HIM, COMPREHEND HIM

7 Av 5751 / July 18, 1991

To B'Rabbi Moshe ben Rabbi Maimon ha-Sfaradi,
Fostat, Egypt

My beloved Master:

You, of all people, shall not argue with the proposition that Man must, always, search for God. We must look for the Lord, try to understand Him and try to emulate Him.

But can one hope to understand Him? And how could one emulate Him, when most of the great Jewish philosophers, yourself included, agreed that what we can know of God's attributes are, at best, negatives: by saying that He is great, for example, all we really mean is that He is not small. Yet we, humans, cannot be such things; so how do we emulate Him?

It would seem to me, Rabbi, that we have been going around in a bit of a circle, not daring to attribute any quality to the Lord (except that of thinking, I believe you once allowed), yet wishing for Man to become more God-like. We can't have it both ways. So let us think again. Can Man come to know, to understand God?

Well, to understand Him fully, no, he cannot. At least, not until the Lord chooses to change Man into something else, into the same substance that He is Himself (but remember, Man is created, if not of the same substance, then at least according to some identical pattern, in God's image; hence such a metamorphosis is not necessarily a practical impossibility, certainly not one destined to happen only in the infinite future).

Yet, at the same time, he has been constantly revealing more and more of Himself to Man. At first, such revelation took the form of voluntary pronouncements by the Lord; lately and increasingly, He has been hiding, as it were, while inviting Man to find Him. The process of revelation has not slowed down, but Man has been forced to become an active participant in the process.

But consider our understanding of the Lord in our 12th century, and contrast it with Man's conception of Him way back in the third: we did understand so much more of His nature and qualities, even while denying to Him any real attributes. And again, do contrast the 3rd century view with the still earlier ones, those in the time of the Prophets, in the time of Moses our Teacher, or that of Jacob our forefather, for example. In Jacob's time, God was viewed as an angry local power; in Moses' time, an extremely powerful God of the Jews; for the prophets, the God of all, but a fickle one. The level of our understanding, the sophistication of our concepts, has increased steadily in all ages.

And that increase stems primarily from our acquired knowledge in a variety of fields. In our days, the branch of science that provided us with new vantage points of the Lord was philosophy, or metaphysics.

We speculated a lot about God as the first principle, the Prime Mover; about His essence, unity, incorporeality; whether He created the world ex-nihilo, or did the Universe exist forever, in some form; about how the world may proceed from Him; about spirits, the soul, intelligences; oh, about free will and divine providence. The tannaic rabbis did touch on some of these topics, but did not have the tools, the language, the concepts for fully exploring them. You and I did, and our contemporaries, in the Jewish and Islamic worlds.

Later, in the Christian theological era, Man speculated a lot more about the nature of God, and that nature has continued to open up for us. Much of the speculation centered on the goodness of God and on His demand that Man be good; those aspects of ancient Greek philosophy that dealt with ethics and morals (some of which were not known to us) were explored to such an extent that those philosophers became almost household names in the west. God became equated primarily with goodness. That process had a seemingly unfortunate result: Man concluded that he also can be good, he can behave morally and ethically, so he *may not need God.* Atheism reached a historically first prominence; and that prominence has been heightened by modern science, a tool consistently misused in the last two centuries in the service of the systematic denial of God.

To the extent that anyone should be blamed for this (for if the whole process was according to the wishes of the Lord, as it undoubtedly was, then why attach blame?), it is organized religion, Jewish as well as Christian and Islamic. These faiths deigned science as something beneath the dignity of the Lord, too practical, too profane, lacking in the preferred tones of sanctimony. In science, every term is defined; it cannot tolerate lofty, meaningless words designed to create awe but no understanding. Religion has been afraid of science.

I think the time has come to eliminate that fear, to re-establish an era in which theologians take full advantage of all findings of modern science, use every tool available to Man. And do so not only in a peripheral manner. I am not thinking of religious congregations using computers for trivial objectives, such as keeping records of their membership, vital dates and annual financial contributions. No, I mean to use the concepts of computing, as well as nuclear physics, cosmology, quantum mechanics, genetic engineering and especially the science of management and control—to use all of these modern sciences, and more, in our understanding of the Holy One, blessed is He.

And by the term "use", I do not only mean utilization as tools; rather, using these sciences as concepts that may explain God to us; concepts that may be part of His make-up, or may serve as practical analogues to such divine attributes that may, still, be beyond our direct understanding.

This will be an exciting exploratory trip then, trying to view the majesty of the Lord in His being and in His actions, especially His actions in creating the Universe, creating life, creating Man—we shall have an entirely new view of Him. Not a complete view, of course; never that, perhaps; but a much more sensible, understandable, acceptable, realistic view. Rabbi, I am sure that you are still with me on this new trip.

Your devoted disciple

Joseph ben Yehudah

APPLICABILITY OF MODERN COMPUTER CONCEPTS

27 Av 5751 / August 7, 1991

To B'Rabbi Moshe ben Rabbi Maimon ha-Sfaradi,
Fostat, Egypt

My beloved Master:

I believe that I mentioned computers to you in an earlier letter. Let me explain the concept to you in some detail.

There are two major elements involved: the hardware and the software. The hardware is a machine, not unlike the human brain, but much more simple (yet enormously complex, impossible to understand by any but a few technical specialists). The software is an idea, intellect, artificially created (again, comparable to the human mind, but incomparably more simple).

(To give you a simplified explanation,) the hardware is primarily made up of many tiny parts, mostly a collection of switches that can direct traffic—in this case weak electric current—in any one of two directions. Depending how the switch is set, you go left or right. Since you are familiar with the enormous numbers one can generate by raising the number 2 to the power of, say, 50 or 100 (really multiplying it by itself that many times), you will not be surprised that the variety of paths the current can take in a hardware is astronomical in a machine with, say, some thousands of such switches (which results in 2 raised to the power of thousands). Actually, there is not even a need for that many switches, as I shall show you.

You can already see, perhaps, how this provides for almost every type of decision and action, even for simulating every human activity short of heavy physical work; for example, translation of a book, composing complex music, planning strategy for an army, and so on.

But the switches are not yet set. The setting of them is done by the software. Any decision-making activity can be broken down into a series of yes-no questions; a set of instructions containing thousands, perhaps millions of such questions. There is no need to limit the questions to the number of switches in the hardware, the same switches can be used for different decisions at different times, say a fraction of a second later.

What kind of questions? If the opposing army has more than 50,000 men, then call it A, otherwise call it B; then, if A and they have a certain type of arms, then if their location is not closer than 60 miles, then we shall use the X type of armoury, otherwise the Y type; but if their size is B, and if the number of their vehicles is not more than one for every ten men, then . . . and so on. Do you get the idea? The instructions would go on for pages, could be of a book-size; it is called a program. When executed on the computer, it might do the calculation in less than a second; a very big program may take a few seconds, even a minute or two. Translating your "Guide for the Perplexed" into a new language might take minutes, for it is a difficult book. A set of coherent programs is the software.

There is still another aspect to both hardware and software: the memory. A part of the hardware stores information in the form, again, of yes-no switches. Like decision-making, information can be broken down into its smallest elements, such yes-no switches, in this case called bits. This is easy to see; after all, the most complex book is just a collection of some 20-odd letter types; and each letter can be stored as unique combination of just five such bits, for 2 to the power of 5 is 32. In practice, seven or eight are used, to allow for the ten numbers and for special characters. So the letter L may be stored as "no-yes-no-no-yes-no-no-no".

One can store, therefore, whole books in the computer memory; as well, anything else can be broken down to small elements: pictures, sounds, smells. The program needs a lot of such information about the subject matter before it can perform its task. The information is either pre-stored in computer memory, or fed in mechanically just prior to executing a particular program.

Now, back to the software. When we "run" a program on a computer, it is never just one program. The user of the computer may write one program, or he may write a complex group of interactive programs, and run them; but they would not work without another set of programs, the "operating system". That is a set of programs that the user does not write. It usually comes with the hardware, "sits there" waiting for the user program. It receives instructions from these programs, and in turn gives instructions to the hardware itself, tells it how to operate at all: how to "read in" the information, or data, that it is fed; how to interpret arithmetic symbols; how to move data in and out of memory; how to sort information; how to handle unexpected situations or problems; how to do more than one task apparently at the same time (really, moving very quickly between several tasks); how to talk to several users, perhaps thousands or more, while still doing other things in the background; how to print out the result, say your book using the symbols of the Chinese language (not the actual translation, that is handled by the user's program; only the instructions regarding the handling of the "output" when being transferred to the printer); and many-many other functions. Each of these situations is handled by a complex program of its own, or a hierarchic series of programs; each is part of the greater hierarchy which is the operating system. When the user runs his program, be it a simple one or a large hierarchy of programs, that program or hierarchy becomes, while he runs it, a part of the operating system at its lowest level.

Now, Master, you do see that the software is intellect. Like the human mind? No, as I said, the mind is far more complex than computer software, even if the brain operates a lot slower than the hardware (probably not really slower; the most simple human task probably involves millions of little decisions, to be made in an instant; or so people have found when trying to program a computer to direct a machine to find and lift a cup of water off a table, move it and set it down on a saucer on another table: an extremely complex task).

Also, software, while not as complex as the human mind, has been increasing in complexity all the time. Do you recall the game of chess? There is software now that can beat all but the best humans at that game (which means that they would have beaten the best players of our age).

But can we compare software to the mind of the Lord? A mind that is almost infinitely more complex than the human mind? I think yes, we can. I want to remind you, again, of the term I used for the software: intelligence or, if you prefer, intellect. Master: remember the Active Intellect of the Greek philosophers! Is God the Active Intellect, or is He still one level higher? That is immaterial: as you admitted yourself, He thinks. For He is The Intellect; and he created us in His image.

Then what are we? We are bodies, including the hardware, the human brain; but we possess the Potential Intellect. That can develop into Acquired Intellect, with the facilitation of the Active Intellect. I am using these Aristotelian terms so you will feel right at home while familiarizing yourself with these modern computer concepts. Aristotle called the overall direction Active Intellect or Agent Intellect; but Plato, or at least the Neo-platonians simply called it the Mind.

Yet we may have a problem. Software, the intellect, the mind, operates on the hardware, a machine, a *substrate* that is relatively unimportant, almost incidental, yet absolutely necessary. That duality may sound familiar to you; that arrangement does describe our understanding of sentient beings; but how can it apply to God? For He is not a created being; He is not supposed to have a material base; He is not allowed to have parts, a structure, a hierarchy—and yet, a hierarchy of celestial beings was considered acceptable. But God

Himself must be indivisible, simple. Simple! The highest level of intelligence is called a simpleton! It is so obvious that God is, far from being simple, the most complex being that there can be.

The reason for calling Him simple was to protect His unity. But surely we have outgrown that requirement of idolatrous times. Of course He is One. So is the computer operating system. It is one; with many parts. We can deal with it as one, or we can address any particular part that we have business with; it does not matter, since we are still, always, dealing with the whole, whether or not through one, two, a dozen or thousands of lower sections, subdivisions.

This should give you something to think about, Rabbi, before moving on to another view of the Lord, blessed be He. And with His help, I shall return to this subject in one of my letters to you in the not too far future.

Your devoted disciple

Joseph ben Yehudah

DIMENSIONS: ONE VIEW

11 Elul 5751 / August 21, 1991

To B'Rabbi Moshe ben Rabbi Maimon ha-Sfaradi,
Fostat, Egypt

My beloved Master:

I have thought a lot about the physical nature of the Holy One,
blessed be He. Given that He is essentially intelligence, yet that
intelligence must have a physical base. But if so, where is it? How
come that we can't see it, yet He can see us and He can manipulate
us whenever he decides to do so? What laws of physics are we subject
to that He is not, and what laws of physics do apply to Him? Do we
share any law with Him?

Perhaps even before worrying about physics, we should consider the
mathematics involved, it may be more relevant to our quest. I think
that perhaps a key to our understanding the Lord and His relation to
us may be found in the dimensions of space.

You were quite familiar with two and three-dimensional geometry.
Two dimensions, perpendicular to each other, define the plane. Three
such dimensions define space. In space, we can deal with such objects
as globes, cubes, cones and indeed, considering combinations of these
and irregular objects, an infinity of others. Those include, of course,
all inanimate and animate objects that we are familiar with on earth
and outside.

People have speculated about a plane, two-dimensional world. Could
it exist? Could there be some kind of life on such a world? It was
concluded that existence, even life, could be possible on the plane;
such theoretical life has even been studied thoroughly and defined in
detail.

One thing that strikes you is that the two-dimensional people would not be aware of the third dimension, could not possibly conceive of it even if it was explained to them; and could not see a three-dimensional object, except to the extent that such an object passes through their plane; in which case the three-dimensional object would be perceived as a two-dimensional one, except that unless it made no motion whatsoever in the third dimension, its shape would appear to change constantly. Such an object would appear, change its shape in rapid succession, and then disappear.

But could a three-dimensional being see, sense the two-dimensional world? I think not. It is possible to see what is written on a piece of paper; but what we see is the three-dimensional ink particles on that paper, no matter how small. I think that with the disappearance of the third dimension, our perception of the object would also disappear.

With this preamble, I ask: could God reside in a four-dimensional world? (I know that you denied the possibility of God's having any dimensions at all; but let us base this discussion on the assumption that while the essence of the Lord, which is intellect, may perhaps have no dimensions, the physical substrate for that intellect must.) I admit that it seems unlikely. If the analogy I just presented holds, He could not see us from the fourth dimension; while every time He appeared in our world, he would take a different form, and a constantly changing form at that. We have no record of such appearances.

Nevertheless, there is more to dimensions than meets the eye. God could have dimensions other than our own. He may have three, four, five, six or any number of dimensions. One, two, three of those may be identical with our own. I think that even among mathematicians, few understand how a space of, say, three dimensions would interact with another space of three different dimensions. They would probably say that those don't interact. But what if one of those three dimensions were shared? What if two were?

Could God reside in dimensions more than ours? Different from ours? Probably not, while still being relevant in this world. Yet in some ways, He is undoubtedly in a different world, albeit one where he can sense and manipulate us. How different? We don't know. So until we can think of a better concept, the best "visualization" we can have may, after all, be a physical base for the Lord, one that is, say, a five-dimensional object, three of those dimensions coinciding with our three.

To complicate matters, the wise men of this age tell us that in addition to our three spatial dimensions, we do have a fourth one, a temporal one: that time is a dimension, perpendicular to the other three. If so, God could have an advantage over us in being able to move consciously in our time dimension, forward or backward. He may even have one or more additional temporal dimensions. But this raises additional difficulties; I think I shall have to think about those, perhaps you will, too; and I hope to write to you about that idea later.

Meanwhile, I just wanted you to see if any twelfth century idea would serve to describe the abode of God in a technically acceptable way. The spheres must, unfortunately, be discarded, even though they would have been so convenient. There is another term that comes to mind; but let me leave that to a subsequent letter of mine, if He will help me, another letter about computer software and hardware in a little while. You may want to think about it, meanwhile.

One more thought about dimensions: could God possibly be spatially two-dimensional? Yet somehow still being able to move through the third dimension, perhaps by some application of an extra temporal dimension?

Your devoted disciple

Joseph ben Yehudah

PROJECT MANAGEMENT

26 Elul 5751 / September 5, 1991

To B'Rabbi Moshe ben Rabbi Maimon ha-Sfaradi,
Fostat, Egypt

My beloved Master:

It is difficult to contemplate the nature, the abode of the Holy One, blessed is He, for our mind is not up to the task. Yet we do need to strive towards understanding Him, or as close to such an understanding as He will permit and encourage us to reach. But we need a respite; so let us think of something a little more easy, more comprehensible by humans: what the Lord has been doing, and how. Of course, he may have been doing many things outside our world, but those things do not concern us. Anything that He has done in our world, on the other hand, is fully visible to us; much of this He has done before our very eyes. From these evidences, it should not be very difficult to draw a rather comprehensive, though by no means complete, set of conclusions about the Lord's objectives as well as His methodology. In this letter, I would like to concentrate on how He has been doing it. Doing what? That is another question. I hope to write to you about that later.

The one most conspicuous fact on how He has been going about His work is that while it has been extremely complex, He has been doing it in a highly organized manner. That is, of course, the only way of achieving a very large and complex objective. In our days, we did not have many such tasks. But today, Man is quite familiar with the idea.

They call them projects. They define a set of tasks as a project, with one or more final objectives; then they plan it, organize it, monitor it, control it until it is done. One major project of the 20th century was putting the first man on the Moon. It was very difficult, involving many sub-projects of still considerable complexity. Other recent projects included building the major waterways, including the Suez Canal: the largest ships can now sail directly from the Mediterranean to the Indian Ocean; and connecting the European continent with England through an under-water tunnel: this project is now nearing completion.

It seems very clear to me that God has been working on a major project. Perhaps irreverently, one could think of Him as a Project Manager.

What does a Project Manager do? Well, having assumed responsibility for a project, he reviews it starting with the expected end-result; he makes sure that he understands what the final outcome should be and also what by-products may be required.

He then determines what the major phases will be towards the achievement of the end product; there should not be too many, or the project will be in danger of getting lost among the details. But each major phase will be a project of its own, with expected end-results and further phases. If the project is very large, there could be a hierarchy of sub-projects at many levels, five or ten or even a hundred.

If a project can be broken up into sub-projects, such that more than one of them may be under way at the same time, then it is advantageous to appoint a project manager for each of those, while the higher level project manager acts as co-ordinator of those projects, especially when conflicts emerge and demand resolution. There are always conflicts: contention for limited resources; interfaces; events that are influenced by two or more sub-projects, perhaps in different order, with conflicting priorities.

So let us consider a sub-project of such complexity as does not require the creation of still lower level sub-projects. It will still have phases, major steps.

The project manager will try to make sure that as far as possible, he understands every phase (if not the smallest details) right at the outset; that he knows how he will do any and all of them. If he was not sure of that, then in one of the phases he might encounter difficulties necessitating the creation of still further sub-projects, perhaps of greater size and complexity than the original sub-project; that could cause (depending on the criteria) the whole project to suffer major delay.

Next, he establishes the necessary resources as well as timing for the project; and takes steps to assure that such resources will be available. Depending on the type of the project, he can acquire those resources on the open market, subject to availability, and his budget; or, more relevant to our consideration here, he may have to request those from his upward hierarchy, in which case he may have to be prepared to contend for the best resources. Still another alternative is for this project manager to develop his own resources; very often, that is a possible and welcome solution.

All of these activities result in a project plan; by the time it is produced, the project manager fully understands all phases of the project.

The resources are then organized for the commencement of the project. This may involve education and training; preparation of tools, establishing the appropriate working environment, and hundreds or thousands of other preparatory activities. The task also includes setting up the monitoring and controlling mechanisms.

The project is then under way, and so is its monitoring function. There are major "milestones" and minor ones; criteria must be met regarding the pace, quality and quantity; the project manager must remain on top of all phases and tasks at all times.

He must also realize that things will go wrong. Yet he must be in full control. How to do that? By foreseeing the unforeseeable. That sounds like a contradiction, yet it is possible. He does not have to know what will cause any particular task or step to malfunction; but he does have to know what to do when it happens, he must have contingency plans; and the lower level of application of such contingencies, the better, for it provides for the possibility of getting back on track without losing valuable time.

Of course, this implies that when considering hierarchically higher level projects, what may go wrong could be an entire sub-project, one hopes a relatively low level one. Obviously, not each project will be equally successful. One's choice of project manager may have been overly optimistic; but every once in a while something may have happened to foil the best-laid plans of the most outstanding project manager. So there will be excellent sub-projects; good ones; acceptable ones; and, every once in a while, a failed sub-project. But the higher level project manager, and certainly the overall one, has provided for that, has had a contingency plan all along, and can take the appropriate corrective action.

My Master, this is how they do big projects in today's very complex world, and there is no reason why the Lord would not use the same, or similar methodology. In fact, there is every reason to believe that He does. He is the overall Project Manager. But who are, then, the Managers of the various sub-projects? Ah, I shall have a lot to say about that in one of my future letters to you.

Your devoted disciple

Joseph ben Yehudah

WHAT HE'S BEEN DOING AND HOW:

DIRECTED EVOLUTION

25 Tishri 5752 / October 3, 1991

To B'Rabbi Moshe ben Rabbi Maimon ha-Sfaradi,
Fostat, Egypt

My beloved Master:

I would like, in this letter, to continue with the study of the methodology of the Holy One, blessed is He; to look at some other aspects of how He has been doing things. I hope that if we go about this carefully, then eventually such study will lead us from methodology to objective.

This time, let us consider the various animal and plant species and how they have come about. We have talked about this earlier, but now I would like to go into some detail.

Modern scientists have dealt, firmly, with the technicalities of the matter. Foremost among these scientist was the Englishman, Charles Darwin, of the 19th century. Let me try to summarize his explanation; and please understand that while these are theories, not yet proven facts, the basic idea, if not the specifics, is sound.

That one species can evolve from another, that has really been known for thousands of years; even the compilers of the Mishnah knew it, while formally denying the concept. In the Midrash, in the Aggadah, there are plenty of references to such concepts.

(It is perhaps understandable that, lacking access to modern and precise scientific instruments or even scientific approach, the great Rabbi Yehudah haNasi and his colleagues had accepted lots of nonsense as feasible facts. They seriously believed, as I mentioned and as you know, that the mouse is not a reproductory animal, but one generated from dirt.)

Still, from Aristotle on, the evolution of animal lifeforms has been accepted by all scientists and philosophers willing to trust their mind and instincts. In fact, a brief overview of such evolution can be obtained by studying the human embryo; it has been said that ontogeny recapitulates phylogeny (the genesis of the individual follows the pattern of the genesis of the race of which he is a member).

Before Darwin, a Swede named Linnaeus catalogued and classified all plant and animal life-forms known at the time. Without intending to prove evolution, he built a "family tree" structure, showing the proper place for each species in the relationship. What he created was the taxonomy of all life-forms.

In Linnaeus' system, there are two "kingdoms", animal and plant. Within each, there are a number of "phyla"; under each "phylum", "classes"; then "orders", "families", "genuses" (or "genera") and finally, under the "genus", "species". If those were not enough, these categories are sometimes enhanced, so that each level can include super- and sub-levels, increasing the number of terms from seven to twenty.

But then, there are over one million animal species known today! (Most of those are insects.)

The earliest known life-form of any kind seems to have developed in the sea. Of 22 phyla within the animal kingdom, twenty are comprised exclusively of sea animals. Only the 18th and 22nd have land (as well as sea) animals. In the 18th phylum one finds the class of insects, some 850,000 species (the next most numerous class is that of mollusks, including snails, clams, octopuses: there are about 80,000 species).

The 22nd phylum is the most interesting because it has all of the vertebrates. Some of the classes within this phylum are those that include all the modern fishes; the amphibians, such as frogs; reptilians; birds; and finally, mammalians, or warm-blooded animals with hair and mammary glands.

Of mammals, there are some 3500 known species. The earlier types still laid eggs; somewhat later, the live-bearing animals developed, pouched animals at first (you would not have heard of these, most of them are found in Australia) and then, placental mammals. To give you an idea of the major types of these (for there are some twenty-five orders of placental mammals), one order has the moles and hedgehogs; another, the whales and dolphins (you did know that these were not fishes, I think). There are the orders of rodents and of rabbits. There is an order for elephants and another for carnivores, including dogs, cats, lions, tigers, bears and others. There is an order for horses, tapirs, rhinoceroses; another includes cattle, deer and pigs.

And most important for us, there is the order of primates. That order includes several families of monkeys and one superfamily of homonoidea, man-like apes and also man. Man! The end-product of a long and complex evolutionary movement.

The Lord has laboured for billions of years to bring forth Man and Woman! For we can now determine the age of animal and plant fossils, remains and imprints found in the earth, buried deep under successive layers of sediment. We have known for a long time that some animals have been around for millions of years. Now even older animals have been identified through fossils, even though most have been extinct for a very long time. But the most simple life-forms can now be determined to be two or three billion years old!

But how did such evolution come about? How can a fish become a chicken or a tiger? Well, it does not quite happen that way. It is really the ancestors of these animals that are related. But evolve they did, one species begot another, always more advanced, more specialized, more suitable for a hostile environment and consistently moving in the direction of the end-product, Man.

Here is how it happens, according to Charles Darwin and others: any plant and animal species is always struggling to survive in an environment that is partly friendly, partly hostile. The degree of hostility fluctuates; for example, in some years there may be worse weather, more predators, less food than in others. In such times, many die; only the strongest survive, mature into adulthood so it can generate offsprings. The strongest is not necessarily the one equipped with the most muscles: it could be the tallest, greenest, spottiest, hairiest, fastest, most sharp-eyed, most intelligent.

The characteristics of any species are determined by chains of chemicals, incomparably smaller than the bacteria or even viruses that I have mentioned earlier. These are called genes, accumulated in chromosomes inside the cells of every living being. Such genes include still smaller elements, codes that specify the manufacturing and deployment of the building elements; these codes also determine the characteristics of the reproduced offsprings. In each of the billions of cells in a human being, for example, there are over forty chromosomes, each including many genes, each genes comprising many individual codes, created from a base of a compound called DNA and coded with another type of chemicals, called "nucleotides", the combination of any three of which determine the next amino acid to be selected, a link in the protein chain, the body building block that is to be created.

In these genes, "random" mutations happen all the time; so every individual is different; this produces the requisite variety that, ideally, ensures the availability of many types of individuals, including some able to survive all but the worst catastrophe; thereby all but guaranteeing the survival of the species. Well, not always; but that is the decision of the Lord. Under normal circumstances, the individuals most fit will adapt to the hostile environment and survive; and will be the most likely to have offsprings. In bi-parental lifeforms, when both parents have such most important characteristics, those will be enhanced in the offsprings, some of whom may then have such new characteristics in excess of the parents, and survive and reproduce in preference even over their own siblings.

Darwin called the process "natural selection". It is achieved through the survival of the fittest. Over many-many generations, subtle changes become pronounced, until a completely different species evolves, one that usually cannot even interbreed with the unchanged members of the progenitor species that may have survived at another location.

But there are some problems with the "requisite variety" that is produced from an accumulation of random mutations and is needed to assure the availability of new features needed for survival in the changed environment. Mr. Darwin and his followers cannot fully answer some embarrassing questions about how gradual evolution could have produced end-results where the intermediate stages were totally useless, and the whole process may have required thousands or millions of generations—such as the development of the complex mechanism that provides sight. I am sure that you and I could provide the answer. We'll talk about that later.

So how does a butterfly, a wasp, a bat or a bird (related only through remote, non-flying ancestors) grow wings in the first place? Possibly through the appearance of an environment causing them to fall out of trees and perish, unless they can move some body appendage fast enough to slow their fall through the generated air resistance; the ones that have the most wing-like appendages will survive and grow larger and larger wings over many generations. Alternately, flapping large appendages may have helped some animals escape from pursuing predators; some such "escapees" may even have managed to lift into the air for a short time; again, this ability would have increased over many generations facing similar predicament. Neither of those explanations are very good; one cannot really "sense" that it happened that way. For one thing, how would the theory account for the development of feathers? Diehard evolutionists claim that in this case the intermediate stage, where feathers were useless in flight, helped the bird keep warm—an unlikely story. But that is the theory.

And this is evolution for you, in a "nutshell". Even apart its problems, and I have alluded to one or two, one needs to understand this question: why is it so? Why has evolution brought forth species of constantly increasing complexities? Why has the process progressed relentlessly in the direction of complexity, of Man, of intelligence? Of course, the real question (and even answer) suggests itself: Who set it up in the first place? Who controls the external environment forcing natural selection in one direction or another?

There are many today, including most (but by no means all) scientists who say that it is all a natural phenomenon: the environment changes, and those who can adapt to the new, hostile environment best, the fittest ones, will survive. That is, in a general sense, correct. Yet it does not account, by itself, for the evolution of complex features, especially in view of the fact that species without them survive in excellent health and large numbers.

It has been calculated that just the development of the genetic basis of the most simple living being, if left to the mechanism proposed by the Neo-Darwinists, would have taken more years than the number of atoms in the universe. There were not that many years available.

Let us look at it again. They say that mutations are entirely random. That is hard to believe. Will such mutations cause certain fishes to develop a highly sophisticated electric system, complete with batteries and insulation, to give electric shock to its enemies or prey, when other fishes are quite well off without it? Will it actually cause sea animals to crawl onto dry land? Develop live birth with mammalian feeding? Evolve intelligence? Will a million, a billion monkeys, given paper and pen (or writing machines) eventually write, by accident, a major work of Aristotle? Perhaps an infinite number of monkeys, over an infinite length of time will; that is meaningless for me. But in finite time, such miraculous things don't happen. And how much more complex is the most simple living being than the greatest work of Aristotle! As I have indicated, even individual features, such as the eye, the electric system of the eel and many other wonders of the animal kingdom involve complexities beyond the understanding of most of humanity. And the transitional stages during the development of such a feature would have been of no use to any animal.

Let me be blunt: the requisite variety could not have emerged on its own, except in the most trivial situations—sizes of limbs, perhaps. Certainly not in the case of advanced features, involving high technology. Random mutations will not produce the requisite variety, not in ten to the power of a hundred years (and you can guess how large that number is.)

But if somebody has been directing the process—yes, that could explain everything. Suppose that this somebody, let me just refer to Him as the Lord, if He manipulated the genes, caused *non-random* mutations, sometimes in generation after generation, even in millions of subsequent generations, until the desired feature was completed; and if, at the same time, He carefully changed the environment to enhance the characteristics He wanted to evolve? If He introduced just the right amount of radiation or chemical changes to cause the extinction of some species or families and make room for another, more advanced one—yes, then, the evolution in the direction of intellect would suddenly make sense. He created plants, simple animals, complex animals and eventually Man; achieved all that through the process of directed evolution.

Yes, Rabbi, that is what the Lord, blessed be His name, has been doing; the evidence is in front of us; and that makes the work of one who is trying to understand Him so much easier, so delightful, so happy, for such a one is observing the handiwork of the Lord, not hidden, not through trying to interpret mysteries, but in plain view of all of us. Great is He and great is His work.

Your devoted disciple

Joseph ben Yehudah

STRIFE, EVIL, SUFFERING: GENERATORS OF PROGRESS

8 Heshvan 5752 / October 16, 1991

To B'Rabbi Moshe ben Rabbi Maimon ha-Sfaradi,
Fostat, Egypt

My beloved Master:

Have you had a chance to reflect on my last letter? I hope I have not
confused you. After all, I first presented a picture that showed a world
where an individual—be it plant, animal or man—is constantly
struggling to survive. To survive and to reproduce itself. Then I
assured you that the current crop of evolutionists are quite wrong in
their reliance on random mutations to accumulate over generations and
produce totally new species and features. Please don't misunderstand
me: the mutations are certainly not random, they are certainly
manipulated and directed by the Holy One, blessed be His name, to
assure the availability of the requisite variety of mutated genes, in the
direction He wants them to be changed; but to take effect, to become
established in the animal kingdom, their possessors must still struggle,
fight for survival and domination.

You could accuse me of painting a grim picture: depicting a world
where an animal, say a graceful gazelle, far from enjoying the sylvan
beauty, the fresh branch water, the ample food found everywhere and
the pleasure of his doe, is in constant fear of his life. He desperately
forages for scraps of food, for drops of water, escapes from lions and
other predators while barely managing to find a doe who will have
him rather than the other, more handsome gazelle. Which picture is
the true one?

I am afraid my bleak one comes closer to the truth, to the extent that there is such a thing. For there are no absolutes in nature: sometimes things are better, sometimes things are worse; you do know that well, for this is no different in case of humans. I think that if things were even worse for gazelles, if they were always in flight, always chased, always threatened, then they would soon collapse, their hearts would give up; certainly there could be no question of reproduction, the species would soon die out.

Nevertheless, the lions do chase the gazelles and catch them and eat them. Only the swiftest will survive and reproduce. And the doe may not like his antlers, or at least the best doe may choose another. It is a life of almost constant contention, strife and struggle. You could almost call it, from the gazelle's standpoint, a horrible life, an evil life.

Is God then not good? My Master, the answer seems to be that He is good, but not to every individual gazelle.

(Yes, Rabbi, I am aware of the implications of that statement; and I shall deal with them quite soon, perhaps in my next letter to you, if the Holy One, blessed be He, permits me.)

And so, where the gazelle is concerned, there is evil in the world. The lion is after him, the cheetah is after him, even Man is after him; while the other gazelle is robbing him of his doe; and there is not enough food. It is a cruel world.

Is God really behind all the evil that befalls the gazelle? I don't think that God particularly wants to hurt the gazelle; but He probably finds it unnecessary to go out of His way to help him. For one thing, the lion has as much right to live as the gazelle.

For another, a more important argument, God may be in the process of developing another life-form, a still swifter, still more alert, more rugged version of the gazelle. But this is not likely; there has been little evidence lately of new evolutionary forms, other than those created by directed evolution by Man, over the last few thousand years.

But even if the Lord is not especially visiting trials on the gazelle, the animal has to cope with the system; for struggle and strife are the very basis of life on earth. Man and beast have always had to cope with adversity, with periods of plenty followed by periods of scarcity; with tolerance followed by intolerance; with peace followed by war.

Why has God created such a system? Why could we not live, Man and beast, all peacefully in the Garden of Eden? Is it because of the forbidden fruit? Of course not.

Strife and struggle are necessary in the world. Only through those means can something better, stronger, more advanced develop, evolve. The best individuals emerge when faced with adversity, threat and suffering. The best species emerge when exposed to a variety of dangers, enemies sufficient to decimate the population, but insufficient to eradicate it.

Trying to understand the Lord, we must observe what He has been doing. Through manipulating the genes as well as the environment, He has been creating new life-forms, new species, genera, families, orders, classes, phyla. The main thrust has been towards complexity and intelligence. Of course, He has had numerous other objectives along the way, perhaps even at apparent odds with the main one, although ultimately in its support. He must have had ecological objectives, to create a balanced, self-sustaining environment on earth. He must have created life-forms in vast abundance, for the simple purpose of burying it under ground, under sea, as reserve fossil fuel a billion years in the future, when Man will need such fuel to make a sudden rapid burst of scientific and social advance possible, to achieve a technological eminence in a short period of a only few hundred years, before he solves the problem of almost unlimited energy requirement through nuclear or other means.

Whether the gazelle needs to struggle because God is still manipulating the species, or simply because the mechanism is left in place after it fulfilled its need, I don't know. (I think the mechanism is necessary to keep the biosphere in ecological balance, a requirement for Man to this day and for some time even into the future.) But I do know that He's created, on the one hand, strong instincts, those of self-preservation and racial preservation; and on the other hand, the threat of extinction; and out of that cauldron of bubbling good and evil emerge ever higher levels of life-forms, complexity and intelligence. That cauldron is the generator of progress.

Your devoted disciple

Joseph ben Yehudah

HOLOCAUST vs. STATE OF ISRAEL

20 Heshvan 5752 / October 28, 1991

To B'Rabbi Moshe ben Rabbi Maimon ha-Sfaradi,
Fostat, Egypt

My beloved Master:

I am sure that a reminder is not necessary, but let me recapitulate what I wrote to you in my last letter. I stated that out of strife, struggle, evil and suffering, progress is generated. I was writing primarily about the animal kingdom, but you must have wondered how this may apply to Man (who is, technically, part of that Kingdom; intellectually, one hopes, Man can at least anticipate being part of a totally different kingdom, that of the Holy One, blessed is He).

I don't think there is any doubt that the system does apply to Man, and not only at the time when new species are being created. The self-preservation instinct is as strong in Man as in any animal and so is, I think, the instinct of racial preservation. When faced with adversity, with threat of suffering and death, Man will go to any distance to prevent such eventuality. He will always try to maximize his chances of survival individually; then, that of the groups he belongs to, in the order of increasing size: first, his family; last, humanity as a whole; in-between, his tribe or nation. Also, he will always try to optimize his lot, which itself is probably a tool towards achieving the best probabilities for survival. He will always migrate from lands of want to those of plenty; from oppression to liberty.

God can, and does use this fact to manipulate Man to do God's bidding. Let me be clear about this, My Master: I am not talking about how He might manage the evolution of a new species of Man (although I might, later); more simply, about how He controls humanity on a day-to-day basis in order to achieve His short-term objectives.

Let us think about how He has been using the system, that of strife, suffering and evil on the one hand, instincts for self-preservation and racial preservation on the other, to manipulate the Jewish people. Two thousand years ago, He dispersed us to various parts of the world —why? As punishment for our sins? Perhaps. One has to be aware of Job before daring to make such a statement firmly. There is, indeed, individual reward and punishment. It is almost always aimed at the future, not the past. God rewards good behaviour in order to encourage it; he punishes sins to goad people back to the path of righteousness. He has done so with an entire people, ours, during the days of our wandering in the desert.

But I would think that the cause of the diaspora was more than a wish to punish. It depends on what we really mean by punishment: whether it is a calculated, objective-directed measure, or merely a vindictive action. (Bearing Job in mind and hazarding only fearful guesses), I would like to think that the Diaspora was definitely established for a purpose, for the future, not the past. After each punishment in the past, the Jewish people became a nation of different characteristics—sometimes better, more God-fearing, other times more united, or militarily stronger, more advanced in a variety of ways. It is reasonable to assume that such results were exactly what the Lord wanted in each of those cases. Is it then likely that He punished the Jews so many times as measures of retribution, or is it more believable that He has visited good and bad things on us over the history to shape us, His chosen people, according to His wishes?

Reward and punishment, or necessary shaping tools—really, this is only a question of semantics, the choice of words. But there is no doubt that He has watched over us, kept us alive against all odds and made something of us, something totally different from what we once were. And that He has done all that through the application of measures, good and bad, as the situation demanded.

Surely, we have moved from country to country because we had to, because He wanted us to. And along the way, we have learned much. We have learned from almost all people of the world, and they have had a lot to teach us. Two millennia ago, we were an isolated people, knowledgable only about the Torah and primitive agriculture; even neighbouring people knew a lot more about astronomy, about philosophy, mathematics, logic, politics, warfare, medicine and other subjects. No, let me not be unfair to ourselves: we had a great gift for justice and ethics; for literature and history. But now, we know everything there is to know in the world; we are, if anything, more knowledgable than any other nation, and perhaps even better equipped to apply theoretical knowledge to practical situations. We have become an intellectual leader of nations. Scientific as well as ethical, artistic, legal, medical and, recently, even military geniuses have emerged from among our ranks. A most prestigious prize is granted annually to the best achievers in the fields of physics, chemistry, medicine, economics and literature. The share of Jews among the prizewinners is several hundred times what could be expected from their population ratio, a relatively small number today. In this century, seventy or eighty of the prizes have been won by our people, out of about 400. This is what the Lord has done to us, and we would not have done it voluntarily; we had to be goaded through good and bad or, if you prefer, through reward and punishment. I don't much like to use those words, though, because of what they imply for the 20th century.

We have learned a lot, against our wishes; and at the same time, we have become stronger, our will to survive has become enhanced. It may be that the Jews are the one people in the world with the highest survival instinct—in practical terms, the ability to do whatever needs to be done to stay alive in adverse circumstances. This, after centuries of persecution, was finally achieved in the most drastic process of—shall I say refinement?—the Holocaust. A better allegory might be "pruning"; the removed leaves and branches will not thank the gardener, but the remaining plant will become stronger.

For surely we have not been so bad as to merit punishment severe enough to cause six million of us, nearly 40% of our people, to perish? Yes, we did become secular; but we are no less secular today; when did the Lord punish ineffectually? And indeed, He has been rewarding us lately, making the State of Israel a small but extremely powerful country.

There is no way to understand the motives of the Lord fully, but I think we must always strive to get closer to Him, to understand Him to the best of our abilities, Job notwithstanding.

It seems to me that the Nazi Holocaust of the 20th century was a horrible but necessary evil, one that achieved two needed objectives: it made the remainder of us stronger, more willing to fight and survive against all odds; and it gave us the final push towards our country. As the result of that horror, Israel was re-established; and the Lord has surely indicated, through the Prophets, that this was exactly what He has intended all along.

But why did we have to wait for the Lord to provide this final push? Why have not hundreds of thousands of Jews, millions, moved to Palestine, as it was then called, with or without permission, and confronted the foreign rulers with an accomplished fact? Well, we would not have done it, because life there was harsh, all facilities of civilization were lacking. One had to start at the agricultural level, and Jews forgot everything they once knew about agriculture. We were used to city living, easy access to all goods and services and to all aspects of the good life. Still, thousands did actually move to Israel during the early days of Zionism, learned to be peasants on small farms or larger ones owned jointly by dozens of Jewish immigrants. But would they have stayed? After all, people have gone up to Israel in every century of the past two millennia; most left soon, as you may recall. A certain critical size of returnees had to be reached, to make the venture viable. And such a mass aliyah could not have happened without the Holocaust.

Yes, the Holocaust was the last necessary evil before the Jewish people, now strong and fully educated in the ways of the world, would re-assume their rightful place in the Land of Israel. That is what the Lord wanted and that is what happened. I said that the pruned-off branches will not thank the gardener. Will the remaining plant, now stronger and healthier, thank Him?

*   *   *   *   *   *   *

I say "last necessary evil": last in the sense of achieving one major historical objective. Surely not the last in the history of the Jews. Surely there is still a long history ahead of us; we can only speculate what plans the Lord may have for the Jews and for all nations. But it would be naive to assume that all suffering is now behind us.

Perhaps we shall, one day, be compensated for the suffering. Man is different from the beast; he has a mind, closely related to the divine Intellect; perhaps he merits something that is finally, permanently good in the World-to-Come.

Your devoted disciple

Joseph ben Yehudah

GOD'S GREAT PROJECT; PHASES

28 Heshvan 5752 / November 5, 1991

To B'Rabbi Moshe ben Rabbi Maimon ha-Sfaradi,
Fostat, Egypt

My beloved Master:

Having gained, perhaps, a little bit of insight into how the Holy One, blessed is He, operates, we may be ready to attempt a definition of what it is that He has been doing.

I wrote to you already about project management. It seems clear that He has been managing a project of such enormous size that human perception will barely permit a general comprehension of it, and at that, a very limited and grossly naive comprehension. Still, can we get an idea of what the project is all about? Perhaps; but how? Ideally, we should start by looking at the end-product; but have we seen it? I should say not. It seems clear to me that God is still working at His project, that the project is by no means complete.

We could speculate about what the desired end-product may be. We could and we shall; I propose to do just that in a letter to you quite soon. But for now, we must be satisfied with the intermediate product that He has created to date, and that is ourselves.

How did the Lord, blessed be His name, go about creating Homo Sapiens? Well, we can discern some of the observable phases of that project.

First, out of nothing, He created the Universe. Starting with "tohu vabohu", the original chaos, He differentiated matter, combined them into clusters of galaxies including our own; brought forth solar systems within those, including our own; planets around some stars, including our own, earth.

Then, He created life on this one planet among the billions.

Then, He created intelligence. And that's it. Sounds easy. But it has not been. Let us consider some of these phases.

We now know that the Universe was actually created about seventeen billion years ago; what was there before? Absolutely nothing. But then, there was no such thing as "before"; we now believe that He created time and space at the same "time", if we can put it that way; or in the same process.

The Universe was created in a so-called "big bang". The total space of the initially created universe was, actually, zero. This particular zero is called a "singularity", a point into which the matter, or energy, of the entire universe is condensed, at infinite density. The temperature of the universe was extremely high, some say infinitely high. The state of the content of this university was chaotic.

This chaos (was this the "Tohu vaBohu"?) immediately began to expand, and the radius of the universe, once there was such a thing, grew by a factor of millions by millions by millions . . . all in a matter of a fraction of a second.

As the universe begun to cool, matter precipitated from energy. This matter eventually coalesced into galaxies and stars within those. Really, Master, I am oversimplifying the process, as I must; frankly, even if I could present for you the technically correct description of the Creation, I am afraid that you could not possibly understand it without deep immersion into 20th century theoretical physics and cosmology.

Creation of life may have been just as difficult, perhaps more so. Self-reproduction was a most critical part of the process. That required an extremely complex structure that involved embedding intricate codes in every cell of all living matter. How did He create the first cell? The first strand of DNA, the molecule that is used for storing and controlling and replicating the genetic code? Even at lower level, how did He create the proteins, which are the building blocks of every species, at least in the animal kingdom?

But He did all that and created one-celled beings that survived and reproduced; and once those were sufficiently stable, He then started to vary them, started to introduce changes in the code to complexify the creature.

Soon (on a divine scale; it may have been a matter of a few hundreds of millions of years) there were a large variety of those beings, first one-celled, then more and more complex, larger and larger, swimming in the ocean, devouring each other and fighting for survival. How He instilled in them the instincts of self-preservation and that of racial preservation, I really could not say. But He certainly has taken maximum advantage of those instincts. By exposing the creatures to hardships, both external (the environment was not always friendly) and internal (they had to fight, constantly, within and without the species), and by providing the appropriate mutations at the gene level, to assure the requisite variety of differentiated individuals, He encouraged the emergence of the desired characteristics, as we have discussed earlier.

And so He created a million species, some in the sea and some on land, some crawling and some flying, some walking on a hundred legs, some on four and some on two. All birds walk on two legs; but I am thinking of Man. He was created last.

What distinguishes Man from all other species? Of course, it is his mind. Intellect. Consciousness. Reflection.

If creation of living matter was vastly complex, think of the complexity of the mind. Perhaps, with all due respect, you cannot; for only in this century has Man developed an understanding of the technical basis of intelligence, of the enormity of the nervous network required, of the connections needed and of the thinking process in logical terms. To design a machine capable of nothing else but writing down this one paragraph is something that Man can do today, yes, but that machine still would not be able to do any original thinking. In another twenty or fifty years from now, Man will be able to design a machine with some very limited thinking ability. But the Lord created such machines, ourselves, millions of years ago! And what a superior machine, compared to our own measly effort!

Still, here we are, intelligent beings, each with a mind of unequal qualities, capabilities, attitudes and standards, yet miraculous all of them; and we know that the Lord created it all. It is, has always been, highly gratifying to know that he has gone to all that effort just to create us; how wonderfully important that makes us feel. And with good reason: God has needed us. But it would be the height of folly to think that He needed us for the end-product of His creation project. What for? What good are we as we are? Sure, we have minds, but to what purpose? We have had it for a long time; yet we don't see that the Lord has taken particular direct advantage of them to date. No doubt He will one day; but we may be quite different by then.

We shall speculate a lot more about these matters, with His help, in several future letters.

Your devoted disciple

Joseph ben Yehudah

NO LIFE OUTSIDE THE EARTH

13 Kislev 5752 / November 20, 1991

To B'Rabbi Moshe ben Rabbi Maimon ha-Sfaradi,
Fostat, Egypt

My beloved Master:

During the last hundred years or so, an idea has emerged, originally among the most intelligent people, one that later has spread to the least intelligent masses. This idea states that on at least some of the other planets circling the Sun—Venus, or Mars, Jupiter, or the others—there must be life, perhaps even intelligent life.

The first powerful—but not powerful enough—telescopes showed formations on Mars that could be interpreted as canals, artificial ditches. Later study rejected those findings, but popular curiosity was by then aroused.

If there is life on the planets of our Sun, why not on planets of the other suns, all the countless stars? For there are billions of stars in our galaxy alone, and there are billions of galaxies. It is a reasonable assumption that all of these stars, or most, have planets; and if so, and if there is life on this one, why not on all of those?

You see, the underlying idea is that life can emerge naturally when conditions are right. Many scientists have thought that even when conditions are wrong, where extreme temperatures or pressures or chemical conditions would make life, as we know it, impossible, there would be other life-forms, based on totally different principles.

And all of these stem from a denial of God. If life can emerge without divine assistance, then there is no need for a God. And if there is no God, then presumably the emergence of life is a natural phenomenon. A circuitous argument, logically fallacious, but it had great attraction for those masses.

A good scientist could easily have shown that all of this is nonsense, for the basic premise is wrong: life cannot emerge without God's assistance, without His involvement, indeed without His active initiation of the process. The laws of physics would make this impossible.

But (with a very few exceptions) no major scientist had the intelligence to say this, or if he had intelligence, he lacked the courage; for things got to the point where an admitted belief in God would generate ridicule and ostracism for a man of science. The most a scientist was allowed to admit to was agnosticism.

Meanwhile, popular science and eventually all instruments of the informative and entertainment industry—for it is a major industry by now—have latched onto the concept and have inundated the population with tales of extraterrestrial beings. Some of these were depicted as bad, dangerous; epic struggles were imagined, with the population of earth, or its heroes, eventually achieving glorious victories. More often, though, the strangers have been shown as superior to us, wise old races who come and teach us how to behave, how to live in peace and with love towards everybody on earth and outside.

Eventually, space travel could be taken seriously, if not outside the solar system (not to this day), then at least within it. Excitement then reached a crescendo: people expected to find life and probably intelligence on the Moon, or the nearby planets and elsewhere.

Man managed, first, to send machines to the Moon and to take pictures of the Moon and send those pictures back to earth. (I have not told you about photography, achieved by a simple machine, you point it, push a button, and it takes an accurate picture of what is in front of it. Simple machine on the earth, but not so simple on the Moon, especially when there is no man to aim and push the button.) No evidence of life was found. Many refused to believe the photos; missions were planned to the Moon; eventually, Man succeeded in landing on the surface of the Moon. A number of trips were made. Anything brought back was treated with the utmost caution in laboratories, least they include some microorganism, a miniature life-form that could perchance invade the earth. But, needless to say, no life-form of any kind has ever been found on the Moon.

At the time of my writing these letters, Man has not yet landed on any of the planets (as I may have told you, the Moon is not a planet of the Sun, it is a satellite of the earth, if you like, a planet of a planet). But we have very accurate photographs of each, taken by machines that have landed there, and there is certainly no evidence of life on any of the planets.

The problem of getting out of the solar system is that the nearest star is over four light years away. That means that if man could travel at the speed of light (which, at 186,000 miles per second, is the theoretical limit of possible speed; practically, even half cannot be achieved), then the round trip would take nearly nine years.

But there is no need to travel that far. If there is intelligent life anywhere in the Universe, and if their intelligence is at least as mature as ours, then those people can communicate with each other through radio waves which can travel through space at the speed of light. Thus even those stars that are ten billion light years away could yield evidence of intelligent population, if the radio waves left ten billion years ago.

Indeed, scientists have been convinced that this must be the case; and have spent enormous amounts of money—public money—to set up scientific equipment that could detect radio waves from great distances. The result? Nothing. Lots of natural radio waves, but no sign of intelligence. Absolutely none.

My Master, without knowing all that today's science teaches, you could have told them that they won't find anything; I could have told them. Creation of life on earth, creation of intelligence on earth have been undertakings of vast size, vast effort. While we cannot fully know the plans of the Holy One, blessed be He, it is reasonable to assume that having spent this huge effort on creating life and intelligence here on earth, He has no need to duplicate the effort elsewhere. He may, of course, have had reasons to do so, anyway, reasons that may be beyond our understanding; although we could guess about some such possible reasons, as I hope to do in my next letter to you, or in the one following that.

In any case, based on the best knowledge and reasoning that we are capable of, I think we have to accept the fact that, for one reason or another, we shall never find life anywhere outside the earth.

Your devoted disciple

Joseph ben Yehudah

INDESTRUCTIBILITY OF HUMANITY

24 Kislev 5752 / December 1, 1991

To B'Rabbi Moshe ben Rabbi Maimon ha-Sfaradi,
Fostat, Egypt

My beloved Master:

In my last letter to you, I indicated a belief that there is no life, much less intelligent life, outside the earth. That is, because the Holy One, blessed be He, has been creating human intelligence purposefully and it does not seem likely that He would need to do so at more than one location (and also because empirical results support the concept of our being alone in the Universe).

But if so, human life becomes very precious. The amount of work, planning and execution that has been expended towards the creation of intelligence is huge; even if we made an effort to view the size of that project through the supposed capabilities of something or somebody billions, trillions (the real number is much, much greater than that) of times larger, more powerful, more knowledgable than ourselves, even from that platform we couldn't help being over-awed by the extent, the magnificence of the Lord's project in creating Homo Sapiens on earth.

We cannot know these things for certain, but it is surely a very reasonable assumption that the Lord would not spend many billions of years creating something and then simply destroy it in a fit of pique, bad mood or disappointment. It is more likely that, were He to see a need for change, improvement, than He would simply effect it.

And if we assume that He won't, whimsically, destroy His creation, how much less likely that He would permit this creation to destroy itself.

You see, certain modern scientists—I may already have indicated to you my assessment of their limited intelligence, apparently well below that of the population on the average, although of course these comments don't apply to many truly intelligent, outstanding scientists of this age—well, these people have got it into their heads that Man is about to destroy himself. How shall he do this? By poisoning the environment, the waters from which he drinks, the air he breathes, the vegetation and animal life he eats; until perpetual illness and early death leads to the extinction of the human race. Ridiculous? Not quite; much of it has actually begun to happen. But if the Lord does not want it to happen, there are many things He can do to prevent it. One option He has, of course, is simply to manipulate Man so he will become aware of the danger and take measures against it; in that case, you see, the doomsayers are fulfilling a most important role.

The destruction of the environment would be a relatively slow process, giving Man a chance to realize the danger and remedy the situation. But another deadly threat the scientists warn against is annihilation of life on earth through a nuclear catastrophe.

You see, a number of nations have stockpiled nuclear arms, atom bombs and hydrogen bombs, thousands of devices any one of which is sufficient to destroy a city of a million. These bombs can be flown from one part of the world to another in a matter of minutes, and there is no effective defense against them yet. Worse, these bombs emit an invisible radiation that can speed through the atmosphere, the air cover of the earth, and be carried to remote areas by dust, clouds, rain. If one nation attacked another with nuclear arms, and the other one retaliated with many of those devices, then in a few hours not only may human life be destroyed in those two nations by the explosions, but radiation may have ended all life everywhere else on the earth.

Since the invention of nuclear arms, nearly fifty years ago, nations having these weapons have been highly aware of the dangers, have set up elaborate mechanisms to prevent accidental firing of even one of the devices. But, theoretically, some mistake could be made. A faulty detector could warn of incoming nuclear missiles, and a counter strike could then be ordered, starting a series of retaliatory actions that could not be stopped until it was too late. Also, now only a handful of nations possess nuclear arms. That is about to change: smaller and smaller countries, perhaps less and less responsible ones, are getting hold of those, perhaps even revolutionary and terrorists movements with no care for what the consequences of using a nuclear weapon may be.

Could such an event occur? I think not. I am not saying that some nuclear accident, whether or not weapon-related, could not happen; some already have. I am writing about a nuclear holocaust, eliminating life on earth. Could that event ever come about? Would the Lord allow His creation to destroy himself? Surely not.

Let me then talk about clergymen, priests, rabbis and ministers of a large variety of religious denominations. They should know better; yet they are at the forefront of the doomsayers.

Of course, warning people of a major threat is not at all harmful; just the opposite, it is an important public service. Just as in the case of ecological danger, such warnings result in heightened awareness of the magnitude of the threat, and therefore in building in more preventive measures into the system; and that is good.

But these clergymen, these so-called "men of God", insist on depicting the Lord as somebody who is grieving over the behaviour, the evil ways of his creation, somebody who is extremely sad seeing that Man is about to destroy himself, yet somebody who is powerless to prevent the catastrophe. Does that sound like the God you and I know?

Where would the world be today if it was managed by such a powerless God? I tell you where: nowhere. Human intelligence would not have emerged; any kind of life would have had no chance of coming into existence; the planets, suns, galaxies would not be around; there would be nothing, or perhaps only chaos, *tohu vabohu*.

No, Rabbi, our God is not a powerless one. If He's created intelligent life on earth, He's had a purpose in doing so; and shall not make the mistake of looking away while at a sensitive phase the creation accidentally destroys itself.

And therefore I believe, my Master, that humanity is indestructible.

Your devoted disciple

Joseph ben Yehudah

EXPERIMENTATION BY GOD

12 Tevet 5752 / December 19, 1991

To B'Rabbi Moshe ben Rabbi Maimon ha-Sfaradi,
Fostat, Egypt

My beloved Master:

In my last letter, I wrote to you about the indestructibility of humanity. I really believe in that. Nevertheless, I shall have to qualify those comments, at least slightly.

We must bear in mind, first of all, that any statement made about the Holy One, blessed is he, must be, by necessity, mere speculation. Even our proofs can never be absolute; we can know Him from His apparent deeds and from logical deductions based on our knowledge of the world; yet our knowledge amounts to so little!

But further, and assuming that our conclusions about His project, about what He has been doing and how, are correct, that still leaves a possibility that things are not exactly as I have stated them. Let me explain.

It seems clear that the Lord has been developing us, human intelligence; and in order to do so, He has performed a number of sub-projects, or phases. I have indicated the major ones:

> Cosmogenesis, the creation of the Universe and everything in it (including this planet)

- Biogenesis, creation of life on this planet

- Noogenesis, creation of intelligence out of earthly life.

Now, as I have also indicated, this must (quite certainly) have been a well-planned, well-organized, well-executed project, and so one could assume that it has progressed smoothly, according to plan, with no problems, no difficulties, no setback.

One could assume that, but I am not sure it would be a reasonable assumption.

We must remember what projects are, what project management is. Projects are a series of tasks, arranged in a primarily hierarchical organization, but with secondary, or network connections (I am sorry to use these terms, they are somewhat common at the end of the 20th century, mainly in computer-related circles; I can't think of good 12th century equivalents). What it really means is that there is one project; then, there are, say, four major phases; then, under each, there may be five or ten or 20 sub-phases; and further and further subdivisions, until the smallest task involves perhaps not more than causing a single quantum fluctuation.

Considering the magnitude of the whole project, it is easy to see that all of these lowest-level sub-phases could not have been planned from the beginning, only the broader sub-divisions. Obviously, God has gone through a series of planning exercises. At the very beginning, He must have decided to create a certain end-product. That meant undertaking a project. Probably soon after that, He determined how to do it; in very general terms, what the major phases are going to be. He then thought about those phases (I assume) and determined, again, how to go about them, and so, what sub-phases should be set up at the next level.

But has He gone into more detail than that at the beginning? Probably, but we cannot know how much detail. Considering the number of the smallest tasks, it is reasonable to assume that at some point He stopped planning and left smaller details to execution time.

Everything does not always go right in a large project. Out of a hundred tasks, perhaps 85 will go the way you want it; five may come in higher and five lower than intended, but still within the acceptable range; while another five must be rejected.

Sure, one can argue about these numbers. God, being what He is, may have achieved an initial success rate of not 85%, but let us say 99.9999%, or whatever number one chooses; yet there must still have been rejects.

When faced with that problem, what does a project manager do? First, he tries to prevent failures, even that of a minute component, through careful monitoring. But he cannot monitor everything constantly (you could say that God, being infinite, can; I shall have more to say about that later). So he will be hit with the news, sometimes, that a component has failed. He can then repair it, replace it with an existing component, if available, or may have to repeat a task, probably with improvements. If so, that may hold up a much larger segment of the project, presumably not a desirable turn of events.

Another way of avoiding problems and delays of this sort is through the concept of redundancy. If the project manager needs four of something, and if it is a critical component, he may decide to make five or six. That is a waste of material, facilities, effort, but sometimes the criticality of the product warrants it.

Still another problem a project manager faces is that what he is doing is usually entirely new, something that has never been done before. While he understands how this innovation is to be done in general terms, nay, while he understands most of its details, there will always be elements that present unexpected difficulties, problems of the type that the project manager, the original planner did not expect. God is great; but so is His project. Let us not assume that He will only undertake trivial work, such that has already been done, such that is easy, routine. It is very reasonable to assume that His project is commensurate with His capabilities, that is, He is undertaking something challenging. And if so, He will encounter difficulties, problems.

If you consider, just for a little while, the evolution phase, that of the various biological species, in the direction of intelligence, you will see the type of problems that the manager of such a project must expect. The line of evolution is not straight. You cannot simply develop larger and larger, increasingly complex brains, capable of supporting intelligence; for such brain must itself be supported by a complex mechanism providing oxygen through blood circulation, blood which must be pumped and filtered and purified through mechanisms that require energy, obtained through still other mechanisms that digest and convert food, obtained through the ingestion of other life-forms, all the while competing for individual and racial survival, and so on.

This kind of development will result in strange lifeforms, animals perhaps with extremely long legs or necks, others built monstrously large, like houses, others protected by armour—we have seen those and other strange species.

But not every developmental direction will always be successful. The Creator may have an idea of how to achieve certain desired objectives, perhaps how to reduce a long series of steps by substituting a simple, brilliant solution—one that may work, or not. Again, he may decide the opposite: to go through many small step in a circuitous route to the desired objective, steps that make little sense by themselves, but increase the probability of a successful outcome for some desired feature or intermediate product.

What I am saying is that the Creator will, by necessity, experiment. He will try certain approaches; if they work, fine; if not, He will close off that approach, that branch of life, and do it another way. Also, He will do some important steps more than one way, perhaps running two or three parallel tasks towards an identical objective, just to assure the availability of at least one successful outcome.

It is unlikely that the Lord, blessed be His name, created several worlds, rather than just one, considering the effort involved. But this Universe quite likely includes innumerable solar systems like ours; while He must have carefully chosen our planet for His purposes, it is not entirely inconceivable that He decided to try two or three more approaches to developing life and intelligence on some other planets of other suns in other galaxies.

But the difficulty, the complexity of the project constantly increases; and so, unless one assumes that God's capacity is also constantly increasing (yes, I know, you will say that He is infinite; we shall discuss that later), then the time would inevitably come, sooner or later, for Him to abandon first some, then all but the most promising of such alternate projects.

We do have evidence that He has experimented with life-forms that may have turned out unsuccessful, and that eventually He has abandoned them. If we assume that we are very close to the intended end-product of the evolution, then we can reasonably expect that by now, even if the Lord had conducted alternate, experimental projects elsewhere, He has abandoned them and chosen us for the best approach to His final objective.

Or so I hope.

Your devoted disciple

Joseph ben Yehudah

WHAT HE IS; WHAT WE ARE:

GOD'S BASIC NATURE

26 Tevet 5752 / January 2, 1992

To B'Rabbi Moshe ben Rabbi Maimon ha-Sfaradi,
Fostat, Egypt

My beloved Master:

We have now spent some time observing the work of the Holy One, blessed is He. I think that we may have learned something about His way of doing things and about His great project. And how else can we hope to know Him, except through His work?

But do we know Him now? Well, of course not; we never shall. Yet perhaps we know Him a little better than before. Or at least we may know something of His intentions, plans, needs; all of these things lead us towards Him, always a little closer.

Let us speculate on the nature of God. Perhaps we may be able to come to some tentative conclusions about what He is. And if we do, we may then begin to understand ourselves a little better.

At this point, I would like to remind you of your long debates with those who insisted on an anthropomorphic depiction of God; their arguments were based on various references in the T'nach, especially on the statement that God created Man in His own image. You were successful in discrediting those arguments by proving that the references are simple allegorical statements; I think that you have come closer than any other philosopher to understanding the similarities and differences between God and Man. But then, you did not dare to go far enough, you pulled back.

It seems to me that we have to accept that statement about God's image without argument (how could we do otherwise?). But let us remember: He created Man in His own image, not the other way. And so, we can deduce what Man is like by comparing him to God; but we cannot draw conclusions about the nature of God by comparing Him to Man!

Having said that, let us think about what God is like. The unfortunate thing is that you knew the exact answer to that question, to the full limit of possible human understanding in the 12th century; yet you were forced to deny that knowledge by substituting the Neoplatonic nonsense (perpetuated by the Muslim thinkers) of the doctrine of negative attributes.

I am not putting down the great philosophers of Islam; always have had the greatest respect for them. But the Neoplatonic idea that God cannot be assigned with any attributes except by negations, that when we say that He is great, all we mean is that He is not small—I think that is silly. Especially when everybody, while mouthing those doctrines, has gone ahead making categorical statements about the Lord; for example, about His unity, omnipotence, omniscience, eternity and so on.

So let us go back to the basics, things that you knew, things that Aristotle knew. He and the other ancient philosophers postulated the Active Intellect (sometimes as Agent Intellect) as a transcendental substance, perhaps located at the outermost "sphere", emanating from God the Prime Mover. This Active Intellect was then supposed, according to your own beliefs, to actualize a potential Intellect in Man, so that he can have an Acquired Intellect. All of these various intellects were interrelated; intellect or mind, *nous*, everywhere in the world, coming from God.

I think that the reality is similar, but more simple. God is the Intellect. Essentially, pure Intellect. There is no need to categorize intellect at various levels; we can do that, if we like, but surely that is where we indulge in pure speculation, making statements about something that we can't possibly understand. God is a vast, overall intellect; how that intellect is organized, what levels or subdivisions it may have, is clearly beyond our current comprehension.

Rabbi, you know me well enough to respond that such limitation won't stop me from speculating about those matters; and you are right, I shall have some comments on it later on. Perhaps the one difference then, between what I am writing about now and what the philosophers of old did, is that they always stated their conclusions categorically; while all I dare to do is propose a tentative possibility, for what do I know? What does any of us know? Unlike our great teachers of blessed memory, I am not wise; but I may have a little advantage over them in recognizing how little I know. And I assure you that, unlike that of Socrates, mine is not false modesty.

Now, when I say that God is pure Intellect, what do I mean by the term? It is not easy to define. We have discussed the matter lightly, a while ago, when we considered the relevance of software for Man and God. I like to use these terms interchangeably: "intellect", "intelligence", "mind" (a 17th century French philosopher named Descartes even equated the term "soul" with these things, probably quite correctly). The Greeks called it "nous". The reasoning facility. More than reasoning, of course. With superior thinking, the Intellect can find the way for doing, for planning and executing. For organizing, monitoring, controlling projects. And so, Intellect is power, capability; not weakness, helplessness.

People have been aware of the superiority of the Intellect for thousands of years. In addition to Aristotle, who felt very comfortable with the idea, Plato was quite familiar with it, and of course, Socrates; even earlier, Pythagoras. Of course, it was difficult for those philosophers to equate the Intellect with the concept of the One God: their background was polytheistic. But Aristotle, at times, came very close to acknowledging the One God and to understanding Him. Unfortunately, he was also confused by false outside factors, such as the "harmony of the spheres", associated with the Pythagorean astronomy (just as those same silly spheres of the later offshoot, the Ptolemaic system, confused you and me even as late as the 12th century).

The Greeks, a little later, did have another word for the Intellect: "Logos". In some ways, the Logos was also Intelligence. "Logos" could perhaps be better translated as "speech", "rational expression", "rational order". But the Neo-platonists thought of it rather as the order of the Universe, or the organizing force behind it. Among the Jewish philosophers, Ben Sirah was familiar with the concept, but he called it "Wisdom"; while Philo posited it between Man and God; he also described it as a "copy of God", while human intelligence was then a "copy of the Logos". The Christians went a step further and identified the Logos, or as they called it, the "Word", with the Son of God, the pre-existent Messiah.

All of these can be confusing. The Logos is, if anything, Torah for the Jews; Christ for the Christians; the Intelligence that governs the world for the Greeks, perhaps even the early philosophers, such as Plato. The Logos seems to be something from God, part of God, intermediary between God and Man, a divine substance. It seems to me that in all of these speculations, we (people willing to reason) have been going around and around the most simple fact, perhaps too simple to accept: that God is it. That He is the Intelligence, Intellect, Mind, Logos —really, just words, human words describing something that we don't understand very well, but are beginning to comprehend just a little better. Intelligence. Thinking, reasoning, knowing. The ultimate spirit, if you like. The Intellect. God.

Blessed be His name, forever.

Your devoted disciple

Joseph ben Yehudah

GOD'S CORPOREALITY

11 Shevat 5752 / January 16, 1992

To B'Rabbi Moshe ben Rabbi Maimon ha-Sfaradi,
Fostat, Egypt

My beloved Master:

Now we have established, with a very reasonable certainty, that the
Holy One, blessed be He, is intelligence, the Intellect. You should
have no problem accepting that concept, for all Jewish and Greek
thinking, including your own, has revolved around some such basic
idea. But I am about to complicate it a little.

Do consider what I said in my last letter, about intelligence translating
into power, about God being able not only to think but to do. To plan,
organize, monitor and control His project. To effect changes. After all,
He is supposed to be omnipotent. Well, but how can pure intellect
effect changes? How can such a thing be potent, even a little bit, let
alone absolutely?

This is where 20th century knowledge comes handy. We are beginning to understand what intelligence is. We are experimenting with
creating artificial intelligence. That is a computer software that, given
a series of facts, can make good decisions, as good or better than a
human would make. If necessary, this software will ask further
questions, and then, based on what it hears (sometimes even making
judgement about the veracity of the information) it "makes its mind
up" about the situation and decides on the appropriate course of
action. This kind of software already exists.

Really, it has existed in the last thirty years in a primitive way. It is getting more sophisticated now. This kind of intelligence is highly specialized; one such software could make excellent medical diagnosis in cases of heart trouble, but would understand nothing of, say, intestinal disorder, let alone the analysis of chemical structures or designing elevators for tall buildings. Some different software, on the other hand, can do exactly that, design elevators and nothing else. If it were necessary, such capabilities could be combined into one, larger software; of course, there is seldom any need for such combination.

But there is one most important requirement for the functioning of any software, simple or complex: the availability of a suitable computer to operate on. A machine, any machine, that can interpret the thousands or millions of instructions embedded in the software, simple instructions such as add A to B, compare C to D, if C is larger, then the next instruction is X, otherwise it is Y—things like that. From the largest to the smallest computers can handle instructions like that, some are very inexpensive, most children have one (although the computers that run artificial intelligence programs tend to be larger, of more advanced design).

The point is that even the most sophisticated software cannot operate without the computer which is the hardware. We can also say, with roughly equal meaning, that the most advanced mind cannot operate without a brain.

I have already referred to that basis, hardware or brain, which supports the thinking principle, as the "substrate". It has to be there, there must be some kind of substrate for every intelligence. For the designer of the intelligence or software, it is not always necessary to understand the particular features of the substrate; he assumes its existence. It must exist.

And so, we can extrapolate the analogy to the intelligence, the Intellect that is God. I have said that, in essence, He is pure intelligence; and so He is. But as such, He still needs a physical base, a substrate to operate on. Not a computer, at least not as we know one. Something. Some physical basis or device; but by physical, I don't mean that it needs to be based on the physics of the earth, of the Universe even, as we know it. There may be laws very different from ours; there may be concepts that we would find very difficult, if not impossible, to understand. But laws there must be, a physical basis there must be for God's Intellect, which is His essence, to operate on.

And that is only the thinking process. When you consider the necessary actions, obviously (to me) there must be other physical components, parts, tools or whatever devices necessary for the actual effecting of changes. And these need to be devices at least partly of this Universe, subject to our laws, to be effective. I shall try to write more about such devices, with the help of the Lord, in one of my future letters to you.

There is one other thought perhaps worth considering: If there is a physical base for God's Intellect, should we be concerned about that? Should we revere it? Pray to it? I would say not: the essence of God is still the Intellect. But we must be aware of it; we should have a term for it. And it has occurred to me that the word "Heaven", the abode of the Lord, clearly not the sky, may be an apt term for that substrate.

Your devoted disciple

Joseph ben Yehudah

SOFTWARE AND THE HUMAN MIND

18 Shevat 5752 / January 23, 1992

To B'Rabbi Moshe ben Rabbi Maimon ha-Sfaradi,
Fostat, Egypt

My beloved Master:

By now, we just about understand ourselves, humans—why we have
been created, what we are; not yet what we are going to be; we shall
deal with that later.

So you could say that what I am writing to you about in this letter,
the essence of God and of Man, is simple and by now, somewhat
obvious. But let us explore it. The Holy One, blessed is He, has
created Man in His own image. By attempting to reverse the analogy,
the Torah exegetes of the past got themselves into deep trouble: they
deduced from the passage I mentioned earlier that God is man-like. To
your great credit, you did show up this argument for the folly it was,
you proved that anthropomorphism is false, a misunderstanding of
allegory used by the Lord; an allegory that was necessary at the time
because the Torah needs to speak in the language of the people.

Yet logical deduction in the other direction is perfectly legitimate. We
must first understand what God is, then we can deduce from that what
we are.

And now we see that He is, essentially, pure Intellect, intelligence,
supported by a substrate that is subject to some laws of physics that
we may know nothing about. Ah, but we do know a lot about

intelligence. How much? We understand the basic concept—*what it is*. We don't understand one trillionth part of God's intelligence, specifically: how it is organized, structured, how it operates logically, let alone physically on the substrate. No, those things we cannot conceive of; but we can make many reasonable assumptions, tentative ones, as we shall see, that should take us closer to understanding the Lord.

But meanwhile, knowing that He is intelligence, and knowing that He's created us in His own image, us but not even the highest animals, we can quite reasonably conclude that Man is essentially intelligence! That is what we are, and any man or woman who is not proud of that fact is a fool (forcing us to consider the inevitable, if apparently paradoxical, concept of the foolish intelligence).

Now our intelligence is obviously at many levels below that of the Lord; we couldn't even estimate the difference of those magnitudes; there must be a number for expressing those levels, and it may be just as well that we cannot know that number, it would dishearten us to realize how far down the scale we are. The important thing is, though, that while the substrates supporting the intelligence of God and those of human beings are quite different in material, nature, even in the applicability of physical laws, yet the intelligences, divine and human, are exactly of the same substance. That, to me, is the most important statement regarding the God-Man relation; notwithstanding the fact that it is technically an incorrect statement, in that no actual substance is involved: there is only logic, translated onto the substrate, a translation that, in the case of Man, takes the form of connections and relations within a very complex nervous map. Our intelligence is a compendium of logical statements and instructions; plus, of course, an attached storehouse of knowledge, facts, memory.

There is every reason to believe that God, being Intellect, is exactly the same: a complex set of logical statements and instructions, plus attached memory, a storehouse of facts. Software, as I've said, is the current, early, term for operative intelligence. In the terms of the 20th century (but certainly not later ones), God is software; and so are we, proudly so.

Now in our case, there is a lot more to us, visible things that are relatively of much lower importance, yet essential, at least at this time. Our software is supported by the substrate which is the human brain, our hardware. That, in turn, is supported and maintained by an extremely complex mechanism which is a marvellous creation of the Lord, yet of a complexity much lower than the intelligence.

Most of the human body is directly of animal origin; after all, that has been the very purpose of creating animal (and plant) life on earth, to develop a form ready to accept intelligence. The higher the level of a species, the closer it is to us. One could think of the highest animals as the most intelligent ones; but that would be misleading, for true intelligence is not possible in even the highest evolutionary levels below our level—not in apes, not in dolphins or any other "intelligent" species. Their brains are clearly more advanced than those of lower species; but those brains are not ready to support intelligence.

Yet I think we should temper our justified pride a little. Justified, for it is a beautiful and great thing to be, essentially, of the same substance that the Lord is of; but, after all, *we* did not create this thing, earthly intelligence: *He* did.

And further, we are obviously not the end-product. Once we understand what such an end-product may be, we shall feel quite small and inadequate; for we are still far from that objective of the Lord's. Although, perhaps, not hopelessly far.

Your devoted disciple

Joseph ben Yehudah

OBJECTIVES OF GOD'S GREAT PROJECT

2 Adar 5752 / February 6, 1992

To B'Rabbi Moshe ben Rabbi Maimon ha-Sfaradi,
Fostat, Egypt

My beloved Master:

Now, I think, we need to move back to our earlier topic: what it is that the Holy One, blessed is He, has been creating. For there is no question that Man (and you know that by that I mean Man and Woman) is the jewel in the crown of His creation to this day, as He has clearly stated in the Torah, yet it would be the height of folly and conceit to imagine that we are it, that He has gone to all that trouble just to create us.

Perhaps you and I have looked at this slightly differently. You considered the Universe, the immense size of the various bodies and how numerous they were; and judged the earth no bigger than a point relative to those (you related it to the diameter of the "spheres"; there are no such spheres, but there certainly are immense bodies dwarfing the earth). And still further, you then contrasted the size of a human to that of the Universe; to deflate not only the individual, but perhaps the human race itself: "How can any of us think that these things exist for his sake, and that they are meant to serve his uses?" you asked.

Nevertheless, Man has been the object of creation; at least, the object up to the current age. Even the scientists of these days are beginning to realize that the Universe, whether or not the work of God (for they are still skeptical) has been created for Man.

And what exactly do we mean by Man? Observing the trend of evolution, it becomes very clear that what has been emerging is consciousness, self-reflection, intelligence. If that is the general direction, we may be justified in ignoring the development of the physical body. While necessary for the support of the mind, the body has not changed very much in the last few million years; really, the human body, while attractive for us, is essentially the same as, say, the canine or feline one, or any of the other mammals. Marvellous creation as such is, let us ignore it and assume that the most important objective has been the mind.

What about the mind? It is new in Homo Sapiens, that is why he is sapient; and while perhaps, this is not observable over just a few generations, it is clearly still evolving. Indeed, there are some who believe that while the mind has existed over millions of years, since our species first made its appearance, yet self-reflection, consciousness is only about three or four thousand years old; that before that, people were under the direct control of something or somebody, they acted upon the bidding of voices, external or possible internal, and that consciousness originated in the breakdown of the bicameral mind around the time of Homer and of our first Kings.

Be that as it may, the Lord has now created an inordinate quantity of intelligence on earth. Some of this intelligence has acted in a highly innovative, creative manner; but interestingly, other blocks of human intelligence, while in no way inferior to the former, have exhibited little originality, preferred to behave as if they were semi-conscious members of a super-conscious whole, a large group of people. The more you think about that kind of organization of minds, the more you come to recognize the reality of group, or collective thinking.

This leads us back to one group of animals that may exhibit traces of God's experimentation with the concept of the collective. I am referring to insects in general, and to several species of insects is particular, such as ants and bees. These species, and doubtless others, live in highly organized collectives. A romantic slogan of men some centuries ago, "one for all and all for one", does not apply to them: it would be, instead, "one for all, yet none for the one". The individual has no importance (except for the queen bee), its only individual role is to be a member of the group. There may be no collective consciousness as such, but the group is extremely capable of defending itself and surviving.

Shall this be the direction of human development? Has God's experimentation in this area a bearing on our future? Has He done it to see if the concept, after suitable refinements, may be viable? I think that may very well be the case.

For if we assume that we are not the end-product, which is a reasonable assumption; and if we then attribute a much higher mental power to our successor, again reasonable: then we shall face a humanity on earth and elsewhere consisting of super-intelligent individuals, and for what purpose? Well, we cannot know the purpose, can only speculate; but it would seem to me that a collective of all human intelligences could be a worthy object of the creation.

There is another way of looking at it: with the advance of technology, the time is probably not far when Man can consciously shed his human body and concentrate on the development of his mind, basing it on an artificial substrate. And having got that far, what is to stop him from experimenting with the combination of two or more of such units into a new whole, more powerful than the sum of its individual components, yet maintaining each individuality separately? (After all, to use an almost trivial analogy, is that not what marriage is all about?)

People have found human organizations useful throughout the known history; there is strength in multitude. The individual can be stronger in the group then alone. Once such conglomeration becomes feasible in a precisely planned and executed mechanism, its advantages will be such that Man will find it irresistible. Certainly, there will be no instant merging of all minds; more likely, two minds might merge at first, probably on a basis approximating our concept of marriage, and that might be quite common for a long time; then later there may be some threes or fours. But competition (for that has always been the driving force behind development, presumably always will be) shall force the individuals and smaller groups to coagulate into ever larger aggregates, until there will be only one.

I shall have to continue speculating about this aspect of our future, and hope to write to you more about it in one of my letters. But meanwhile, let us consider, as a hypothesis, that the objective of the creation is exactly what we have been talking about here, the aggregation of all human minds, something that I tend to think of as the Universal Mind. Would that be a worthwhile end-product of the creation project? I would think yes.

Or, perhaps, not really the end; there may be a step beyond that. Will that Universal Mind be *the* Intellect? Will it be *an* intellect? Or will it be both of those things, an intellect first, on its way to developing into *the* Intellect? And then, will it merge with God? Or what purpose would He have with such new intellect? Oh, Rabbi, how much thinking, reasoning, speculation is still ahead of us!

Your devoted disciple

Joseph ben Yehudah

HOW HE WORKS:

GOD'S UNITY: MODERN INTERPRETATION

15 Adar 5752 / February 19, 1992

To B'Rabbi Moshe ben Rabbi Maimon ha-Sfaradi,
Fostat, Egypt

My beloved Master:

So far, all we have said about the Holy One, blessed be He, is that He is essentially the Intellect, operating on some quasi-physical substrate. I would like to explore, with you, some of the attributes (tangible, positive attributes!) and modus operandi of the Lord.

We used to know a lot about Him, or thought we did. Later, as I have commented, we became impressed about the majesty of God and our relative insignificance; became afraid of insulting Him through the attribution of human characteristics to Him; and ended up with the paranoid doctrine of negative attributes.

Nevertheless, we have believed, throughout these centuries and millennia, a few basic things about the Lord: that He exists; that He is One; that He created the Universe and everything within; that He is eternal; that He is infinite, omnipotent and omniscient.

I shall, with His help, deal with those last attributes in one of my next few letters to you. Right now, I would like to investigate only one of them: His unity. That has been an article of faith established by you and by others before and after you. (Much as Jews have respected you over the centuries, a number of wise scholars developed their versions of the articles; each set was somewhat different, with obligatory and optional beliefs varying in a confusing way. Eventually, your version became incorporated in the daily prayer book, the siddur, but has remained a subject for arguments to this day.) Our most important prayer is the Shema: Hear, oh Israel, the LORD is our God, the LORD is One.

But this Oneness, like everything else, was discussed thoroughly in olden days, and the discussion led to strange conclusions. It seems that for logical reasons, it became necessary to interpret this Unity to include some associated attributes: simplicity, incorporeality and indivisibility.

What you said was that God is not only One, but His Unity is different from any other unity in the world: for example, a species which comprises of sub-species, or a physical body which consists of parts and dimensions, may each be one, but not One the way the Lord is. In other words, he cannot have sub-elements, parts or dimensions.

I have already commented on the aspect of incorporeality, when discussing the difference between God's essential nature on the one hand, which is pure intelligence, and on the other hand, His necessary substrate based on some laws of physics, and therefore, clearly corporeal (unless we restrict the term to bodies responding to laws of physics peculiar to our Universe).

We have already talked about dimensions. So let us now consider simplicity. You know, Rabbi, the more I think about that, the angrier I become. Why does Oneness require simplicity? How dare we attribute simplicity to Him who created us all? What do we know about Him? So little! Yet arrogantly we claim to know so much, we so easily attribute simplicity to Him, even as we piously talk about negative attributes. Why should He be simple? There is every reason to suppose (if one is willing to overcome his paranoia at least sufficiently to dare to attribute tentative characteristics to the Lord) that He is extremely complex, more complex than anything we can possibly conceive of.

No, we have no reason to consider Him simple, nor incorporeal and, let me assure you, not indivisible either.

What do we mean by indivisibility? I don't think that the unity of humans is normally questioned. A man is a man, one. A woman is a woman, one. For that matter, so is a dog, one; or a bird, a fish, even an apple.

Are they divisible? Yes and no. They can be cut into portions, but the portions will be different in essential characteristics from the original: a halved or chopped-up man or dog or apple will no longer be a man or dog or apple.

I grant you, this is not true or everything. A halved stone will become two stones, while a living cell may split into two halves, resulting in two identical cells. But with higher, more advanced living organizations, those that no longer reproduce through division (except at the cell level), divisibility does not compromise unity.

Sure, I understand some of the old concerns. If God is corporeal, then He may have a left and a right side, a front and back, a top and bottom. Which is God? Does He consist of many parts, each of which is the deity? Or worse, each being a deity, all of which being parts of nothing more than an association of gods? Olympos? The idea would be revulsive to a religion that has just recently succeeded in conquering polytheism.

Yet it almost appears that God Himself has encouraged this kind of thinking. Throughout the Torah He refers to His front and back, left and right, and so on. I know, you have refuted anthropomorphism by stating that it is all allegorical, for the easy understanding of primitive man, and so it was. But where does the Lord deny having a structure? Organization? Complexity?

If God, as Intellect, as software, operates on a substrate, hardware, that hardware is clearly divisible; whether its parts could operate independently, we don't know; but the substrate should not concern us at all, for it is not an integral part of God's essence.

His essence is the intelligence, which, again, is software (though, let me remind you, not necessarily software as we know the concept today). Is that divisible? Well let me just talk about software for a minute. According to our current understanding, it typically consists of a very large number of logical statements and instructions. They are all part of one whole structure; but in order to be efficient, nay, maintainable, they must be organized in a hierarchical modular structure. There are a certain number of hierarchical levels; at each level, logic modules handle functions of a level of complexity that is broken up to its constituents, which are handled at the next hierarchically lower level. I have already proposed that such structure, were it to apply to the Deity, would have, at its lowest levels, units that would have simple responsibilities dealing with one type of condition, upon which one type of action would be effected.

Clearly, it would be inappropriate, or at least futile, to think of those truly simple end-units as God. But let us consider the very high-level modules. Could those high-level modules be considered God? I think that if one likes to think of them as such, it may be permissible; yet we should always remember that they are only parts of the divine structure.

Perhaps we may be excused if we tried to approach one such high-level unit, turning to it in certain circumstances, if the supplication and the desired response is such that it is not likely to involve any other hierarchically identical or higher units. But then, how are we to know that?

You could say that it would not make much sense to apply to such a "subdivision" of God, and I would agree. Still, there are people who, for some reason, may feel more comfortable with such a lower-level unit than with the deity as a whole; and as long as the wholeness of the structure is recognized, I don't see that such an attempt to relate to God through a part only would be harmful.

One thought: perhaps we Jews, who know the Lord better than others, who have known Him for longer, have some justification in attempting to communicate with God as One; while others, not feeling that close to Him, being rightly over-awed, are correct in trying to deal with a unit less than the whole of the Deity.

And so, bearing in mind that all of this is only speculation, I would like to propose a view of God as One, unique, organized and structured, modular, essentially incorporeal but based on a substrate of a necessary (but for us irrelevant) corporeality. This is the only way modern, 20th century Man can accept the reality of God; and yet, He is very real, very evident, more now than ever before.

Your devoted disciple

Joseph ben Yehudah

GOD'S ORGANIZATION, STRUCTURE, MODUS OPERANDI

23 Adar 5752 / February 27, 1992

To B'Rabbi Moshe ben Rabbi Maimon ha-Sfaradi,
Fostat, Egypt

My beloved Master:

Having developed some tentative understanding of the Holy One, blessed is He, particularly about His essence, His secondary physical aspects and, most important for us, His great project, the time has come to develop postulates about His actual organization, structure, modus operandi. I shall attempt to describe to you, not how the Lord is structured, not how the Lord operates, but how He *may* be structured, how He *may* operate, conceivably and approximately. The truth is quite certain to be different; it is quite certain to include concepts that we couldn't possibly understand today; but the basics of His structure and His operation may still be similar to what I am postulating here. So let us begin (and let me warn you that this letter may be a little difficult for you to follow, being based on so many 20th century concepts; yet I am sure you will be able to make enough reasonable assumptions for it to begin to make sense).

In understanding how God may operate, we must use the concepts of *cybernetics*, the science of control. More specifically, automatic control, using automatic actions based on the results of automatic feedback mechanisms. Try to imagine a machine that keeps opening and closing the window depending on the information provided by a sensor about the temperature inside the room: that is cybernetics at its most simple.

The above example indicates the necessary presence of two types of basic elements, and something in-between. The basic elements are sensors and effectors, or in current usage, input and output trans-ducers. They are then connected through a control node, or switch, one that in its most simple version merely orders the effecting of one action, or not, depending on the information received. Opening and closing a window already requires a somewhat more complex switch, as two different actions are needed (unless the window closes by a spring when not opened and kept open by the effector). Really, the control node is an extremely simple device.

But the control nodes, in addition to performing their simple duties, report on them to the next higher level. There, decisions are made about how the lower controls are to operate: exactly as before, or should the parameters change? Should the setting be altered? Should more, or less of the controls be activated?

At the next higher level, already decisions of some complexity may be required. The problem is that all of these elements are to be interconnected, not only hierarchically but often sideways, in what is called a network configuration. This is required for efficiency. And the number of those connections, even in relatively simple organisms, become astronomical by the fourth or fifth lowest levels. This problem is alleviated in a viable organization through two means: intelligence in the control nodes, from the third lowest level up; and constant re-structuring of the organization, dynamically, according to the changing need.

So the control nodes become intelligence nodes. That way, any aspect of the organization can be controlled and operated by complex intelligence, as opposed to simple rules.

Let us look at a typical organization. Let us call it a business or, if you prefer, a government. At the lowest level, section and department employees are operating in a routine manner; they are controlled by supervisors and department managers who perform relatively simple roles, depending on the size and specific function of the department.

Above these managers, at one or three or maybe ten hierarchical elevation is the company's general management, co-ordinating the functions of all department managers. And it performs this co-ordinating role upon the dictates of the policy-making body, say the company's board of directors, or in the case of a government the House of Representatives, Parliament, which represents the people, the voters (assuming a democratic system).

To generalize, there is the control of the operating units; then, ignoring intermediate levels, there is the co-ordinating control of all units, which is operational management; and at the top, the overall direction and long-range goal-setting function.

At the lowest level, all that happens is that a balanced situation—the technical term is homeostasis—is maintained through feedback. Such feedback is also necessary at the highest levels; indeed, there are always direct lines connecting some of the lowest and intermediate levels to the highest levels, bypassing the hierarchy, to assure overall stability and to provide for emergency warning.

And so a hierarchical organizational control is achieved; but as I have said, the number of connections soon becomes astronomical, so that internal reorganization is always necessary. A viable organization is a dynamic one, in a constant state of re-structuring; and consisting of a very large number of intelligence nodes and other related, necessary units (multiplexors and specialized connectors, for example), all parts of a lively, throbbing organization. Such a description will apply to a business, an army, a religious or cultural organization and, with not much change, a man, a cat, a fish.

I believe, my Master, that this is how the Holy One, blessed be He, operates. Of course, the size, the complexity of the intelligence units, the grouping of those units, the number of levels between the transducers at the bottom and the policy-setting at top are hardly comparable; yet the concept would be the same. And that concept is an organization which is a highly complex composite, but without the possibility that either the number of its elements or their interrelations would compromise the Unity of the organization.

And so, Rabbi, I may have, coarsely, described the conceptual organization of the structure which is God.

Your devoted disciple

Joseph ben Yehudah

ANGELS, DEMONS, ETC.

4 Adar II, 5752 / March 9, 1992

To B'Rabbi Moshe ben Rabbi Maimon ha-Sfaradi,
Fostat, Egypt

My beloved Master:

Now that we are beginning to understand how the Holy One, blessed be he, operates, how He may be organized, many things that used to be mysterious become clear. Let me comment on one of those mysteries, on the age- old question of the angels.

As you know, Aristotle considered these separate intelligences, and so did most of the Islamic and Jewish philosophers of our age. Specifically, ibn Sena described two hierarchies for the angels, intelligences and celestial souls. These were involved in moving the "spheres". Ibn Rushd, your contemporary, rejected the second of these hierarchies; yet you had no problem with it, if I remember correctly.

You described ten categories of angels, from Hayoth near the top, to Ishim at the lowest level; and were quite sure of their rights and responsibilities. So were the other sages; it has always amazed me that with how much certainty our wise men have stated unknowable things, such as the number of archangels—some said four, others said seven—let alone their names, jobs and their histories, how and when they were created. How we knew everything, yet everybody differently; how the other sage who miscounted some type of angel was, necessarily, an ignoramus.

The weirdest, yet most prevalent, of our opinions was the assignment of purpose to the angels. While they were supposed to have a variety of jobs, mostly acting as some kinds of intermediaries between God and Man, yet the primary angelic function seemed to be the praise of the Lord. They were constantly singing (not only as a manner of speech, but real songs, words, melodies) His praises. In one version, He created a new host of angels every day, just for that purpose, to sing His praises; they then perished at the end of the day.

My Master, I protest! What kind of God are we supposed to have? Is He so unsure of Himself that He needs the constant reminder of His greatness? We are not supposed to endow Him with positive attributes; yet without any hesitation, we assign to Him the quality of vanity!

Actually, in biblical times, our ancestors did not worry much about angels. In the early part of the first millennium B.C.E., we inherited, from Zoroastrian and Babylonian sources, the concept of the angel of darkness, sons of evil, demons; this was the beginning of the gnostic notion of duality, two deities, one good, one bad, in constant struggle. We have actually incorporated into our faith, at least in the aggadaic literature, the idea of fallen angels, using them as support for explaining some more obscure chapters of Genesis.

Then, during the Babylonian exile, polytheism gained strength, it had to be fought, although not as vigorously as idolatry. Perhaps transcendental gods were slightly more acceptable to our leaders. And so, as a solution, we simply converted some of those gods into angels. Greek polytheism probably intensified the need for such manoeuvres: so long as their gods, all subordinate to a chief god, become angels, then that faith is considered semi-respectable. (We actually allowed the notion of some angels assuming the shape of animals or men—straight out of Greek mythology!)

Mysticism has always been a strong streak within Judaism; it became almost dominant starting about our time, the 12th century. While, to your credit, you rejected any direct appeal to angels, there was a group in the 16th century, in Safed, which insisted on including new prayers in the Siddur, prayers supplicating to angels.

With the coming of rationalism, Jews have thrown those prayers out of the prayer book. The few references still remaining are interpreted symbolically. I think that there are few Jews left today who believe in angels with any seriousness.

Yet, in a sense, they may be wrong. There is now a way of reconciling the old beliefs with the modern scientific understanding of the Deity. Even your views of angelic hierarchy seem to be justifiable (I shall refrain from commenting on the specifically defined levels and functions).

God's structure (as proposed in my previous letters), that of a vast hierarchy of intelligence, allows for, indeed demands, the presence of discrete modules of concentrated intellect, executive units, if you like. Those must be transcendental as the whole of the Deity is transcendental: pure intelligences, yet supported by a material base. That base may be of the material of God's physical substrate, at the higher levels; while at the lowest levels, it may be the matter of our Universe, or something in-between, if possible; for at the very lowest level the actual sensors and effectors must exist. I assume that such transducers would operate on the sub-atomic or quantum mechanistic principles.

The Torah certainly supports this view, even without the painful twisting that we are so good at. It does not always distinguish clearly between God and His messengers; sometimes, He and His angel are mixed up in the same passage.

Considering also, at lower levels, the movement of the input and output signals, ascending and descending throughout the hierarchy, information gathered moving up, instructions for action moving down, how apt is the description of Jacob about the angels ascending and descending the ladder in his dream. I remarked earlier about the Torah being full of messages for later generations, descriptions that remain obscure for a long time, but there for the enlightenment of people in the future. I think Jacob's dream is for the late 20th century.

And so, we can envision the Deity with incorporating, at levels below the Godhead itself, a hierarchy of high and low angels, each with unique responsibilities. But we must be careful not to identify God with only the very top level: He is the whole structure, top to bottom: for He is One!

This is why it was important to pretend that He was unstructured, simple. For there is great danger that people without thorough study and many years of thinking acquire a partial understanding of His structure, they may then identify independent parts, or modules, as the Deity, or as a deity, consider that unit as their god.

Again, should men pray to angelic units? No, one should not, as you said. Still, if they understood that they were turning to a lower-level unit only as a measure of convenience, as it were, because it is perhaps less awe-inspiring, less fearsome, than the entire divine structure, and through that unit they are really praying to God as a whole, one could argue that there may be no harm done.

That is all I wanted to write to you on this subject; I think there is enough in here for at least a few hours' worth of speculation.

Your devoted disciple

Joseph ben Yehudah

GOD'S ATTRIBUTES, SIZE, POWER

18 Adar II 5752 / March 23, 1992

To B'Rabbi Moshe ben Rabbi Maimon ha-Sfaradi,
Fostat, Egypt

My beloved Master:

What objection could be raised to the postulate that states that the Holy One, blessed be He, while essentially intelligence, still uses a material base? Well, the doctrine of His immateriality is certainly one. But the main problem most theologians would have with the concept is that it would conflict with the doctrine of His infinity. It would be hard to argue that such a material base could be infinite in size. Nothing material can be infinitely large; nor can be anything else that is real (numbers can be, of course, so long as they don't represent anything other than themselves). Even if the Lord could be, somehow, pure intelligence without a material substrate, He would still not be infinitely large.

Where did this idea of His infinity come from, anyway? He is vast, surely, if size means anything when describing Him. But I think that Man's assigning the quality of infinity to God is simply a cowardly device, a subterfuge: were we forced to contemplate just how great He really is, in human terms, we would quickly come to be afraid and humbled, rightly terrified of the Lord. Saying that He is infinite removes the necessity of thinking about His magnitude.

You may ask about God's infinity in time: is He not eternal then? I would almost prefer not to answer that question; for if I deny such eternity, then you shall ask how God came about, who created Him? Is there a still larger being above God, one existing before and after Him? And then, perhaps still another? An infinite chain? And if there is such a chain, does it not add up to a Supreme Being infinite in every respect, anyway? Let me just say this much: I don't know. I would like to know; I would like to find out as much as possible about the Lord, but I do recognize that there are limits to our comprehension. Let us deal with one set of questions at one time; once we fully understand God, we can perhaps begin to contemplate the next question; even then, the next *one* question, not every possible questions all at once.

This idea then, a finite God, takes us into the necessity of discussing some of His related attributes. What does He know? What can He do?

Well, He is not omniscient; reading the T'nach, we should have realized this long ago. He sees everything important that happens; He does not care about the unimportant. Let me give you an example. If five hungry lions attack a herd of gazelles and kill, say, two of them, that fact may or may not be important for the Lord to know about. If the entire herd of hundreds or thousands of gazelles get into some unexpected trouble, that is more likely to be brought to His attention. He may take protective measures to prevent the disaster (conversely, the calamity may be His doing; it may be necessary for some purpose well beyond our understanding).

But take a cloud of mosquitos, millions of them. Say something unexpected happens to one of them, it dies of an internal illness, a non-infectious disease. Far from planning it, far from trying to prevent it, I would venture to guess that the Lord does not know about it, and does not want to know. It simply does not matter. If the entire cloud of mosquitos were about to be driven into a blaze and burned up, that may or may not be important, we cannot say.

But what about foreknowledge? No doubt, He has that: He can predict the future: but not completely. Let me explain: You can predict the future; I can predict the future; every man and woman can. I release a book and I predict that it will fall—and lo, it does. Winter comes in the north, I predict cold and snow—and sure enough, it turns cold, snow begins to fall. I predict that eventually I will die—it turns out that my prediction is absolutely correct.

I am not trying to be flippant about this, Rabbi; but I have to show that the future is, to a certain extent, knowable. Yet there are some factors involved. First of all, how far into the future can we predict? Not very far; I could not say, for certain, that ten thousand years from now people will still live and die on earth; or even if there will be an earth. I could not predict what summer and winter are going to be like at that time. I could predict that, if there will be an earth, a book dropped on it will still fall—unless objects will be equipped with anti-gravity devices, quite possible.

But the Lord obviously does foresee major events far into the future; ten thousand years for Him is probably like a minute for us. Still, I venture to say that He does not foresee the infinity of time, certainly not well; that He is more certain what is going to happen in ten thousand years than in one billion.

Then, the second factor in prediction is the certainty of the expectation of the event; while the third is the amount of detail foreseen. Let me comment on those two together. Since He is not infinite, He has to allocate His resources carefully. He will assign sensors, if that is what He is using, to groups of things, rather than individuals (I am talking about unimportant inanimate objects and very small units of life). He can predict that a certain school of fish will swim from Point A to Point B and will arrive there in about two days time. He does not know, or care, about any individual fish in the school; or about what happens to them; but He knows, if we assume that it is important to Him, that of the school of, say, five thousand, a number between thirty-eight hundred and forty-two hundred will arrive, within 45 and 50 hours.

But He is not absolutely certain in this knowledge. He can calculate the probability, and in this case, it may turn out to be, say 94%. With higher probability, He can be certain of less accuracy. For example,

He may be 98% sure that the school will arrive in between thirty-five and sixty hours, or that the number of fish making the journey safely will be between 3,500 and 4,500.

If their number, or time of arrival, is important as a factor in one of His plans, then He will install warning devices. Should He find that an attack of larger fish on this school is likely to damage the school more than intended, more than within the scope allowed, outside a certain range, then it may be important for Him to institute certain measures for the defense of the school. Otherwise, He may activate whatever back-up plans He may have, to compensate for the late arrival, for the fewer fish than originally expected. Or it may not matter at all; but even then, it may be a factor influencing the calculation for predicting some major event, such as the temperature change of the sea and through that, wind condition, weather, storms, burning down of a forest, and so on.

So you see what I mean about His foreseeing events at certain detail, with confidence that is never one-hundred percent, but usually very close. The less important a detail, the less confidence requirement specified. He may consider, if He cares at all, that a certain fish in the school will probably arrive at Point B, within thirty-five and sixty hours, with a probability, or confidence of, say, 40%; and that will be quite good enough. The likelihood of the school arriving at all may be 99.2 percent; while the forest burning down may have been planned with a 99.995 percent confidence.

If He watches a man, say, and has important plans for this man in twenty years' time, then how likely is it that the man will survive twenty years, will not fall victim to an unforeseen accident? Very likely, of course; not absolute; and that is where the second point, that of omnipotence, comes in.

For He is obviously not omnipotent; but He is more powerful than anything that we can conceive of. And by power, I mean both the magnitude of His acts and also the multitude and details.

My Master, it is very easy to prove logically that nobody, not even God, not even an infinite God, if such a thing were possible, could be omnipotent and omniscient at the same time. Omniscience precludes omnipotence, and vice versa. Those are mutually exclusive notions. If He knows for certain what He shall do, then He has no freedom of action; while if He can do anything He wishes, at any time, than He has no certain foreknowledge.

Now if we talked about multiscience and multipotence, that would be different. That would be entirely feasible. What does a multipotent God do if the task at hand is to assure the survival of a person? He will then assign enough sensors and effectors to almost guarantee that outcome. If the task is smaller, say it is to prevent the accidental destruction of the school of fish we discussed, then He will assign sufficient sensors and effectors, perhaps for the attacking sharks, to make such an outcome unlikely, with the appropriate confidence of, say, 97%, or whatever the necessity dictates. If the task is to prevent the destruction of life on earth through an accidental nuclear holocaust, then we can be assured that such an event will be prevented; the confidence, while not absolute, never absolute, will be something like 99.9999999999999 percent, or higher.

Our Lord, blessed be His name, is great, knowledgable and powerful. If you prefer to interpret these comments in the Neo-platonic negative sense, that of Him not being small, ignorant and weak, do so. But I don't see any reason for withholding from ourselves and from each other any knowledge about Him; for God knows that what we know is little enough; let us at least use that much for our own understanding of Him, for the understanding of others who may want to know Him.

Your devoted disciple

Joseph ben Yehudah

ARISTOTELIAN CONCEPTS vs. MODERN VIEWS

3 Nisan 5752 / April 6, 1992

To B'Rabbi Moshe ben Rabbi Maimon ha-Sfaradi,
Fostat, Egypt

My beloved Master:

We do understand now, don't we, many important things about the Holy One, blessed be he: how He operates, what he really is. Now it may be worthwhile to review the earlier concepts, not only yours and mine, but still further back, those of Aristotle, your "Chief of the Philosophers".

Every day I am surprised by how much he knew in certain areas, what a great biologist he was. How much better he understood the essentials of life than his colleagues in the two millennia to come.

For one thing, he realized (unlike his teacher Plato) that the Universe is dynamic, it is in constant state of development, change. He also understood, to a great extent, the evolution of the species. He even knew of the main instrument towards that end: the mechanism of the survival of the fittest, what they now call natural selection.

He also threw out Plato's ideas about the duality of the world: a sensible but unreal world plus a real but transcendental world, to Aristotle, made no sense; he stated that the world is simply real.

Still more relevant to what we are discussing in these letters, he realized that the Universe is in the process of creating something greater than it has so far; indeed, he stated that the entire evolutionary process exists for the sake of the thing that is finally evolved, and not this for the sake of the process. That is a most important concept that is still not understood by most of the intellectual leaders even today.

He also saw that everything that has been created had a purpose. And he understood project management: he said that every major human activity is for the purpose of a plan or a "form".

A comment on that term, "form": while nobody views objects and living being the way Plato and Aristotle did, as consisting of matter and form, yet regarding life, the concept may have some validity. I have used, on numerous occasions, the expression "life-form". And indeed, all living beings are made of the same basic materials, similar proteins and quite identical elements; what they are, the actual specificity, is determined by the genetic code. It is the genetic definition of the species that gives pattern and character to an individual; and in that respect, the genetic definition may approximate the Platonian "form" quite closely, at least for living beings.

Still another thing: Aristotle, like Plato and Socrates before him, understood the immortality of the soul, even though he did not directly identify it with the mind, as Descartes did some two thousand years later. But he stated that thought is what elevates Man, for he shares that facility with God!

He had deep faith, all the more remarkable because of his polytheistic background. Yet he dared to state that reason and faith need to be separated, considered individually and then, from positions of knowledge, reconciled! I wish people understood that idea today!

His approach to scientific—no, only biological—investigation was far superior to that of most scientists and philosophers for the next two thousand years: he learned through detailed observation, experimentation, research. He may indeed be considered the father of systematic logic; and his ethics are formidable even today. How much he would have discovered with access to modern scientific tools, measuring instruments, microscopes, telescopes! But none of those things were invented for some 1900 years after his death.

Even his concept of "motion", not used in that sense today, is very close to the modern scientific term of "energy".

Yet Aristotle was not infallible. Many of his ideas have been proven wrong, even pure nonsense. So have those of many other outstanding men. It is interesting to speculate that generally, those ideas that you accept ready-made, rather than develop by your own reasoning, are most vulnerable, most likely to be discredited.

What ideas am I criticizing? I have already mentioned, more than once, his totally wrong concept (and that of many other illustrious philosophers) of the celestial spheres, animated, intelligent beings surrounding the earth and influencing it various ways. There are, of course, no such things. But Aristotle should receive less blame for this blunder than his followers; for he did not have access to the words of the Lord, the Bible, words that later philosophers knew by heart; nowhere does the Lord claim to have created celestial spheres. Do you see how dangerous it is to try to explain things into His words?

Aristotle studied animals, understood a lot about the various species and genera (for one thing, he knew that whales and dolphins were mammals, not fish!) but had no idea about how and why the blood circulates; not recognizing that the heart is a pump, he attributed to that organ the *situs* of thinking and feeling. The brain, according to his opinions, was simply a cooling organ. (But again, he had no access to scientific instruments.)

But let me be frank: Aristotle was an awful physicist and an extremely poor astronomer. It had never occurred to him to use mathematics in the service of those sciences. He totally misunderstood the concept of motion, never realizing that a moving object will continue to move while it can—the concept of momentum; a discus or javelin flew, without anyone moving it, until air friction slowed it down. He missed that completely. Hence his need for a series of "movers", and finally the "prime mover", proving God's existence on the wrong premises.

And his astronomical views, even apart from the animated spheres moving each other were disastrous. He assumed that the planets, sun and moon revolved around the earth; yet his contemporary Heracleides already postulated that at least some planets moved around the sun. Barely two generations later, Aristarchus of Samos understood the fully heliocentric solar system (he called it "universe"), stated that all planets, excepting only the moon, revolved around the sun. His views were oppressed, by doctrinaire Neo-Platonists, by the Church and by just about everyone else for two millennia.

Aristotle's social views were no better. One typical area of misconception: his views on women were archaic and, frankly, wrong. Here, his teacher Plato was ahead of him: Plato provided good education for women; Aristotle considered them uneducable. Nor did he treat tradesmen and labourers fairly: he would not give them, or to artisans, the right to vote. Financial businessmen were considered by him as people with no interest in the good of the community, and therefore were to be similarly disenfranchised. And he considered slaves below contempt, by definition stupid, a lower race. You know, Rabbi, in many ways your Chief of Philosophers was a rather unpleasant person. What would he say if told that democracy, real democracy, is now considered the highest form of government? And that we learned that form from ancient Athens? What would *you* say?

In other areas where Aristotle was wrong, you corrected him. My Master, I am proud of you. He wrote about the natural necessity for development, evolution; you pointed out that it is all by divine design, not necessity. Interestingly, there are very brilliant philosophers and theologians today who still follow Aristotle in that respect.

Also, he stated, correctly I think, that God provides for each species, but not for each individual within the species—with some qualification, I would call it a true statement: He made no distinction between plants, animals of different levels of advancement on the evolutionary scale, and Homo Sapiens. Yet surely, the more advanced a species, the more divine attention and providence it rates.

Your formulation on this is a classic: you stated that in case of humans, God's providence depends on the intellectual perfection of the person. That may very well be so. Yet I wish you did not put it quite that firmly; for what do we know? We can only guess about His intentions. He may provide for, may watch a certain person of lower intellectual perfection in preference to one of higher achievement, for reasons of His own.

I also think that your definition of the nature of the soul provides significant clarification to that of Aristotle: you have accepted its immortality, but only its potentiality at inception. You also thought that the immortality of the soul may be collective, not individual. While in my concept of the Universal Mind, it is indeed a collective immortality that I envision, I surely hope that you are wrong about the individual mind, or soul: I would like to retain my individuality even while part of that great collective.

The major argument between yourself and Aristotle concerned the origins of the Universe: has it been eternal, or a temporal creation? Aristotle believed in its eternity, since he considered it impossible to create prime matter. Islamic philosophers modified this by the theory—under Neoplatonic influence—of constant creation through eternity, by means of divine emanation. But you rejected this, insisting instead on temporal creation, as specifically stated in the Torah; and how right you were!

Interestingly, though, you added that while the Existence and Unity of God can be proven scientifically, His *creatio ex nihilo* of the Universe cannot. Today the situation is almost the opposite. Your proofs for the existence of God cannot quite stand up to logical scrutiny (although the probability is very strongly on the side of your proofs). At the same time, the theory of eternal Universe has fallen: Even the atheists (and I have told you that most of today's scientists are in that class) admit that the Universe has not existed eternally, but was created suddenly in something they call the "big bang" some seventeen billion years ago. Created by whom? They won't say; or rather, they will claim that it just happened, accidentally. A stupid opinion? I agree with you.

Your devoted disciple

Joseph ben Yehudah

DIMENSIONS: ANOTHER VIEW

23 Nisan 5752 / April 26, 1992

To B'Rabbi Moshe ben Rabbi Maimon ha-Sfaradi,
Fostat, Egypt

My beloved Master:

In an earlier letter to you, I have stated that the Holy One, blessed be
he, is very real, some ways even physical (at least with regard to the
substrate that supports His essential intelligence), yet not of this world.
That His physical substrate may be subject to laws quite different
from ours. I alluded to one possibility for this, that His dimensions
may differ from ours; that He may occupy more spatial dimensions
than we, perhaps even temporal dimensions; that this may account for
His superiority, our being like Him and yet being so inferior to Him.

I would like, in this letter, to explore that concept with you, to analyze
the spatial and temporal dimensions as they may relate to God and
Man.

First, about spatial dimensions. It is easy to speculate about a
two-dimensional world; but if one existed, we could not see it, hear
it, sense it, conceive of it. We hardly see a thin pane of glass; if it
were only a few molecules thick, we would not see it; if it were of
zero thickness, it would not exist for us.

Would we exist for such a world? Perhaps. They could sense us if we
were motionless in that third dimension of ours that did not exists for
them; that may be practically impossible. Otherwise, at best, we would

appear as a blur, and perhaps not even that, for at the smallest sub-atomic level, at any one time the number of such particles appearing on a plane may be near zero.

In any case, even if the lower dimension could conceive of the higher one, it could not possibly influence it, act on it.

Similarly, two three-dimensional worlds, sharing only two common dimensions, could not conceive of each other, let alone exert influence; for the non-shared dimensions are mutually non-existent, while the two shared ones are like a plane passing through an object, unseen and unsensed by the object and probably by the plane.

Concerning temporal dimensions, first I have to note that by necessity, such a dimension must be unidirectional, in sharp contrast to spatial dimensions. It may be that this is the one thing that distinguishes it.

Could two worlds co-exist with the identical time dimensions, but operating in opposite directions? Yes; but they would be totally irrelevant to each other.

Of course, worlds of totally different time dimensions would be mutually non-existent. But could two worlds co-exist and influence each other if one had more than one temporal dimensions? Perhaps; a second time dimension is very difficult for us to understand. More likely, just as in the case of spatial dimensions, the two-time world could not conceive of the one-time world.

Up to now, we seem to be saying, in effect, that God's dimensions, spatial and temporal, cannot be different from ours, if the term "dimension" has any meaning similar to ours in His world.

But there is another possibility that we must consider. Could the temporal dimension of one world become the spatial one of the other?

Well, yes, there are some real possibilities here. Try to imagine a two-dimensional world. Let us limit the extents of their two dimensions to manageable sizes, say the size of a wall of your room. So at any time, this world can be imagined as a plane, a square. We can then take a series of that Universe, that wall, as it changes through discrete time units; remembering that time is perpendicular to the other dimensions, these "snapshots" will be planes parallel to the original, very close to it; until enough of the "time" elapses to fill up, say, our room. We end up with a solid block, a cube. If we are able to penetrate it, which is not difficult, we then have a view of a solid that represents a plane world gradually changing through time. We can, at any point, see their future as well as their past.

We can not only conceive of such a thing, we could have created it. We do create such worlds, easily: any block built may be considered such a two-dimensional world, with the third one a temporal dimension for it. What we cannot do is build it with a complex set of physical laws included, so that the time dimension reflects an unending series of causes and effects; let alone other major achievement, such as life.

Could God have created our world that way? Could His world consist of four spatial dimensions, one coinciding with our temporal one? Of course, in that case, He would have to have a fifth dimension, a temporal one of His own: existence is not possible without one.

Yes, he could have. In that case, he would have our past and future laid out in front of Him; He would indeed be omniscient. But He would not be omnipotent: His potency would be zero, at least so far as it affects our world.

You see, if He then made any change, He would make it in His own time, which is not our time; so any change made in our future or past, would simply create another version of us that would exist later in God's time, but never in ours. Our future would be fixed permanently; God would know it, but would be effectively powerless to change it.

I think I may just have described the Ash`arite view of the world: where God knows all, where there is no free will, where fatalism is the only sensible approach to human existence, since it is all pre-ordained, there is nothing we or anyone else can do to change a thing.

But if that picture was correct, there would be no point in our praying to God; for He could not respond to such supplication. Even though He would be our Creator, for all practical purposes He would be non-existent for us.

My Master, I reject the Ash`arite Kalam, I reject fatalism. God is real in our world; He not only created us, but is with us every day; He acts on our world, listens to our prayers and if he wants to, helps us, changes things for us. This is not a permanently frozen world; it is alive with the God-Man relation, a dynamic and vibrant relation that sustains us, so be it.

But then, what is the solution to God's "whereabouts"? If He is not in different dimensions, then where is He?

Well, while difference of dimensions is not the only possible answer—indeed, the answer is quite likely to be non-comprehensible to humans—yet let us not discard the concept of dimensions too fast. Let us consider the difference between God's essence, which is intelligence, and His substrate. The latter is necessarily physical (though, as I have said, not necessarily according to our physics, our laws); but its dimensions are somewhat irrelevant, even misleading. A software may easily run on a computer of 2, 3, 4 dimensions or more. And that software itself has no dimensions at all, at least not spatial ones.

So we can envision God, His intelligence, as a dimensionless structure of logic, operating on some substrate of unknown dimensions.

Yet the lowest levels of that logical structure must control physical devices, sensors and effectors, that can interface with our world. These must be three- dimensional devices. So the only question is, can there be a substrate supporting the Lord's Intellect, a substrate that is, at its lowest level, three-dimensional, while elsewhere perhaps more?

Yes, there can be! Dimensions, as mathematicians have recently discovered, do not need to be integral. There may be a fractional dimension. God could have both the same dimensions as we do, and also more, in that at the lowest levels the number of spatial dimensions could be something like 3.001; this number would gradually increase at the higher hierarchical levels, reaching eventually four, or some other number at the Godhead. Such a minute difference between any two levels may still permit interaction.

But one more thought: If the essence of the Lord is software, which has no spatial dimensions, what about time? I think that software must have a temporal dimension: the logical statements follow each other in time of some kind. And, again, God can only be relevant to us if His logical time dimension is identical to ours (at least "substantially" identical; for we do not know whether a fractionally higher time dimension would permit interaction).

But could it be bi-directional? I have said no, but perhaps that may be not quite true for a structure which is software. Perhaps it is, somehow, possible for a superior set of logic to move in both directions temporally.

If so, then we have two aspects of God, of which only one is relevant to us: He sees the future, but can change it; He is therefore multipotent and multiscient, a relevant God. He can also move back in our past and change it; but that is almost irrelevant for us, because then the previous version will have never happened. It would be possible to pray to the Lord to change the past, effectively through His "undo/redo" facility. He could do that. But we could never thank Him for it; for we would never know that a different, less desirable present has ever existed.

Well, I am sorry, Rabbi, if having explored these ideas, I can only show you some possibilities, instead of presenting for you a simple and clear answer to the problem of where God is, how His world is different from ours, how the two interact, how He senses and controls us. We can think more about these ideas; perhaps one day, He will see it fit to enlighten us.

Your devoted disciple

Joseph ben Yehudah

FROM CHAOS TO CHAOS:

LAWS CREATED AND NOT CREATED BY GOD

2 Iyyar 5752 / May 5, 1992

To B'Rabbi Moshe ben Rabbi Maimon ha-Sfaradi,
Fostat, Egypt

My beloved Master:

If we accept, as I feel we must, the hypothesis about the Holy One, blessed is He, that while He is essentially intelligence, yet is still based on a material substrate, then there is some speculation in order about the nature of that matter. We have done so recently, in discussing the possible relevance of dimensions, both to the hardware and the software aspects of the divine structure. That exploratory adventure has yielded only limited results: a vague understanding about what the Lord's domain may and may not be; for soon we have found ourselves running into the brick wall of incomprehension.

But then, most of the scientific ideas that we are taking for granted today could not even be imagined a hundred years ago; so who knows what another hundred years may bring to our comprehension? Just to give you a somewhat outrageous possibility: we may find that things really great are to be found among things very small: among the sub-sub-sub-sub-atomic particles, we may find enough power and intelligence to make our earthly size totally irrelevant, to make us feel like dwarfs. Who knows?

Yet there is one thing that we do know, and that is that nothing physical can exist without it being subject to the laws of physics. In our world, we may count on heavy things to stay on the ground; on liquids to flow into deep cavities, on gases to disperse, on objects to expand when heated, and so on. These laws are what make all things behave as they do, and hence useful to us in thousands of ways.

A computer substrate for some software operates through making use of countless physical laws, another instance of Man taking advantage of those laws. Without laws, nothing could work.

There is no question in my mind that the substrate that supports God is also subject to many laws, although by no means the same ones as our laws. Some laws of physics. But that raises a question: who created *those* laws?

Now, Master, we again are on dangerous grounds. By assuming that the Lord created them, we'll have to ask ourselves what He did before, what He was before, how He could exist without that physical substrate. We can envision perhaps an older, smaller, more primitive substrate, supporting a smaller intelligence; carrying the regress further and further back, we may reach an image of God as a very small deity at first, perhaps a child; but we are fighting a never-ending series of questions involving God's eternity and creation.

Of course, if our answer to that earlier question is that God did not create the laws to which His physical substrate is subject, then who did? We are back into the quagmire of an infinite regress of questions.

(Rabbi, I would prefer not even to speculate about those things. Not because I think there is anything intrinsically wrong about such speculations, anything irreverent, blasphemous—no, none of those things. It is that the answers to those questions are so far beyond our ability of comprehension, that any attempt to reason in those areas is bound to be a waste of time. Yet I would not want to discourage others from trying to find some of those answers, even while I am struggling with nearer ones, such that may just barely be within our ability of understanding and only if we are willing to apply our current knowledge, rather than millennia-old concepts.)

Nevertheless, we must accept the fact that God, as He is in His physical aspects, is subject to certain laws; whether or not he could change them, we don't know.

But do we know that He can change *our* laws of physics? No, we don't know that. Has He created those laws? We believe so. He certainly created our Universe; but how much discretion did He have in setting up this Universe, how much was He able to manipulate its physics, how difficult it may have been to "fine tune" it so that a life-supporting granular world would emerge, and how inflexibly that requirement may have defined the necessary laws that were to apply here, we really cannot say. My guess is that the process of creation involved unimaginable levels of difficulties, perhaps also a long series of trials and errors, until the "fine tuning" produced a viable Universe capable of sustaining life and intelligence.

It is possible that the laws of the Universe to be created had to be such and such. It is probable that the options that the Lord had at His disposal were severely limited.

But I think that there was one law, above all others, that God must have accepted as given; the law that may stamp unidirectionality on the time dimension; a law that He may or may not have liked, but had no choice in the matter; and that was the law of entropy.

(There may have been another very basic law, that of quantum physics. This is a very complicated matter, with deep philosophical implications; let us not discuss is within this series of letters. If the Lord, blessed be His name, encourages me to do so, I may write to you about it at some future time.)

With regards to entropy, I have already mentioned it to you; and hope to write to you more about it in my next letter.

Your devoted disciple

Joseph ben Yehudah

ENTROPY

15 Iyyar 5752 / May 18, 1992

To B'Rabbi Moshe ben Rabbi Maimon ha-Sfaradi,
Fostat, Egypt

My beloved Master:

I made a brief reference to entropy in my last letter, and in earlier letters as well. I should discuss it in some detail, I think, for it is highly relevant to our thinking about the Holy One, blessed is he.

Physics, in the 19th and 20th centuries, has sprouted many new branches. One major branch is thermodynamics, the science that studies heat and its effects on matter; as well, the conversion of various forms of energy from one form into another, especially thermal energy into kinetic energy and motion; and also the reverse. (Do you realize that there is a law that states that energy changes format, but the total amount, in a closed system, remains constant? Another says that matter also remains constant. And now, in the 20th century, we recognize the fact that matter can be converted to energy, a tremendous amount of energy: thermonuclear power, which provides both electricity and devastating nuclear explosions.)

Well, thermodynamics has several laws; we only need to concern ourselves with the second. It resulted from studies of the conditions that make a steam engine possible; it is restricted to conditions prevailing in closed systems. The original studies were aimed at discovering whether or not it may be possible to construct a machine that will move by itself, forever, and perhaps even produce useful energy, or motion, for the external world.

Such a perpetual motion machine, in a closed system, is theoretically possible, under ideal conditions. However, those conditions cannot exist in the real world. Since in reality, motion always produces heat, and since heat, according to the law, will not move from lower to higher level, or even between two objects of equal temperature, therefore the produced heat cannot be fully re-converted to motion. Hence a "perpetuum mobile" cannot exist in the real world (let alone a machine that produces motion for the use of the external environment, yet maintains its internal balance without change and without input of energy from the external world.)

The key to the law is that energy always flows from the higher to the lower level; in effect, it runs down eventually. In the process, higher level of organization gives way to lack of organization, chaos. The measure of this disorganization is entropy. In any spontaneous change, entropy (of a closed system) always increases. It cannot be reversed. If we view the entire Universe as a closed system, then the amount of entropy in it is constantly increasing, whether we like it or not.

To put it another way, energy differential constantly dissipates, while structures change from complex to simple. What is complex? An elaborate mechanism constructed for some special purpose is complex. What is simple? The components of that mechanism are more simple, even though they may be complex on their own. Such components fallen apart, no longer able to fulfill their functions, odd pieces of metal and wood, that is more simple; yet still far from the ultimate simplicity.

Everything falls apart, organization changes into disorganization, complexity changes into simplicity —that is the law of nature. One feels instinctively that it is true; but a very simple demonstration can be made. Drop an egg, or shake one in a glass bottle: it will break up. That is natural. But then shake the broken egg in the glass bottle as long as you like, in the hope that eventually, by coincidence, by random action, its pieces will come together in such a way that a complete, unbroken, whole egg will result. Of course, it is impossible. It will never happen.

There are many other examples of the organization-to-disorganization, complexity-to-simplicity process. Everything falls apart. The best machines will cease to operate without constant maintenance activity. Human organization, so difficult to create, will disintegrate in no time at all. Buildings will crumble, artifacts will be chipped and chipped again until nothing remains. And bodies, human and animal bodies —well, you know what happens to them. Even during the lifetime of the being, it begins to malfunction; once animation disappears, the body decomposes to its lowest components in very little time.

That is entropy. It constantly increases. According to the classical law of entropy (and I shall soon tell you why I refer to it in such terms), the only way to create anything in a closed system is by decomposing something else (say you create steam by burning wood). In the long run, there is more decomposition than creation; everything in the closed system falls apart, as it has no access to external energy. Inevitably, all matter must reach its lowest level of complexity, meaning a total decomposition to the smallest, most basic components, with no energy differential at all. That state possesses no complexity, no organization; but it does possess order. It is smooth, orderly, uncluttered. The Universe is complex, uneven, disordered. A galaxy is clumpy, and so are the elementary particles.

The name we have for that ultimately ordered state is *chaos*.

Rabbi, the world is rapidly moving to a state of absolute chaos. We come from dust and we shall become dust, not only as individual persons, but collectively, the entire world.

But, you may object, the law of entropy should not at all apply to the earth, for it is not a closed system: it receives energy from the Sun, radiation from the entire Universe; it radiates in turn; not to mention the effects of gravity. Indeed, there *is no closed system*, other than the Universe itself.

It seems to me that there are at least two aspects to the Law of Entropy. The aspect dealing with the rundown of energy differential seems to apply to the Universe, if nothing else, as stated. This is what I mean by the classical formulation of the Law. However, complexity is another matter entirely. Things move from complex to simple, never the other way, except by intelligent manipulation. Energy, while necessary for complexification, does not by itself convert to complexity (breakdown of complexity does, of course, generate energy). I would like to deal only with the "second law of entropy" (my invention), that which defines the relation of complexity to simplicity. Perhaps this is the "third law of entropy": a major scientist of this century, one John von Neumann, already established a second application: he extended the law of entropy to *information*, stating that it, like energy differential, always dissipates. Information could, perhaps, be equated with complexity; but let us not worry about that now. Let us simply base our speculation on this third law of entropy, or as I prefer to call it, the *"Law of Entropic Simplicity"*: Left to themselves, all things move from complex to simple.

And having postulated that, let us contemplate what the Lord has done. He decided to create the world, our Universe, out of nothing. Let us assume that creation of some material, some elementary particles out of nothing, through quantum fluctuation, does not conflict with the law of entropy; it probably does, but we don't know enough about that, at least I don't. What He had then was chaos, primordial matter, Tohu vaBohu. This matter was at the maximum state of disorganization; at absolute entropy. Yet He reversed that entropy. How? He brought it all together (I have mentioned the "big bang") in a way that the system was suddenly alive with the tension of energy differential, matter differential. (What is that? Well, for every smallest sub-atomic particle there is an anti-particle, identical yet opposite; if the two meet, they annihilate each other, leaving energy in their wake). After the annihilation of matter with antimatter, what was left, it was a form of energy that may also be matter, particles or waves called photons, the smallest units of light.

Matter solidified in seconds or milliseconds. That matter (clouds of swirling gases, consisting mainly of protons, the nuclei of hydrogen) eventually contracted to protogalaxies and galaxies and stars. Systems within systems were created, increasingly organized, if not particularly complex at first. There were the billions of galaxies. There were the billions of solar systems within each, all the (presumed) planets and satellites. But all of those were built up from marvellous elementary particles. Molecules and atoms and so on. Consider the protons and electrons and neutrons and other sub-atomic components, and still further down, the quarks and leptons, the "strange and charmed" particles—oh, so hard to comprehend those. That is what He's created.

Yet that was only the first step. We have already considered God's major project; but let us think about it now from the viewpoint of the Law of Entropic Simplicity.

As you will recall, the second major phase of creation was that of life on earth. Life! Now that we are beginning to understand what it is, we are over-awed about the complexity of the process. The well-control-led chemical reactions, converting food to energy and supplying the living being with thousands of needed components! The provision of oxygen for that conversion! The circulation of oxygen through the blood vessels! The purification system for the blood! The nervous system! The lymphatic system! The reproductive system! The senses! The hundreds, thousands of components, all working, all co-operating smoothly in an overall structure so complex that modern science still does not understand it all!

Too many exclamation marks, Rabbi, I know. You think that I am getting over-excited about this view of life as complexity upon complexity. Yes, I am. But wait, you have not yet heard me describe the internal control mechanism, the computer code that regulates the production of proteins and determines the specific and individual characteristics of the being produced or maintained. Or I may have mentioned it in an earlier letter; but it is impossible to say enough in the praise of that system, the genetic code, determined through the combination of nucleotides embedded in desoxynucleic acid chains, what they call DNA, and the transfer of that information through ribonucleic acid segments, and the copying of the DNA chains, and all that established billions of years before Man invented copying mechanisms; not to mention the interpreting mechanism for the code, tiny computers embedded in every living cell—can you think of complexity higher than that? *Is this entropy?* To me, it does not sound like entropy at all!

Having encountered such a marvel, such complexity, such an antithesis of entropy, one should perhaps be content in his admiration, not even consider still further examples of the Lord's creations of the kind; yet there is more! There is still a further paragon of complexity, the next major phase of the creation project: thinking, reflection, consciousness!

For human thought, the complex interrelation of concepts and facts in a constantly changing, evolving mode, resulting in discoveries of laws, invention of machines, creation of books and poems and symphonies and paintings and millions of new things, wonderful things—well, that is levels above life itself in complexity. Does entropy create life and thinking? Of course not. It destroys those things, takes them apart, breaks them down, attempts to show how little value there is: a handful of carbon, some oxygen and nitrogen, as if there were not enough in the air; some hydrogen as if the oceans could use more; sulphur and phosphorous and other elements, all apparently unimportant. But we know how important it all was while it lasted.

Yes, it all does break down eventually. But while it lasts, how beautiful it is, how complex! Entropy could not have created it. Nature itself, the amassment of all laws of chemistry and physics, could not have created it. Only the Lord could!

And so, He's created a system with layer upon layer of increasing, law-defying complexity. How do we know that He had to contend with that law? That He's found the law and could not simply cancel it? We don't know, but we are almost certain; for we see that law all around us, its effects are the greatest on us of all physical laws, on us and on all of God's creations. The law is still here, it is still a force waiting to destroy us and everything around us, all of our creations and all of God's. We are His creation and we do fall apart.

Or do we?

Let me try to explore that question in my next letter, my Master.

Your devoted disciple

Joseph ben Yehudah

LIFE AS NEGATIVE ENTROPY

3 Sivan 5752 / June 3, 1992

To B'Rabbi Moshe ben Rabbi Maimon ha-Sfaradi,
Fostat, Egypt

My beloved Master:

I have more to say about entropy, about the fact that everything
—ourselves included—will be falling apart, decomposing eventually.
Yes, everything will. But let us marvel, first, about the miracle that
everything that eventually returns to its most simple, most ordered,
least organized state, was nevertheless once highly organized,
extremely complex. How is that possible? How did that happen?

Well, of course, the Holy One, blessed be He, created it all. But as we
have seen, He had to contend with the forces of entropy. Introducing
complexity reduces the overall entropy; yet we have learned that
entropy cannot be reduced. Not without external introduction of
negative entropy. Clearly, that is what He had to do.

All right, we can visualize how, in order to bring all the just created
primordial matter together and bring about the "big bang", He
provided the necessary energy differential, perhaps by simply creating
negative and positive energies out of nothing—it seems that such a
move is within the realm of scientific possibilities. And so, there was
differentiation, matter and antimatter in the cosmos; perhaps the
correct way to state this is that the cosmos itself was created in that
process. And with the cosmos, an increasingly organized system of
galaxies, suns, planets and so on. But that was not the end of the story.

Left to itself, the cosmos would have expanded for a while; stabilized; and then begun to collapse again, until all energy differentials dissipated and nothing but chaos remained. That would have happened; indeed, that may be exactly what will happen. Yet on one planet, meanwhile, further miracles came forth. Life appeared.

Now life is of such high-level complexity that the intricacy within a single living being exceeds that of the entire inanimate Universe. How did that happen? Again, something had to be introduced externally.

What was this introduced factor? Again, I like to use the term "negative entropy". Its effect is certainly the negation of the Law of Entropy, or at least that of the Law of Entropic Simplicity. Through that reversal, it became possible to create complex, self-reproducing life-forms on earth. But more than that: considering that life-forms have evolved ever since, under God's direction, constantly reaching higher and higher levels of complexity, it must be assumed that negative entropy has been added to the system throughout.

I would be tempted to consider life itself as a form of negative entropy.

Let me be strictly technical here. According to the latest state of physics, this negative entropy did not necessarily have to come from outside the system which is the Universe. "Basic entropy" (as opposed to my suggested concept of "entropic simplicity") can be re-arranged so it is reduced at one place, increased at another, with a net change of a small increase of entropy within the closed system. (But we don't have a closed system, anywhere in the Universe! Gravitation, for one thing, permeates all.)

Scientists explain that a complex new thing, such as a hundred-story building, can only be produced at the cost of increasing disorganization somewhere else, say at the disrupted mine where the building materials were extracted from the ground. Let us accept that view provisionally. Could anyone honestly imply that, therefore, the erection of such a building can be explained as a natural phenomenon? I hope no scientist would want us to believe that; even though, technically, it is within the realm of statistical possibilities, so long as the reduction of entropy is offset by a corresponding increase somewhere else.

And so, technically, a skyscraper, a Moon-rocket, a magnificent bridge, could be naturally occuring features of the earth.

That is why I think that the Law of Entropy (finally removed from the confines of thermodynamics), should be extended, to specifically exclude the possibility of increased complexity without *intelligent* intervention, whether or not offset by decomposition, dismantling or decay somewhere else within a closed system. And this is what I mean by the Law of Entropic Simplicity. I am no scientist, so I should leave the formulation of the law to others; but it should say something simple, such as the formulation in my last letter to you; or perhaps "complexification of anything (as opposed to entanglement) is not possible without intelligent intervention".

And thus, we can consider negative entropy as the intelligent intervention, sometimes by God, at other times by Man. To be more precise, I would define it as planned organization, which is the product of energy and intelligence.

For what happened next? Intelligence appeared on earth. And again, the intelligence of one human being may be at a level of complexity that dwarfs that of all lifeforms put together. And so, created intelligence required the introduction of still more intelligent intervention, still more negative entropy.

And that is where we are now; but let us not forget that we are not the end-product. Still higher levels are to come, at least one, maybe more. The next level, as I've suggested, is the Universal Mind, which will be the collective intelligence of all human beings. So much more complex shall that be than our individual intelligences today! More negative entropy; for surely, that phase will not come about without His making it happen, using whatever resources that takes. Remember, the natural tendency of everything, presumably including intelligence structures, conglomerates, is to fall apart, not to get organized further and further.

And so, assuming that the Universal Mind is the end- product, the final object of the creation, then we can contemplate that product (or, if applicable, perhaps a product of still further complexification beyond that) as the result of vast amounts of negative entropy, layer upon layer; and consider that by the laws of physics, as we know them, *all of that effort, all of the negative entropy is for naught;* for introducing negative entropy into a system only delays its eventual falling apart; ultimately, all must end in the so-called "heat-death" of the Universe, when all energy runs down, everything falls apart and all things end as cosmic dust, chaos again, Tohu vaBohu.

Did God not know that? Silly question! Of course He knew. Then why did He bother? Why did He waste His time and efforts? Well, some people will say that perhaps He had nothing better to do, He has just been amusing Himself; and distasteful as that answer is, we cannot prove that it is not so. That is where faith and hope come in.

I believe, Master, that what the Lord has been doing is creating intelligence, super-intelligence, perhaps at a level approaching that of His own, in a cosmic system subject to the laws of entropy; He needed to introduce negative entropy to the system to do this; and just as He could introduce that (substance? force?) from external sources, *He will be able to remove* something from the system in the same way. You could argue that such "window" of God's would disqualify the Universe as a closed system, if it ever was; I'll respond that the window is apparently not subject to our physics.

What would the Lord remove from the Universe? I believe that He will remove the Universal Mind, or whatever the end-product will be, once completed. He will remove that from the confines of our doomed Universe, from the effects of our laws of physics, from heat death.

What laws will that final intelligence then follow at the "place" of God? We cannot know that; but it may be reasonable to expect to find no entropy there, or at least not in the form we know it—it is so easy, Rabbi, to get involved in idle speculations, totally useless; let us guard against it. But let us be happy that the Lord has been creating us and what will come from us in the future, in order that He can eventually take us into His own realm. Perhaps, some way, we shall all see and come to understand that realm. There can be no greater hope than that. Amen.

Your devoted disciple

Joseph ben Yehudah

CREATION—A STORY

24 Sivan 5752 / June 24, 1992

To B'Rabbi Moshe ben Rabbi Maimon ha-Sfaradi,
Fostat, Egypt

My beloved Master:

I hope you will agree with me that by now we really understand, as far as possible with the 20th century mind and knowledge, how the Holy One, blessed is he, created the Universe, life, intelligence: by the word understand, I mean that we can make rough guesses.

Let us pretend that we really see, clearly and fully, the past and present. If so, and therefore admittedly on less than the firmest of bases, we can move on to expand our preliminary speculation about the future.

But before doing so, I would like to make an attempt at summarizing the history of the world, God's creation to date, in a very brief statement, one obviously different from the first chapter of Genesis, yet still echoing it, reverberating with it; expressed in the language of late 20th century Man. The following is one possible version of how we would express that story today (for we still don't know enough of those first few miliseconds; scientists are still arguing what really happened in the "big bang"):

CREATION: A STORY

In the beginning, God created matter and energy. Matter was a formless chaos, in a singularity at infinite temperature and density. Outside that, God existed as essentially pure Intellect.

God brought differentiation to the chaos, and as matter and antimatter mutually annihilated, radiated energy in a "big bang", which expanded the new universe at a tremendous rate. He coagulated the energy into particles, created photons first of all: particles of light. The first era ended: it was to last a fraction of a second.

And God nucleosynthesized hydrogen and deuterium and some helium from energy, thermalized radiation in three minutes; and then the Universe became matter-dominated. The second era came to a close: it lasted three hundred thousand years.

And God gradually made the Universe transparent and granular. Through the effects of gravitation, galaxies formed from swirling clouds of hydrogen gas, and clustered. He created quasars and Population II stars and then Population I stars. And these stars were nuclear furnaces that produced heavy elements, including carbon, and these heavy elements were later dispersed throughout the Universe. And God formed the protosolar nebula and from it, He created the Sun. And God caused planets to be captured by the Sun and to revolve around it. Rocks begun to solidify; the earth began to cool down. The third era ended: it lasted sixteen billion years.

And on earth God negated entropy and created life: an amino-acid-based organization that could replicate itself from basic ingredients. And He controlled the form of the creature through a ribonucleic-acid-based coding structure. And He endowed the creature with an urge to reproduce and preserve the individual and species: the instinct of survival. And He provided an oxygen-rich atmosphere for the creature.

And He provided mutation, and there was a variety of the creatures. And God changed the environment and circumstances, so that only the fittest would survive: directed evolution. And thus the fourth era ended: two billion years.

Micro life-forms were followed by macro life-forms. And God differentiated the life-forms into flora and fauna. Early land plants were created and then developed into ferns and connifers. In the seas, He developed increasingly advanced marine life approaching the form of early fishes. And He created land animals: reptiles, birds, mammals and other beings, always through directed evolution. And so, the fifth era ended; it lasted one billion years.

And God varied the mammals to evolve primates. And He then increased their brain capacities, and improved their features and bearing, and brought forth Homo Erectus. And He provided a very complex and powerful brain for this creature, so it could begin to use language and think simple thoughts; and this was Homo Sapiens. And then, through reversing entropy still further, He gave consciousness to the creature, and it could think for itself and reflect, and had to do so in order to survive. And so He created Homo Sapiens Sapiens: a creature with a mind, capable from birth of acquiring the Intellect. And the sixth era ended: a hundred million years.

(And God rested in the seventh era: it lasted a fraction of a second.)

Yes, Rabbi, it is still full of speculation. I would have liked to present the story in more chapters, more eras; for example, I could have shown a long era of a million years, while He created Homo Erectus; a shorter one, of a hundred thousand years, for Homo Sapiens; and a very short one, of only a few thousand years, for Homo Sapiens Sapiens, the truly conscious, self-reflecting Man. But that way, we may have ended up with ten or twelve eras; perhaps sensible, but we feel more comfortable with six. Incidentally, I am not sure how He found time to rest on the "seventh day". I suggested only a fraction of a second; His time seems to be on a different scale than ours, anyway.

The important thing, for us, is the eighth day: for He is clearly working still, creating still; if not creating the world, then developing that which has been the real objective all along. And I think that He will do so for many days yet.

My Master, I have now completed the third group of letters to you. Blessed be the Merciful, who has aided us. I hope to start the fourth and last series next, with the help of Shaddai.

Your devoted disciple

Joseph ben Yehudah

BOOK IV.

The Future

JOSEPH BEN-YEHUDAH'S LETTER TO RAMBAM

25 Tishri 5753 / October 22, 1992

To B'Rabbi Moshe ben Rabbi Maimon ha-Sfaradi,
Fostat, Egypt

My beloved Master:

The time has come for us to consider the future. In a sense I am
pleased that we now realize what we are, we know that we are only
an intermediate product in the Lord's great project; it dulls the edge
of our conceit. And yet, the fact remains that we are the object of all
of His past work, if not the future. Let us admit to ourselves: we are
important to Him. But we are here not for ourselves but for that which
is still to come.

I have already told you what I thought was the likely end-product of
the Lord's project: the Universal Mind. If not end-product, it is so advanced that we may not be able to reach much further in our imagination; at least I may not be able, perhaps better minds will.

But I would like to think a lot more about what this Universal Mind
is all about: how it evolves, how it behaves, how it relates to God
Himself; questions like that, many questions.

Of more immediate concern to us, I would like to understand how we,
people living today, relate to the Universal Mind. Will we be part of
it? Will that happen when we are resurrected? What about the
World-to-Come? I know that you thought about those subjects, and it
seems to me that you were quite right in most of your comments;
perhaps not all.

And I would also like to explore the role of the Jews in that future. How shall we expect to fit in? What shall we do? Are we going to be treated differently from the others? Will that difference be to our advantage, or otherwise? Clearly, these are important questions; and I am sure that any answer to them, even if based only on intelligent guesswork, is going to be welcome by you and perhaps by others reading these letters.

And so, with the help of Shaddai, let us move on to the future.

Your devoted disciple

Joseph Ben-Yehudah

THE FUTURE FOR HUMANITY, FOR JEWRY AND FOR THE INDIVIDUAL

WORLD-TO-COME; RESURRECTION; THE MESSIAH

9 Heshvan 5753 / November 5, 1992

To B'Rabbi Moshe ben Rabbi Maimon ha-Sfaradi,
Fostat, Egypt

My beloved Master:

What will happen to us once we die? To our body, to our soul? Oh, what we would do, what we would give to know the answer. Man has tried to learn it, from revelation and through reason, for thousands of years; and has become increasingly confused in the process. You were one of the most important of the explicators and oracles; yet I know that you were never quite satisfied with your own answers.

Let us remind ourselves of what has been said. Our sages argued endlessly; yet on the whole they seemed to believe that after death, the soul stays with the body until it decomposes, or for a year. Then, the righteous souls go to paradise. In Messianic times, the soul returns to dust and is resurrected with the body. Eventually, in the World-to-Come, all but the really sinful will participate in eternal beatitude.

Your own views were not radically different. You believed in the immortality of the soul, following not only our sages, but Plato and Aristotle. The Neo-Platonist philosophers expected the soul to ascend to God in stages; they had no interest in the body. Aristotle defined the immortal element as the Acquired Intellect, which is to join the Agent Intellect, a divine substance. Actually, he said "re-join", for the human intellect was supposed to be of divine origin.

You did not quite agree with that concept. To you, a child was born with potential intellect only. I think you believed with Aristotle that acquired intellect is the immortal substance of Man. But what happens to it after death? There, you confused many of us. You wrote to me that all human intellect will be saved and united with the divine substance, *collectively*. Elsewhere, though, you said that such intellects will be saved *individually*.

Apart from the immortality of the soul (or intellect), you truly believed in the resurrection of the dead, in a physical sense, with body. Truly believed, as an article of faith; but not rationally, not deep down. You described the Messianic age in purely political terms, with the Messiah as a human king and head of a dynasty; a mortal! And then, you stated that the dead would be resurrected bodily in the Messianic age, only to die again, presumably to await the World-to-Come. Master, I am having a little trouble with that concept; it is not rational. Of course, you knew that.

What have the Christians said? That upon death, each person is judged and sent to Heaven or Hell, or to Purgatory for cleansing (many of our rabbis were of similar opinion). But then, when the Messiah comes, upon His second coming, all souls will return for the final judgement, and will be re-united with the bodies, for eternal life (if merited) in the Kingdom of Heaven. Not that different from the rabbinic view.

The Muslims have similar beliefs, at least about burning in eternal hell-fire, or participating in the joys of heaven forever; they tended to describe those joys in great detail.

Yet an honest consideration of all of those views—whether convergent or divergent—should convince us that they are all confusing and entirely irrational. They cannot even be based solidly on Scriptures, for so many of the holy writings, so many prophets gave quite different answers to those questions.

But we can attempt to reconstruct the solution rationally, based on our new understanding of God and His grand plan.

Let us take the concepts one-by-one. Most important, I think, is the immortality of the soul, or the acquired intellect, or the mind. Yes, that must be of the greatest value to God, and it is entirely reasonable to expect on that basis (even apart from revelations and promises, which are to be taken seriously) that He will save all those minds that merit it.

But what do we mean by acquired intellect? Modern computer concepts teach us that in computing there are, apart from the hardware, two main elements: thinking pattern (or software) and memory. For a meaningful "hereafter", both of those things are to be saved, even though I think that only the first, the thinking pattern, is to be equated with the acquired intellect (and is therefore of any value to God). Your conception of the collective intellect in the World-to-Come would use all individual software, but presumably no memories. I would like to believe that He will grant us the retention of our memories, so that we each shall know who we are, where we come from; and we shall have relationships to certain others, even in that other world. But I am jumping ahead of myself. Let us assume that my expectation is within reason.

So the mind is to be saved, along with the memory. What happens to it? Well, first of all, nothing needs to happen right away; after all, time is of no importance to these minds in a state of suspension. Technically, I expect them to reside on some physical medium (not "substrate", for they are not operative). As an analogy, we could use our current computer storage devices, such as magnetic or optical disks.

But at some point—and I don't claim to know whether upon death, or later, at resurrection time—God certainly makes a judgment. Is this mind worth saving? If not, all He needs to do is discard it, wipe it off the storage device.

And so, we have the modern definition of salvation and damnation: saving or scratching the record.

Which record? I think that He takes back-up recording of every mind and every memory at regular intervals. The frequency would be quite high in early age, while less and less frequent mental recording would be needed later, corresponding to the increasing stability of the mind. Memory recording frequency is probably higher; the recording, on the other hand, may be easier, as only facts need to be recorded, not a complex network of logical connections. (Perhaps he uses the sleeping period, the deepest sleep, as the ideal time for recording. Perhaps dreams are secondary symptoms of the transfer of the information?)

And so, the time comes to resurrect the dead. I tend to think that it shall happen either in Messianic times, or shortly before, for reasons I shall give you.

The bodily resurrection is really an unimportant stage, unimportant for God; but very important for Man. If God only wanted to utilize the human intellect, He would not bother with this step. But it would be a great shock for any mind to find itself in that new environment; it would be looking for something familiar to which it can relate; looking for other persons, its loved ones. And that is why I think that God will resurrect the dead, "soul and body".

Yet you were concerned about how the body can be resurrected, when it is long since decomposed. You were right. It will not be the actual human body, often deformed by illness even before death. I think that the mind and memory will be encased in a pseudo-body, to be provided temporarily, to smooth the transition for Man.

But more than that is needed for that "smoothing" process. God will have to find a way to reconcile the age differences of the resurrected persons. What about the loved one remembered by somebody as his grandchild, a baby, while another remembers him as a beloved grandparent? At different times, each mind may be temporarily "clothed" in bodies as of different ages; and then gradually brought up or down, during a "re-education" process, until everybody is at an average age, typically thirty or forty years, except those who died young. All people will understand the need for and the nature of this gradual adjustment—it may take years, even centuries may be necessary, perhaps less time for some, more for others.

And what will be the object of the exercise? Why re-educate? Well, perhaps the object is the eventual removal of the pseudo-body, having people adjusted to the idea of relating to others without specific bodies, and without the confining concept of chronological age. And why?

Because then, I think, these minds, or souls if you prefer, will be ready to join the Universal Mind, or Intellect, which may or may not be united by then with the divine Intellect. I will tell you more about the Universal Mind, and how it may come about, in my next letter, with the help of the Lord. I think it will come to exist with the assistance of the Messiah. And you see, that is why I've said that the resurrection needs to await the arrival of the Messianic age, or could happen just before that time.

Another thought: while I am convinced that everybody but the worst sinners will participate in the resurrection of the dead, it is not equally certain that there shall be room, or need, for all human intellects in the Universal Mind. I said earlier that it is the mind, the acquired intellect, that God needs. Yet perhaps that structure is only for the superior intellects of the *future*, and the Lord, or the Universal Mind itself, shall only accept, or "invite", those minds from the past (if any at all) that are above a certain level? Perhaps just a few, ones that can contribute something unusual, a different feature? Perhaps the others shall continue their existence as resurrected, with or without pseudo-bodies as long as they like? This is a rather pessimistic thought; nevertheless, we cannot rule it out entirely. But, again, we have reached a level of speculation where no rational answer can be given; at least not by me, not now.

But assuming that a soul, perhaps most souls, will have joined the Universal Mind, and through that having been united with the Godhead, either immediately or later, (or perhaps having become adjacent to It), can we then say that the World-to-Come will have arrived complete with eternal bliss? Well, eternal bliss may be a bit too fanciful; it would be more prudent, I think, to state that we have no idea what it will be like to be united with God, or being very close to Him; what tasks He may have for the human mind, in what situations we may find ourselves—there is no way to say. But I am sure that we are all looking forward to that state; for human aspiration knows no higher pinnacle than that, finally reaching the Holy One, blessed is He.

May it be God's will.

Your devoted disciple

Joseph Ben-Yehudah

UNIVERSAL MIND

20 Heshvan 5753 / November 16, 1992

To B'Rabbi Moshe ben Rabbi Maimon ha-Sfaradi,
Fostat, Egypt

My beloved Master:

We discussed, in my last letter, whether or not the dead, having been resurrected in pseudo-bodies, and having gone through a period of readjustment, may join the Universal Mind; let us hope that it will be so. But how does that organization come about in the first place? Clearly, it is one created not by the dead but by the living, the "quick" as they used to say. Collective and supreme intelligence has been the object, final or nearly final, of Creation. But does it simply emerge, naturally? If not, what does it take to make it a reality?

As before, we can only guess. I shall propose two alternate approaches, an easier one and another, more difficult. There may be other ways, there probably are many possibilities. Perhaps you will develop some of your own; but please, if you do, don't make it an article of faith!

In my first scenario, the process is entirely voluntary. As I may already have told you, parts of the human body are now being replaced by artificial pieces. In our days, we've already had artificial teeth or hair, although today they are better than in those days, so good that the wearer can often forget about their artificiality. So, also, we have artificial knee-joints and hips and other replacement parts for the skeletal structure. People severely burned get artificial skin grafts. Limbs are available, although not yet permanently installed or indistinguishable from the real arm or leg. For that, we'll need another twenty or thirty years.

More important, some vital organs can now be replaced by artificial devices; again, admittedly, further development is still needed, to miniaturize these in order to fit completely into the body frame. People now live with artificial hearts, lungs and kidneys.

Do you see where I am heading? Once all parts of the body can be replaced by superior (that is, more stable, less subject to disease) substitutes, then people will want to do so even in advance of the real need. Why? To prevent debilitating or fatal disease, of course; but later, also for reasons that have to do with vanity. Why be stuck with an ugly body when an attractive one can be obtained for nothing more than some inconvenience, and lots of money? At first, only certain parts would be replaced, as are today; later, it may be thought more simple, perhaps even more safe, to move the whole person into a completely new body. With one exception, of course.

The exception is the brain, and probably, for a long time, the head housing it. I think that finding a replacement for the brain, an artificial substrate to support the software which is the individual mind, will take a very long time. But it will happen. At first, it may be limited in its facilities; the first recipients of artificial brains will encounter serious problems, setbacks in the program are quite likely, lasting years or decades. But eventually, there will be a replacement that will match the capabilities of the human brain in every respect.

That is to say, it will do not less than the human organ. But it will also be able to do so much more. For one thing it will certainly be able to provide most, if not all, of the capabilities of a modern computer system, including millions of calculations per second, as well as knowledgable instantaneous decision-making. A person with such a brain will have insurmountable advantage over those without it; and it will then become imperative to undertake a program for the provision of such brains for everybody, a social necessity. (We are pretending, in this scenario, that all of these things will occur smoothly, without social upheavals, without violence; in reality, it is naive to expect that, I know; but we shall deal with more problematic predictions in the second alternative.)

You may object to the concept of the artificial bodies on the grounds of irreparable loss of bodily pleasures. (No, let me correct that: *others* are likely to voice such objections, not you. If I know you well, I would say that of all people, you are one of the last to complain about the loss of those human privileges.) But those losses can easily be overcome. Even today, we are reaching the stage where the pleasure of eating, for example, can be separated from the digestion and metabolism of food, for those in need of obesity control. In the future, artificial bodies may ingest food and drink, obtaining stimulation of the artificial taste buds as before. The same principle will apply to other pleasures: they can be achieved through stimulation of the appropriate artificial nerves.

Having thus completely discarded the human body, (but you will ask, what about reproduction? Must I have all answers? It will be done somehow. Even today, fertilization can take place *in vitro*; soon, there should be artificial wombs entirely outside the body; real babies may be created through manipulation of stored genetic material, for instance) people will be free to do things they could not before. They will have shed, along with the body, constraints relating to the necessity of food and drink, as well as protection from the elements. Real enjoyment of life will then commence; one would hope (vainly, I suppose) that it will be mainly intellectual enjoyment.

Up to this point, we are still envisioning individuals, with their minds now supported by superior brains. But *joining* such minds, temporarily or permanently, will be quite possible; and there will be people who will want to do so. Why? At first, out of love, wanting to be fully united with the other person. But soon after that, out of need: they will find that a double mind is more powerful than two single ones; competition will necessitate forming alliances through joint minds.

Threes and fours cannot then be far behind, those will be still more powerful, perhaps exponentially so. This will naturally lead the way to larger and larger alliances, eventually resulting in the joint mind of the entire humanity, the Universal Mind.

Easy and nice, is it not? But I fear that things won't happen that smoothly. So let me then present to you the second scenario, the one I think God may find necessary to choose (would choose, probably, if He only had these two choices at His disposal; for surely He has many others, some similar, others perhaps vastly different).

The technical aspects of my second scenario are similar to the first. But at every single step it is dire, brutal necessity that forces the human decision towards artificial parts, towards the completely artificial body, towards the artificial brain, towards joint minds of twos and fives and millions.

The first steps are clear: People not wishing to die or live crippled will ask for the artificial parts. But here comes a new tool: people being forced to such devices by new situations not heretofore encountered. Let me name just three such possibilities: there may be a major environmental disaster, say the destruction of the tropical rain forests in South America, resulting in an excess of carbon dioxide and a lack of oxygen in the air. Not wanting to suffocate, people may install artificial lung replacements in their chest cavities.

A second possibility concerns the current epidemic, AIDS, if it proves to be transmittable by insect bites. (So far, thank the Lord, it does not seem to be the case.) That would force people to escape from the biological bodies as much as possible. And a third disaster scenario, further out: a nuclear catastrophe—and remember, I have stated that such a calamity would not eliminate human life—but it could force people into completely artificial bodies, to protect against the effects of radioactivity and to eliminate the need to ingest organic radioactive food.

These examples are based on problems we are currently discussing, some of them on a daily basis; I am sure there will be others later on. But believe me, if the Lord wants to force Man into a new direction, He knows how to do it. He has used the technique for a few billion years now; it is called the survival of the fittest.

The joining of minds would probably start for amorous reasons, as I have suggested. But the trend towards larger and larger conglomeration is likely to be vicious. I could almost guarantee for you that it will not take the form of friendly competition.

I am envisioning something like the street gangs of today, powerful conglomerations attacking weaker individuals and smaller groups, who is to say why? Perhaps for financial gain, perhaps for power, possibly just, as they say today, "for the fun of it". Self-defense will then dictate protective organizations, counter-conglomerations of minds, ever larger.

Let us just consider two aspects: nationalistic chauvinism and religious intolerance. Surely, in today's terms, the conglomeration of Protestant Ulster minds will fight the Catholic Irish group; surely the Tamil minds will attack the Singhalese ones in Sri Lanka, and the Sikh mental group will plot against the Hindu one. And I have not yet made reference to Israeli and Arab groups; I shall discuss that subject in my next letter to you, with the help of the Lord.

Eventually, after disasters that some will call more horrible than if Man never gave up his organic body at all, he will be forced into very large families or clans, perhaps culminating in just two or three global blocks of intelligence, fighting each other bitterly. How to bring these groups together? Each of those centers of intelligence is likely to claim that it represents God's will, presume to serve Him and brand the other group as the Satan or Antichrist. Gnosticism is likely to re-appear. It will be a bitter and painful era. But when the time is ripe, the Holy One, blessed is He, will step in.

What I am going to say now, perhaps the first thing in these series of letters, is based on faith more than reason and science. I foresee that God sends in the Messiah to unite humankind. Will this Messiah be of human or divine substance? Both, of course: the substance will be *Intellect*. He will order all human minds who want to be with God to gather around Him, to join Him in the formation of a new, united conglomeration of intelligence. The Messiah will be the seed around which this new sparkling crystal, the Universal Mind, shall form.

Those minds which refuse to take part in the new structure will disappear from the world forever; but for the rest, the Messianic age will then begin. Please don't ask me about the functions of this great collective of minds specifically: I don't know what they will actually do, except that they will do the Lord's bidding. One thing that they may get involved in: coordinating the resurrection of all of those who died before their time, arranging for the pseudo-bodies and the re-education procedure. To the extent that this will be appropriate, they will probably also take care of the eventual acceptance of some or most of those resurrected persons into the Universal Mind itself.

Is that what we call the "Olam haBa", the World-to-Come? Quite likely. Or, perhaps not yet: perhaps it starts only later, when the Universal Mind unites with the Intellect that is God. It is possible that what you said about that time will prove correct: that personal intellects, acquired intellects will merit a part of the World-to-Come (those that do merit it), but only jointly, participating in a collective intellect. If so, then, the participating minds would be less and less interested in their respective individuality, more and more in being part of the collective whole, working with God, being part of God. And that would be a fitting Olam haBa.

May it be God's will.

Your devoted disciple

Joseph Ben-Yehudah

THE CHOSEN PEOPLE:
MEANING, IN THE PAST AND IN THE FUTURE

6 Kislev 5753 / December 10, 1992

To B'Rabbi Moshe ben Rabbi Maimon ha-Sfaradi,
Fostat, Egypt

My beloved Master:

You would ask me, what will be the role of our people, the Jews, in the apocalyptic vision of my last letter. What does the Holy One, blessed is He, want with us? Are we still the chosen people? What will we be chosen for in the future?

Or perhaps you would not ask those questions; I have had the feeling that our election was not central to your thinking; that you could not reconcile that concept with the thinking of your favourite philosopher, Aristotle.

Yet you acknowledged the fact that we are the guardians of the Torah. We accepted the Torah and entered into an eternal covenant with the Lord. Is that covenant still in force? Will it remain in force in the future? Yes, I am convinced that it will, at least until the days of the World-to-Come.

But what does it mean? Generally, we use the definition that we are supposed to be a light onto the nations. That means, in view of our new understanding, that we must always be, as we always have been, at the forefront of development, leading all human progress, nudging the human race along the path of its ultimate development.

Jews have always understood this, but their enemies have not. They thought that by claiming chosen status, we are also laying claim to privileges. No, there are no privileges, only obligations, responsibilities; and suffering. Yehudah Halevy thought that we had an inherited privilege, our ability to enter into communion with the Lord directly; and we may have that. But you rejected the concept of inheritance, at least on genetic basis: you said that acceptance of the Torah makes a proselyte a full-fledged Jew with no distinction from a born one.

Yet if there are no privileges, are there at least rewards? Not visible to us, no. If there are any, they are hidden in the future. For no reward has ever been explicitly promised. The only promise made was multiplying Abraham's seed, which has been fulfilled; and giving us the Land of Israel, which now also has been fulfilled, blessed be His name.

And so we should pay no heed to any potential future reward, but do our duty, our obligation. And what is that? To me, at least, it is clear: lead the way towards the World-to-Come, by moving humanity closer to the establishment of the Universal Mind.

How can we do that? Well, if the first steps in that direction involve the development and utilization of ever increasing mechanization and automation of the human body, replacement of organic parts with artificial ones, then that must be the direction of our leadership. We must encourage the development of those parts and the acceptance of them.

But why would we want to do so? I suppose that if the obligation was stated by God explicitly, that would leave no option but to do His bidding. Yet He has not talked to Man directly for a long time now, and there is no reason to think that He will. Short of that, what will make us give up perfectly good parts of our bodies for artificial components? At the moment, probably nothing. But in the future, perhaps soon . . .

You see, if we accept my proposed events towards the development of the Universal Mind, as I've described it recently, then we are forced to believe that it will develop through necessity. That will be our reason for rapid acceptance of artificial body parts. It may be that the necessity might apply to us, Jews, more than to other people: it may be stronger perhaps, or may come earlier; so we may be more ready than others to do what needs to be done.

We have changed through the ages. Even in the last eight centuries, we have changed. It was the years of suffering that changed us. Suffering and trial have developed in us a very strong innate ability to *survive*. And I am convinced that this is exactly what the Lord wanted.

You do recall, I am sure, my description of how He modified the various species through harsh conditions which encouraged the survival of the fittest. That is exactly what He has been doing during the last two thousand years; and now we are very fit to survive under difficult conditions. We *want* to survive, probably more than any other people on earth. All Jews know this; all but those who really should, the professional scientists.

(It is almost possible to exonerate our enemies for inflicting suffering on us. You could argue that they understood their duty, or at least grasped it subconsciously. God wanted to temper us, to make us stronger through the evolutionary process; so they have done their part by torturing us and murdering us, in the service of God. But then, perhaps, He has always chosen already damned people to do those things to us. Be that it were so; that their minds, their souls should be scratched from the recordings and even their memories be wiped off from the human consciousness.)

Having the ability to survive, what happens next? Well, one of two things could happen.

Either a chain of events will come forth, perhaps something along the lines of my earlier description: everybody will be threatened by an epidemic, by radioactivity, by lack of oxygen; the only way out will be a move towards automation. We should then be among the first to take that route, the ones who offer the least resistance. For it shall be very common among all peoples to refuse the escape, to prefer death to the strange new way of life.

But there is another possibility. We may be forced into the new mode of living ahead of everyone else through the usual way, through special persecution; we are used to that. Or Israel itself may be threatened by its enemies; all Israelis may find the only way to survive: rapid adoption of body mechanization measures.

In either case, we must be prepared for the eventuality. Do we have all we need, in order to be so prepared? I think so. We have our intelligence, our abilities, perhaps not higher than those of other people, but more practical; specifically, we have our survival instinct; and especially, we now have a strong nation, Israel, a power base for all Jews to cope with a threat that can no longer be averted by moving from country to country as we have done for two millennia. Now we shall be able to survive with that power base that the Lord has granted to us again, in accordance to His covenant with us. We have it, we must use it to survive and, thereby, to move ourselves and all nations closer to the World-to-Come.

May it be God's will.

Your devoted disciple

Joseph Ben-Yehudah

NECESSITY FOR HUMAN INVOLVEMENT
IN GOD'S PROJECT

15 Kislev 5753 / December 10, 1992

To B'Rabbi Moshe ben Rabbi Maimon ha-Sfaradi,
Fostat, Egypt

My beloved Master:

Suggesting, as I have, that we get prepared for the inevitable automation phase that leads the way to the establishment of the Universal Mind may appear, on the surface, to be a bold step for Man. Bold not only in itself; I am thinking about how it may be interpreted. It could be called daring; also pretentious, even impertinent, Man suddenly deciding to actively participate in God's project. Is it arrogant? Is it unseemly? I don't think so.

You see, we always have participated in the Lord's project, even if unwittingly at times. In every step of human history, He used people to further His objectives; some did what needed to be done without thinking, some complained (for major moves never happen without pain), some accepted the inevitable as God's will. In a few instances, people tried to anticipate God's wishes and did accordingly, without waiting for forcing circumstances.

And that is as it should be. The Lord, blessed is His name, is great; vast but not infinite. His resources are beyond imagination, but finite. Presumably, He makes more of those resources, as He needs them; it is reasonable to assume that all are used, a large storehouse of permanently unused resources does not exist.

We are such resources ourselves! He has always used us, always furthered His objectives through us; and shall continue to do so. But now there is a significant difference:

From now on, we can be more than resource, more than intermediate product. We can become God's partners! I think He is inviting us to help Him consciously in His great project, to go into partnership with Him, to do more and more of the planning, organizing, monitoring and controlling activities. As the project is getting increasingly complex, He may welcome our relieving Him from looking after every single step in the project. He will still watch it, keep records, obtain reporting or whatever He uses for monitoring; but as long as history evolves within a range acceptable to Him, He will let us handle many tasks.

Another reason of His letting us involved is, of course, to educate us, train us in the high level managerial process that He has been doing alone until now. Once the Universal Mind is established, we may expect to be called upon to be explicit partners of the Lord, even if that phase precedes the World-to-Come, in which we may perhaps be united with the Godhead. And so an informal partnership is certainly reasonable at the point when Man is conscious not only of himself but of his relation to God.

Accepting the responsibility of being an assistant to God, even a junior partner, what should Man specifically do? I do not claim to have a detailed set of instructions, a plan. The project is very complex; it will require more knowledge than I possess to assemble such a plan. Let those who put Man on the Moon, who can co-ordinate Man's greatest projects, let them plan our next move.

Short of that, it may be enough to be conscious of our role as God's partners; to be very proud of that role; and for all humanity (and especially for Jews, as I wrote to you in my last letter) to be ready for the inevitable next move, so when we see it coming, we should not be caught unprepared.

May it be God's will.

Your devoted disciple

Joseph Ben-Yehudah

JUDAISM OF THE NEAR FUTURE

21 Kislev 5753 / December 16, 1992

To B'Rabbi Moshe ben Rabbi Maimon ha-Sfaradi,
Fostat, Egypt

My beloved Master:

Let us, finally, resolve what Judaism should be about in this modern age. We have already considered the mid-term: the trials we may face and our obligations towards the World-to-Come; once past those turbulent times, once the Universal Mind has been achieved and surpassed, I would think that the role of Judaism will have been fulfilled, all covenants completed, and there will be no need for a distinct Jewry after that. But what about the near future? What about the present?

Well, let us consider this question in an orderly manner. There will be no need for Jewry as such in the World-to-Come. Then how about in the Universal Mind itself, assuming that it may be a distinct earlier phase? Will there be a role for Judaism within that? I have already told you that I expect our people to play a major role, probably a painful one, in its creation. But once it is finally established, what shall we be within the scope of that structure: shall we still be Jews?

I think yes; for in the Universal Mind everyone maintains his or her individual identity, and with that, presumably his or her national, ethnic and racial background. That is, at the beginning. Over the history of the Universal Mind, however, those things may gradually fade; it may be that the Universal Mind will be ready for the next, final stage when those individual and group identifications disappear, or at least move into the background at a level comparable to pre-historic mythology today.

Still, one other thing to remember about the Universal Mind: it will be created, it will crystallize, around a seed provided by God, and that seed will be the Messiah. To date, nobody willing to accept the concept of the Messiah has seriously questioned the assertion that the Messiah will be a Man (whether or not of divine substance will be irrelevant by then: the substance will be Intellect), and a Man of Jewish extraction, probably from the house of David. I fully expect that to happen. A seed of David will finally become the seed of all humanity, bringing it to fulfillment.

And what should Judaism be like until the beginning of the Universal Mind, until the approach of the Messianic age?

No doubt Ultra-orthodoxy will remain strong, will even gain ground. For a long time, it will remain separate from other branches of Judaism, the separation may likely be more pronounced; yet I would hope that there will be no distinct branches left by the days of the Universal Mind.

But meanwhile, I would like to see all others—Conservatives, Reform, Reconstruction—to come together in an understanding of God and His purpose with humanity, His plans for the Jews. How? Ideally, under the leadership of a strong leader who becomes prominent, perhaps a leader of the State of Israel, one who rises above sectarian squabbling, and will succeed in uniting all of the Jews, Israelis as well as those in the diaspora, as truly one people.

If we all were to come together, we could plan rationally, prepare ourselves for the eventualities that can be expected based on all the old teachings and our new understanding. Be in readiness to act when the time comes.

We shall, I hope, have a clear conception of humanity's role as God's creation, as His servants, as His junior partners. As for the Jewish people, without elitism, without putting ourselves on a pedestal, we should search our minds about His will for us, and be ready to move without worrying about the rest of humanity: they will follow. We must be ready for whatever painful historic step the Lord assigns to us; for that has been our role all along, that is what the covenant is all about: providing the world with light, with leadership, with direction as we always have.

Israel, as a country, a nation, a people, strong in its struggle against its enemies, yet humble in front of the Lord: Israel, the servant of God leading the world towards the Messianic age—that is the role of Judaism. I am sure that we shall fulfill that role with honour.

May it be the will of God.

For God is very near to all who call Him, who call Him in truth and turn only to Him. He is found by every one who seeks Him, if such a one always goes forward and does not go astray. Amen.

I have now completed the fourth and last series of letters to you, my honoured Master. Blessed be the Merciful who has aided us.

Your disciple and friend

Joseph Ben-Yehuda

About the Author

Andrew Sanders lives in Toronto, Canada, and in Haifa, Israel. His books, in addition to *Dear Maimonides*, include *Hanina, My Son*, an historical novel of the first century, which presents the story of a handful of tannaic rabbis and their families, and *The Galilean Schism*, a critical study of Christianity from a strictly Jewish viewpoint, as he puts it, "with a twist."